RICHARD COEUR DE LION

Richard Coeur de Lion, from the early 13th century
effigy at Fontevrault

RICHARD
COEUR DE LION

A Biography

by
PHILIP HENDERSON

Illustrated

GREENWOOD PRESS, PUBLISHERS
WESTPORT, CONNECTICUT

Library of Congress Cataloging in Publication Data

Henderson, Philip, 1906-
  Richard, Coeur de Lion : a biography.

  Reprint of the 1959 ed. published by Norton, New York.
  1. Richard I, King of England, 1157-1199.
[DA207.H4 1976]   942.03'2'0924 [B]   76-000004
ISBN 0-8371-8724-9

Originally published in 1958 by W. W. Norton & Company,
Inc., New York

Reprinted with the permission of Philip Henderson

Reprinted in 1976 by Greenwood Press,
a division of Williamhouse-Regency Inc.

Library of Congress Catalog Card Number 76-000004

ISBN 0-8371-8724-9

Printed in United States of America

ACKNOWLEDGEMENTS

THE author is most grateful to the following individuals, institutions and publishers: the Dean and Chapter of Canterbury Cathedral for the Great Seal of Richard I; the National Buildings Record for Sydney Pitcher's photograph of the effigy of King John at Worcester Cathedral; Messrs Walter Scott (Bradford) for their photograph of the effigy of the so-called Geoffrey de Magnaville from the Temple Church, London; the Victoria and Albert Museum for their photograph of the effigy of William Marechel; B. Arthaud of Grenoble for the plate from Marcel Aubert's *La Cathédrale de Chartres*; Librarie Hachette and Bibliothèque Nationale for the Jongleur; the German Tourist Information Bureau for the Bamberg Rider; the Trustees of the British Museum for the reproductions from David Roberts's *The Holy Land*; Messrs Constable & Co. for Henry Adams's translation of Richard Coeur de Lion's Prison Song from *Mont-Saint-Michel and Chatres*; Mr John Harvey and B. T. Batsford Ltd. for the translation of Richard Coeur de Lion's Sirvente to the Dauphin of Auvergne; Messrs Peter Owen for a quotation from Ezra Pound's *The Spirit of Romance*; the University of Washington Press for numerous quotations from Dr Stone's translation of Ambroise's *l'Estoire de la guerre sainte* from *Three Old French Chronicles of the Crusades*; Janet Freer for redrawing the map of the Kingdom of Jerusalem from John L. La Monte's *The World of the Middle Ages* (Appleton-Century-Croft, 1949) and Messrs Longmans, Green for the map of the Angevin Empire from G. M. Trevelyan's *History of England*.

Finally, I have once more to thank Miss Phyl Hayter for typing my manuscript.

CONTENTS

LIST OF ILLUSTRATIONS

Map of Angevin Empire missing from this edition

- Iconium

A R M E N I A

E D E S S A

Lost 1144

Edessa•

- Tarsus

• Adalia

•Seleucia

Alexandretta•

•Aleppo

Antioch•

A N T I O C H

Kyrenia•

Nicosia•

•Famagusta

Margat•

Tortosa•

C Y P R U S

Limassol

Tripoli•

Djebail•

SALJUQ
TURKS

Beirut•

M E D I T E R R A N I A N

Sidon•

•Damascus

S E A

Tyre•

Acre• •Hattin

SEA OF GALILEE

Haifa• •Tiberias

Athlit• Nazareth

Caesarea•

Naplouse

Arsur•

Jaffa• Lydda•

Ibelin• Ramlah•

•Jerusalem

Ascalon• Beit
Gaza• Nuba
Daron•

DEAD
SEA

E G Y P T

Nile R.

• Cairo

RED
SEA

I knew the man, my dear master and a great king, who brought the leopards into the shield of England, more proper to do it than his father, being more the thing he signified. Of him, therefore . . . the hymned and reviled, the loved and loathed, spendthrift and a miser, king and a beggar, the bond and the free, god and man; of King Richard Yea-and-Nay, so made, so called, and by that unmade, I thus prepare my account.

MAURICE HEWLETT, *The Life and Death of Richard Yea-and-Nay.*

Prologue

APART from a sporting little book by Clennell Wilkinson, and Maurice Hewlett's romantic novel, Coeur de Lion's life, so far as the present century is concerned, has been for the most part written by lady admirers. Of these Kate Norgate's *Richard the Lion Heart* (1924) is by far the most scholarly and detailed. For those who wish to follow all the battles and unravel all the diplomatic tangles of the twelfth century it is indispensable. But one battle and one conference is very like another, the battles ending in the ransom of the rich and the slaughter of the poor. Looked at like this, medieval history is a bore, till we can get at the men and women behind the dates and the place names.

Even from the beginning when, as his mother's spoiled darling, the golden Count of Poitou, Richard aroused the bitter jealousy of his father, men have always been less indulgent to him than women. "God grant I may not die, before I have had my revenge on you!" hissed the old king when Richard came to receive his father's kiss of peace, after hounding him to death at Chinon. His most recent critic, Steven Runciman, in his great *History of the Crusades*, is positively hostile, as is René Grousset in his *Histoire des Croisades* of 1935. The nineteenth century, in the person of Bishop Stubbs, is more severe still. "English writers," Stubbs remarks caustically, "seem to have thought it possible to show that, although in every relation of life he was found grievously wanting, he was, on the whole, a great and glorious king to be defended against the calumnies of the world," whereas in reality he was "a bad son, a bad husband, a selfish ruler, and a vicious man." Yet, Stubbs concedes, "he possessed some qualities which the men of his time accepted as better than the wicked wisdom of his father and which made his tyranny less intolerable than his brother's weakness."[1] To Sir Winston Churchill, who devotes a stirring chapter to Richard in the first volume of his *History of the English Speaking*

[1] *Memorials of the Reign of Richard I: Historical Introductions to the Rolls Series*, collected and edited by Arthur Hassall, pp. 315-8.

Peoples, he is a glorious paladin whose life was "one magnificent parade, which when ended left only an empty plain." The octingentenary of his birth would seem, therefore, an opportune moment for reappraisal.

So Richard rides triumphantly flourishing his sword outside the Houses of Parliament at Westminster, widely acknowledged as a national hero, in spite of the fact that he was a Frenchman, of mixed Norman and Angevin stock, who never learned to speak the language of the country he ruled at second hand. He spent no more than six months of his ten years' reign in England and only came here to be crowned and to raise money for his foreign wars and his ransom, after trying to sneak back from the Holy Land in disguise. It is true that one of the wars for which he bled the country was the Third Crusade, and one might suppose that in the Age of Faith the country was only too glad to be bled white in so worthy a cause. But the number of those who paid scutage to get themselves exempted is quite surprising.

Richard's life, as everyone knows, was dominated by a passion for war, which, together with hunting, was then considered the only occupation fit for a gentleman. Everybody is agreed that he was a superb soldier. With his long reach it was always the other fellow's head that fell. He was also outstanding as a tactician and a military engineer. He is said to have introduced the cross-bow into France and he brought fortification to a pitch it had never known in the West. Ballistas, mangonels and the various forms of medieval artillery for hurling stones, Greek fire and cross-bow bolts, obsessed him and he worked hard at their improvement. For, unlike most *preux chevaliers*, he could use his brains as well as his weapons. This martial enthusiasm was not, of course, shared to the same extent by the mass of the people, who lost their limbs and their lives, their wives and their homes in the never-ending wars of their feudal overlords, who perpetually chased one another across the countryside, leaving ruin and desolation in their wake.

But Richard was also a poet, a troubadour, trained at his mother's court in Poitou. We know all about his battles, but unfortunately only two of his poems have survived, the prison song, two versions of which exist, in French and Provençal, and the scornful poem addressed to the Dauphin of Auvergne in the Poitevin dialect. These are evidently the work of a skilful and practised writer. Richard had other tastes, too, a little surprising in a warrior. He loved to assist in the decoration of his chapel for feast days and also took great pains with the music. He used to walk up and down conducting, we are told, and encouraging his choir to sing in the most elevated tone. He was fastidious and had an almost feminine love of clothes. When he dined, he did so in the most solemn state. Everything on his table had to be of the finest workmanship, the cloth and each goblet and knife and fork had to be scrupulously clean. He could not bear disorder or any kind of sordidness and was famed for his courtesy and good manners. As we should say, he had a highly developed aesthetic sense, and in all this we may see the influence of his mother, the brilliant and accomplished Eleanor of Aquitaine. In short, Coeur de Lion belonged to the old, highly developed civilization of Southern France, which disappeared in the Albigensian Crusade early in the next century, when Simon de Montfort and his Anglo-Norman knights overran Languedoc and Provence with fire and sword. What they left the Inquisition finished off.

Richard has been seen as the very pattern of the Christian hero who dedicated his life to the rescue of the Holy Sepulchre. In fact, most of his life was spent trying to hold down the rebellious and quarrelsome barons of Aquitaine and to containing the King of France within the narrow strip of his royal domain. Altogether, Richard spent only eighteen months in the Holy Land, though it is true that he vowed to return and continue the war for the liberation of Jerusalem, and might even have done so had he not had more pressing affairs to attend to at home. For throughout the Middle Ages Europe was obsessed with the Holy Land as the home of their faith, and theoretically everyone's ambition was to rescue the Sepulchre of Christ or die in the attempt.

Today the Crusades may appear to us as more or less lunatic expeditions, when they were not simply a pretext of the Italian maritime cities to further their trading interests in the Levant. The ship owners of Genoa, Pisa and Venice made fortunes from the pilgrim traffic alone, and Venice led the Sack of Constantinople. To the Moslems, the Crusades were no more than insignificant skirmishes on the western frontier of their empire, till Saladin proclaimed a holy war in his turn to put an end to the nuisance for good. But those who were most dismayed by each fresh wave of crusaders from the West were the impoverished knights and younger sons who had carved out domains for themselves in Syria and Palestine and were living on the very best of terms with their Moslem neighbours. For them each new Crusade upset everything and was an unmitigated disaster. It was not much more for those who remained at home,

for one result of the Crusades, as far as Europe was concerned, was
the enormous increase in leprosy and other unpleasant diseases,
which the pilgrims brought back with them. Soon there were leper
hospitals in all the big towns.

It was indeed fortunate for Richard that he had his mother behind him to hold the fort in England while he was in the East
fighting for Christ. For he never had much talent as an administrator. His father had left the machinery of government in good working order and Richard, with his nefarious methods of raising money,
did his best to wreck it. Like other counts of Poitou, gay, brilliant
fellows and great crusaders, he was not much use at the more hum-
drum things of life. But he was the very incarnation of the knightly
ideal and at least looked every inch a king.

✦ He was lofty in stature, of a shapely build, with hair half way
between red and yellow. His limbs were straight and flexible, his
arms somewhat long and, for this very reason, better fitted than
those of most folk to draw or wield the sword. Moreover, he had
long legs, matching the character of his whole frame. His features
showed the ruler, while his manners and his bearing added not a
little to his general presence. Not only could he claim the loftiest
position and praise in virtue of his noble birth, but also by reason
of his virtues. He far surpassed other men in the courtesy of his
manners and the vastness of his strength: memorable was he for
his warlike deeds and power, while his splendid achievements
would throw a shade over the greatest praise we could give
them ... The lord of the ages had given him such generosity of
soul and endued him with such virtues that he seemed rather to
belong to earlier times than these.... His was the valour of
Hector, the magnanimity of Achilles; he was no whit less inferior
to Alexander, or less than Roland in manhood.

Thus the author of the *Itinerarium Regis Ricardi*, thought to be
Richard Canon of Holy Trinity in Aldgate, who accompanied the
king as his chaplain on the Third Crusade. He evidently loved
Richard this side adolatry. Other contemporary English sources are
not quite so eulogistic, though all take a national pride in their hero
king. What is more remarkable is that the Moslem historian
Bohardin, Saladin's secretary and biographer, is just as loud in his
praises as Richard of Aldgate. It is the French and German chroniclers who, from sordid political motives, paint everything Richard
did in the blackest colours, for already the old ideal of the unity of

Christendom was going down before emergent nationalities. It was largely national jealousy, and Richard's determination to have the glory of being the undisputed leader of the Christian host, that brought about the failure of the Third Crusade, though it was not such a dismal failure as those that followed.

⚜What nineteenth-century historians could not forgive Richard for was his irresponsible attitude to money and sex. But then the twelfth century, though it built the cathedrals and brought European poetry to birth, did not feel itself to be so virtuous as Victorian England, which built the industrial cities and the slums. "The standard of morality was indeed so low," says Stubbs, "that even if historians were altogether, as they are for the most part, silent as to his personal vices, their silence could not be taken for a negation. Unhappily what little is said is dark and condemnatory." Darker, perhaps, by official nineteenth-century standards, than Stubbs is prepared to admit, though he hints at a parallel between Richard and William Rufus—another redhead of unconventional sexual habits. It would seem, however, that the pattern of Richard's emotional nature was determined by his hatred of his father and his lifelong attachment to his mother, resulting in neglect of and indifference to his wife and an overriding compulsion to prove his virility, if not by begetting an heir, then by spectacular deeds of prowess. He was, we are told, "no squire of dames". We could have guessed as much, though presumably he broke a lance or two in some lady's honour during the course of his life, if only for form's sake, for we hear of him jousting at Pamplona, where he evidently met his future wife, Berengaria of Navarre.

⚜"The evidence is clear," writes John Harvey, "that Richard, like many other warriors and also some most unwarlike men, was the victim of homosexuality. In this his case differs from those of William Rufus, Edward II and James I, where volumes of rumour seem to be unsubstantiated by any real proof."[1] One would have thought that there was not much doubt about the other kings. But Richard is known to have made a most embarrassing confession before his assembled bishops and barons at Messina on the way to the Holy Land, and after his return, when he was married but not living with his wife, he was cautioned by a hermit to remember the fate of Sodom and to "refrain from what is unlawful".

⚜ As to money, Sir James Ramsay writes: "Of Richard's personal intervention in matters of finance it is impossible to speak too

[1] *The Plantagenets*, p. 33.

strongly. He begins with wanton alienations of Crown property; he then proceeds still further to cripple the future by selling sheriff-doms and other offices to the highest bidder, thus opening a wide door to official malversation. When the day of need comes, convis-cation and re-sale are again the only expedients."[2] But what he accumulated by means fair or foul, Richard gave away again just as lightly, with what Ramsay calls "a fatuous generosity". It was not so fatuous, really, because he found that this was the best way to make and to keep friends. When his munificent presents ceased, his friends and allies melted away, as he points out himself in his *sir-vente* to the Dauphin of Auvergne. "Judged by the most moderate standards," Ramsay concludes, "he must be pronounced a bad king and a vicious man." The best that can be said of him is that he was an overgrown schoolboy who meant no harm.[3] There is indeed a kind of innocence in the very openness and directness of Richard's dealings, but he was certainly no innocent himself. Most knights at that time were pretty foul-mouthed, and Richard in particular was famed for his picturesque oaths. There were no Galahads or "pure knights" in a Tennysonian sense in the twelfth century. Thus we find John of Salisbury writing: "For he whose mouth is defiled with the foulest words, whose oaths are most detestable, who least fears God, who vilifies God's ministers, who feareth not the Church—that man nowadays is reputed bravest and most renowned of the knightly band."

✱ We are told that Richard had the power to enchant and won the love and admiration of even his enemies. His overtures to Saladin, who had the greatest admiration for him, were certainly warm enough, and to Saladin's brother, El Malek el Adil, he offered his sister Joan in marriage. At one time his friendship with Philip Augustus of France—the inveterate enemy of his house— was such that the two men, not content with spending all their time together by day and eating from the same plate, could not even bear to be parted at night—"insomuch that all men wondered what this might mean," says the puzzled chronicler.

✱ All his life Richard was the victim of bad health; malaria caught while campaigning in the south of France. These fits of fever, which set him trembling uncontrollably, were combined with eruptions of the skin, so that at times he was unable either to walk or ride. When he went on crusade at the age of thirty-three few people ever

[2] *Revenues of the Kings of England*, p. 226.
[3] *Angevin Empire*, p.367.

expected to see him again. Indeed the wearing of heavy chain mail in the heat of a Levantine summer must have been torture to such a constitution. But Richard mastered all such weaknesses of the flesh by the violence of his will, possibly even deriving satisfaction from this additional penance. For on the whole, his life was dissolute. When lying wounded at Chaluz in the Limousin, he hastened his end by refusing to moderate in the least his usual habits of drinking and love-making.

And yet, when all is said, the kind of man he was can be seen from the effigy at Fontevrault, which appears to be early thirteenth-century work. Looking down at that noble battered face, one feels instinctively in the presence of greatness. The set of the head on the thick sturdy neck, the wide shoulders, the deep chest are eloquent of masculine energy and strength. The face, in its stern concentration, with its splendid brow, finely formed nose, high cheek bones and firm small mouth with pouting underlip, combines in a unique degree the qualities of warrior and poet.

PART ONE

COUNT OF POITOU

"Swerve to the left, son Roger," he said,
  "When you catch his eyes through the
    helmet-slit,
Swerve to the left, then out at his head,
  And the Lord God give you the joy of it!"

WILLIAM MORRIS, *The Judgement of God*.

I

ANGEVIN INHERITANCE

THE ANGEVIN inheritance was a dark and violent one. In the closing years of the tenth century, when a general expectation of the end of the world filled the air with superstitious dread, it is related that Fulk Nerra, or Fulk the Black, Count of Anjou, had espoused a lady of unknown origin "only for the fairness of her body". This lady had a rooted objection to going to church. When prevailed upon to do so, she positively refused to stay for the Consecration of the Host, which created such a scandal that at last her husband resolved to compel her to stay. So next time, as his wife was leaving the church as usual four knights stationed at the door laid hold of her mantel. But the lady, quickly disengaging herself, flew out of the window, taking with her the two children she had been sheltering with her left hand, and was never seen again. "What wonder," Richard Coeur de Lion was in the habit of exclaiming, "if we lack the natural affections of mankind—we who come from the Devil, and must needs go back to the Devil?"

After the peculiar disappearance of his wife, Fulk Nerra made the first of his four pilgrimages to the Holy Land, thus establishing that connexion of his house with the Kingdom of Jerusalem which later resulted in the foundation there of the Angevin dynasty in the person of his great-grandson, Fulk V. Another wife Fulk Nerra burnt at the stake, either for adultery or witchcraft, and as an old man on his fourth pilgrimage to the Holy Land had himself dragged about Jerusalem in the sight of the Turks, a halter round his neck, while another servant scourged his naked back as he howled to high heaven for mercy. History repeated itself to some extent when that Count of Anjou who became Henry II of England walked barefoot across the rough cobbles of Canterbury and submitted to be scourged at Becket's tomb. The pattern recurred again when Richard I, his son, on his way to the Holy Land, came before the assembled bishops at Messina, half-naked in sackcloth and with a scourge in his hand, and embarrassed them all by publicly confessing to the most unseemly sins. But whatever the Angevins did, they did with their whole mind and soul, and when they repented they repented thoroughly.)

On his mother's side Richard's great-grandfather was the first of the Troubadours, that William Count of Poitou and Duke of Aquitaine who ruled over more of France than the French king, who seduced and carried off the wife of his vassal, the Viscount of Chatellerault, and paid for it with a hermit's curse upon his whole line. William of Malmesbury tells us that William took pride in denying the existence of God, and when in 1101 he led a huge army to the Holy Land it was utterly routed by the Turks. "Now this Count of Poitiers was one of the most courteous men in the world and one of the greatest deceivers of ladies, and valiant in warfare, and bounteous in love and gallantry. And he knew well to sing and to make poetry, and long time went through the world beguiling ladies. And his son had to wife the Duchess of Normandy, by whom he had a daughter, the which was wife to King Henry of England, and mother to the Young King, and of Lord Richard, and of Count Geoffrey of Brittany."[1]

William the Troubadour's granddaughter Eleanor of Aquitaine, the wife of our Henry II and the mother of Coeur de Lion, was one of the most remarkable women of the Middle Ages. She is given a very dubious reputation by the historians of her time, who describe her as "light and unstable, though very intelligent". For it was at Antioch during the disastrous Second Crusade, on which she accompanied her pious first husband Louis VII of France, that Eleanor created such a scandal by flirting (if not more) with her uncle Raymond of Poitiers, reputed to be the handsomest man of his time. As for her husband, she told him contemptuously that he was "not worth a rotten apple", and no better than a monk. Soon she was trying to get a divorce on the convenient grounds of consanguinity. "At this the king was deeply moved," writes John of Salisbury, "and although he loved the queen almost beyond reason, he consented to divorce her if his counsellors and the French nobility would allow it."[2]

Having got rid of her husband, Eleanor offered herself, as well as her vast estates, to young Henry Plantagenet, whom she knew to be a very different sort of man from Louis, though she was nearly thirty at the time and he but eighteen. She had already had an

[1] Ida Farnell, *Lives of the Troubadours.*
[2] *Historia Pontificalis*, trans. by Marjorie Chibnall.

affair with Henry's father, Geoffrey of Anjou, and he had warned his son to have nothing to do with her. But Eleanor's irresistible allure, combined with the whole of south-western France, was too much for Henry, and he married her barely a month after the divorce arranged by an accommodating conclave of bishops at Sens in 1152. Two years later, Henry, Duke of Normandy and Count of Anjou, was crowned King of England and the royal pair went to live in Bermondsey, while the palace of Westminster was rebuilt on a magnificent scale under the energetic direction of the young chancellor and the king's best friend Thomas Becket.

Of Henry II it was said that all human virtues and vices seemed to exist in him at their fullest power. And there is indeed something over-life-sized about these people of the twelfth century. Their passions are unrestrained and like madness, their energy prodigious. Henry had been a soldier since the age of fourteen, when he first invaded England to fight his cousin Stephen of Blois and to establish his claim as Henry I's rightful heir. A Frenchman, born at Le Mans, he inherited his father's reverence for learning and was himself consumed with an insatiable intellectual hunger. With his close-cropped leonine head, bull-neck and freckled face, and clear grey eyes that in moments of anger appeared a flaming red, but which yet could be as soft as a dove's, and his short barrel-chested body, Henry was the incarnation of will power. Fearing to grow fat, like his great-great-grandfather the Conqueror, he was ever on the move. From morning till night he never sat down and exhausted everyone around him. Indifferent to food or drink, or to bodily comforts of any kind, he usually ate standing up, cramming his mouth with filthy hands, just as he came in from hunting. Often as not, the food served at his table was quite bad. Henry was too absorbed in his thoughts to notice, but his courtiers complained that they had to filter the wine and beer through their teeth, it was so thick and muddy. His Court was the most slovenly in Europe and must have been a sore trial to Eleanor, with her delicate and luxurious habits.

The king was quite without ceremony and perfectly familiar with everyone. St Hugh of Lincoln found him one day at Woodstock sitting on the ground surrounded by a ring of courtiers sewing a finger-stall. When St Hugh amused him, he rolled over on his back and gave himself up to uncontrollable laughter. Henry had a nice sense of humour. Riding one day through London in mid-winter with Becket, his chancellor, and seeing an old man in rags shivering by the roadside, he turned to his friend and said, "Would it not be a meritorious act to give that poor man a warm cloak?" Becket agreed that it would. So, laying his hands on the chancellor's furred cloak, he flung it to the beggar, saying, "Your's be the merit, then." He was above many of the prejudices and superstitions of his age, refusing to join in the rabid persecution of the Jews and opening his dominions as a refuge for the persecuted Albigenses, who were already being chased from place to place by the Church in southern France. "No man," says Walter Map, one of the king's most intimate councellors, "surpassed him in gentleness and friendliness. As often as he went abroad he was seized by the crowds and carried by force from place to place whether he would or not, and what is remarkable he gave an ear patiently to each man singly and though assailed at one time by the shouts of the mob, and at another violently dragged and pulled about, yet for this he brought no charge against any man nor used it as an excuse for anger. He did nought insolently or pompously ... when he was too hard-pressed he fled to havens of peace." One of these havens was Woodstock, where, it is said, Henry built a labyrinth to shelter his mistress Rosamond Clifford from the queen's jealousy.

Beside this rumbustious, headlong, choleric, libidinous, learned man, Eleanor, for the first time felt somehow of less account. And when he had two sons by Rosamond Clifford she grew to hate him and taught her sons to hate him, too. Gerald of Wales describes a fresco that the king had painted at the palace of Winchester representing a great eagle with wings outspread as if to shelter its young, but the young ones are attacking him furiously—one digs at his vitals, another claws at his eyes, and two more wound his wings. "Thus will they pursue me till I die," Henry is reported to have said, "and the least one, whom I now cherish with so much affection"—that is to say, John—"will be the most malignant of them all."

The year of Richard's birth saw Henry at the height of his power. Indeed he was the most powerful and accomplished prince in Europe. His domain stretched from the Cheviots to the Pyrenees. Inheriting the chaos left by Stephen, he gave England peace and order, making both bishops and barons subject to the common law. While his reign inaugurated a new age, his family grew apace.

Richard, his third (legitimate) son was born on 8 September 1157, at Beaumont Palace, just within the walls of Oxford near the north gate. Beaumont Street is now built on the site and the parish seal of St Mary Magdalene, with its star and crescent, Richard's badge, still commemorates the birth of its greatest parishioner. The palace had been built twenty-five years before by Henry I, "for the great pleasure of the seat, the sweetness and delectableness of the air", says Anthony à Wood. But a year seldom passed without Eleanor giving birth to another child. The youngest, William, had been born in Normandy before her husband's accession, and had died in 1156, the year in which Matilda was born. Henry had already arrived in February 1155; then came Richard, then Geoffrey in 1158, then Eleanor in 1161, Joan in 1165 (Richard's favourite sister), and then John Lackland last of all in 1166. From Rosamond, Henry had William Longsword and Geoffrey, whom he made his chancellor. Richard, always his mother's favourite, seems to have been intended from the first as heir to her duchy of Aquitaine, so named by Caesar because of its many rivers. Young Henry was to succeed his father to the English throne and Geoffrey was to have Brittany. It is likely, therefore, that after being nursed by Hodierna, the woman of St Albans, Richard was brought up at his mother's court at Poitiers or Bordeaux.

In any case, Henry's restless, disorderly Court was no place for young children. Henry was what one would now call bohemian in his habits and Walter Map says that from the scholar's point of view there was little to choose between his court and hell, except that you could get away from it, whereas there was no escape from hell. Yet, he tells us, the king always found time to read or to work out some intricate problem with his clerks. He patronised both the trouvères of the north and the troubadours of the south and it was from the marriage of these two strains that French lyric poetry was born. "With the King of England," says Map, "there was school every day, continual conversation of the finest scholars and discussion of problems." At other times pandemonium reigned. Peter of Blois says that after deciding the night before to remain at a particular place, Henry would wake early next morning and order everything to be got ready for an immediate start—"whereby," says Peter, "it cometh frequently to pass that such courtiers as have had themselves bled, or have taken some purgative, must yet follow their prince forthwith without regard to their own bodies. Then may ye see men rush forth like mad-men, sumpter-mules jostling sumpter-mules and chariots clashing against chariots in frantic confusion, a very Pandemonium made visible. Or again, if the Prince have proclaimed his purpose of setting out for a certain place with the morrow's dawn, then will he surely change his purpose; doubt not but that he will lie abed till mid-day.... Men flock round the court, prostitutes and vintners, to get tidings of the king's journey. For the king's train swarms with play-actors and washerwomen [a medieval euphemism for prostitutes], dicers, and flatterers, taverners, waferers [panders, male prostitutes][3] buffoons, barbers, tumblers and all kinds of that feather." When everything was at last ready and the whole motley Court was set in motion, "the abyss seemed to have been opened, and hell to vomit forth his legions." Then, after travelling all day, the king would decide to stay the night in some desolate part of the country where there was neither food nor lodging to be had, so that his courtiers were constrained to wander three or four miles through unknown forests, and oftentimes in the black darkness, "esteeming themselves fortunate if perchance they fell upon some vile and sordid hovel. Oftentimes the courtiers would fight bitterly and obstinately for mere huts, and contend with drawn swords for a lair which had been unworthy of contention among swine." And Peter prays God that He may turn the king's heart from "this pestilent custom, that he may know himself to be but a man."[4]

The Middle Ages were nothing if not lively. Even in Church people behaved as though they were at the theatre, clapping and applauding any passage in the sermon that particularly pleased them. Painted all over with the gayest colours, with funny and often lewd faces peeping out from every every coign and corner—what went on in the roof on the bosses God only saw—church was altogether a far more entertaining place than it has become since our Puritan revolution. True, the pictures on the walls sometimes had a more sobering effect, for Holy Church, like the Greek drama before it, purged the people with pity and terror. Nevertheless, considering the amount of scepticism and heresy abroad at this time, one wonders whether its power over men's minds was quite as great in the centuries of faith as it is usually represented to be.

After all, the south, with its memories of Greek civilization and

[3] Waferers, the sellers of the wafers that were taken with wine, had an unsavoury reputation in the Middle Ages.

> Singers with harps, baudes, wafereres,
> Which been the verray develes officeres
> To kindle and blowe the fyr of lecherye . . .

says Chaucer in the Pardoner's Tale.

[4] Quoted by G. G. Coulton, *Life in the Middle Ages* III. 3–4.

its great Roman remains, was still half-pagan.[5] Besides, the doc-
trines of the Cathars, the so-called Albigenses, had taken a firm hold
upon the Midi and Toulouse was a stronghold of the Catharist faith.
It was a strange doctrine, founded upon a hatred of the flesh, and
seemingly quite at variance with the luxurious and pleasure-loving
lives led by the southern nobles. For the Cathars held that the world
as we know it is the creation of the devil, that all life is evil, most
evil of all being the love between men and women which results in
children, for children, they said, were of the devil too. Better than
marriage, therefore, were adultery and sodomy—at least that is what
their opponents tell us they believed and practised. In fact the Albigenses came to be known as Bulgars—the doctrine seemingly having
originated in Bulgaria and Eastern Europe—a name which soon
degenerated into a more familiar form of abuse. Possibly it was
from them that Richard inherited his Bulgarian tastes, for few
people living in the Midi remained unaffected by the Cathars. The
truly Christian lives of service to the sick and poor led by the *per-
fecti* of the faith were a constant reproach to the worldly bishops of
the orthodox Church, whom they regularly worsted in argument.
In the end they set up an alternative church of their own and abused
and beat and spat upon the Roman clergy. Something of the feeling
against the Church that existed in the south may be seen from the
writings of the troubadour Peire Cardinal of Puy. "If Black Friars
may win salvation of God by much eating and by the keeping of
women, White Friars by fraudulent encroachments, Templars and
Hospitallers by pride, canons by lending money at usury—if these
come thus to salvation, for fools I hold St Peter and St Andrew,
who suffered for God such grievous torments . . . Kings, emperors,
dukes, counts and knights were wont to rule the world: but now I
see clerks holding dominion over it by robbery, deceit, hypocricy,
force and extortion . . . The priests call themselves shepherds, but are
in truth murderers." This was written in the Age of Faith early in
the thirteenth century. But the Roman Church had its revenge in
the Albigensian Crusade, just as the northern nobility who led it
were only too eager at the prospect of plunder, loot and carnage
offered by the rich and "decadent" civilization of the south. "Kill
all," Simon de Montfort is reported to have said, "God will know
his own."

[5] The Romans still seem the most important inhabitants of the south.
Their influence at such places as Orange, Arles and Nîmes is quite in-
effaceable.

There is no evidence that Richard was affected by Catharist beliefs. His father, being sceptical in religious matters, evidently kept an open mind, or he would not have given asylum to Catharist refugees, but Richard always appears strictly orthodox. It was his mother, with her Courts of Love at Poitiers, who introduced the cult of courtly love to the north, while his half-sister, Marie de Champagne, patronized its principal exponent Chrestien de Troyes, whose long poetical romances were the very fountainhead of chivalrous love.

But the most interesting thing about this peculiar cult is that, contrary to all their frenzied protestations and the green and yellow melancholy in which they pined away for each other, the very last thing these lovers really wanted was the realization of their love. Anything so mundane would be sheer desecration of their ideal, and (in literature at any rate), lovers adored their ladies from afar as they worshipped, or should have worshipped, the Virgin. It was in fact a religion of love with its own fantastic rites. But if, carried away by their madness, a pair of lovers ever came together like Tristram and Isolt or Lancelot and Guenevere, then ruin and disaster followed and they suffered the tortures of the damned. What they really desired was self-immolation, death itself, as Wagner realized in *Tristan und Isolde* when he resolved the theme of sickly love-longing into that of no less sickly death-longing. Though this may seem typically German, Denis de Rougemont has shown in his *L'Amour et l'Occident* that it was the actual basis of chivalrous love.[6]

Farther north, the *trouvères* were more realistic. "Sir," says Charlemagne's daughter to the knight who is staying at her father's palace, "I love none but you. Summon me into your bed some night, my whole body will be at your disposal." And though Sir Amales politely declines, Amis nevertheless gets into bed with him, reflecting, as she does so: "I do not care what people think nor if my father beats me daily, for he is too handsome a man."[7] Such an avowal would have been unthinkable in the south, where the Cathars preached their Manichaean condemnation of the flesh. Courtly love did, however, express one side of the intense idealism of the Middle

[6] "I do not wish to be cured of the pain of love," wrote Guiraut d'Espanha, "on the contrary, the more I suffer, the greater my delight." In this, chivalrous love differed from the poetry of romantic love that was being written in India at this time, in such works as Jayadeva's *Gita Govinda*, where, to say the least, frustration is not the lover's goal. See W. G. Archer, *The Loves of Krishna*.

[7] Sidney Painter, *French Chivalry*.

Ages, just as gothic architecture and the Crusades were expressive of the more orthodox side. For the twelfth century was the most creative and romantic of the medieval centuries. To it we owe the whole Arthurian cycle, a great part of Chartres and many other cathedrals—for the building of which princes and nobles harnessed themselves to the stone masons' carts and worked with the labourers; the *Tristan* of Béroul (which in its freshness and innocence is so very different from Wagner), the half-pagan songs of the wandering scholars and that passion for enlightenment which sent thousands of young men walking the roads that led to Paris, where the *Quartier Latin* soon grew up on the left bank of the Seine and where Abelard, the divine doctor, preached. For during the twelfth century the threatening figure of God the Father, and the no less ominous Son, was already giving way before the tender smile of the Virgin, just as mystery, massiveness and weight were giving place to light and ever more light, to soaring clusters of slender pillars and the flying-rib vaulting of the new gothic style. It was the century during which Europe was reborn, the first and perhaps the greatest renaissance.

What part Richard Coeur de Lion had in this twelfth-century renaissance we do not know, for posterity has chosen to remember the warrior in him rather than the poet.[8] But this was nevertheless the world that was coming to birth around him as he grew up. He was far more than the plain blunt soldier of tradition, or even the over-grown schoolboy of Sir James Ramsay. The kind of greatness he achieved, however, is another matter. Fielding writes of it in *Jonathan Wild the Great*—the ability to bring the greatest amount of misery and suffering upon mankind. It is the kind of greatness Richard shares with most military heroes. For unless the medieval knight had someone to fight and people to kill there was no point in his existence. One might say of him, as Marlowe says of Tamburlaine, that his "honour consists in shedding blood". This was glory, and in military glory, Gerald of Wales tells us, the knights of France surpassed those of all other nations. They met their match, however, in the Turkish light horsemen in Palestine; but on their own

[8] The Troubadours' eulogies of the Plantagenets were, of course entirely conventional, like those of other court poets, and though music and poetry were regarded as obligatory at every feast, it is questionable, as M. Jeanroy remarks, whether those who were lavishly eating and drinking were in a fit state to appreciate either, or to distinguish the original from the banale. Jeanroy doubts whether Richard ever wrote in Provençal, though of course he must have understood it. (*Poésie lyrique des Troubadours,* I, Chap. 3, La Conts de Poitiers.)

field they were irresistible, till put out of action by the English longbowmen at Crécy. Women, in spite of being idealized in literature, were in an inferior position in the Middle Ages because they could not fight—at least they were not encouraged to do so, though many women went on the crusades and even bore arms—and fighters and prayers, knights and clerks, were the two most honourable classes in medieval society. The function of the rest was to work and obey. During a lord's absence on crusade, however, his wife was left in charge of his property, though, since she was the most vulnerable part of it, he was careful to secure her in a chastity belt before going. Not being similarly impeded himself, he could enjoy the Arabic arts of love while rescuing the Holy Sepulchre.

It is well known that the civilization of the south of France owed much to Moorish Spain, where the Courts of the Moslem princes were the great centres of learning and poetry and where ladies were held in high honour.[9] This being so, Richard's first introduction to the Moslems must have been as harbingers of courtesy, poetry and enlightment—for in nearly all ways they were at this date far in advance of their Christian neighbours. His awareness of this would account for his eagerness to make personal contact with Saladin as soon as he reached the Holy Land, where the warmth and courtesy of his relations with Malek el Adil, or Saphadin, as the Crusaders called him, was something that the French and German knights could never understand. Being plain, blunt men, for them the only good Saracen was a dead Saracen.

The principal attribute of medieval chivalry was prowess, a quality for which the condition of twelfth-century France was itself a forcing ground. When there was, for the moment, no war, tourneys were organized by the nobility, in which the men fought in earnest, watched by the ladies. Unlike the tournaments of the next century, weapons were not blunted and there were actual battles between cavalry and infantry, without any of the rules that later kept jousting in the lists on a more gentlemanly level. The "meaner sort" were slaughtered wholesale. But a low-class soldier who killed a noble on the other side was afterwards hanged by his own overlord.

There was usually no lack of real war, however, and the war of the twelfth century, with its catapults and siege towers, had not changed very much since the time of the Romans. About the only

---

[9] The Arab chronicler Ousâma was disgusted at seeing the Christian knights amusing themselves by setting old women to run after a greased pig. Their manners, he said, were appalling. Coulton, *Mediaeval Panorama*, p. 244.

innovation was the crossbow. The balista was an outsize crossbow which fired an iron bolt "feathered" with wood, four times as thick as an ordinary arrow, and worked by a crew. Armour had changed, of course, mounted knights wearing a hood, loose shirt (hauberk) and stockings of chain mail, as they appear in the Bayeux tapestry, and carrying a long iron-tipped lance, long sword, battle-axe and triangular shaped shield. Foot-soldiers wore padded leather or quilted coats, and sometimes even steel hauberks. Helmets had changed considerably since early Norman times; some were flat topped, some round, with an extra piece of iron to protect cheeks and chin. On his second Great Seal Richard is shown wearing a complete flat-topped helm, plumed with *planta genesta*, with the face completely shut in except for eye-slits and air-holes. Worn on top of a leather pad and over the mail coif, it must have been very hot indeed, especially in the Midi and the Holy Land. A surcoat was worn over the hauberk to keep it from the wet and as a protection against the heat during the Crusades, and underneath all this was a long skirted garment. By the end of the twelfth century the shield had become quite small.

Apart from the melée, which was a kind of free for all, medieval warfare consisted chiefly of laying siege to towns and almost impregnable castles, when the walls were mined by sappers and battered till they cracked with bores and battering rams—huge tree trunks slung on a framework between uprights. The ram was wheeled to the town or castle walls and a team of men, often as many as sixty, under cover of a penthouse, swung the great beam backwards and forwards against the wall until the mortar loosened. In time the stoutest wall gave way, though the garrison would lower mattresses and baulks of timber to take the shock, or would try to catch the ram and pin it as it swung backwards and forwards, or set it on fire with burning pitch or smash it to bits with great stones. In the assault the attacking army swarmed up ladders or breached the walls from huge wooden towers on wheels, while the defenders shot at them with arrows and barrels of burning pitch and dropped stones and fire through the machicolations. It was all savage and primitive enough, and the wounded usually died of their wounds, howling in agony. Nevertheless war went on more or less incessantly. When castles were not being attacked, the land round about was ravaged and all cultivation systematically destroyed. And since there was a limit to the length of time that feudal vassals could be called upon to serve away from their homes, each noble or prince enlisted armies of mercenary troops, who, having no feelings of responsibility either towards the countries or the people over whose homes they fought, were usually guilty of every sort of atrocity. For some reason, these mercenaries were called Brabantines, though most of them did not come from Brabant, but were recruited from desperate characters of all kinds, outlaws, renegade monks, who, in lieu of pay, were given a free hand to plunder. They were much used by Richard and his brothers in their wars against each other and against their father.

The chief *causus belli* at this time in France was the resentment of the southern nobles at the overlordship of an Angevin, and they took advantage of Henry's difficulties with France during his quarrel with Becket, which began almost as soon as his appointment as archbishop in 1162. It was to secure the Count of Barcelona's help against Raymond of Toulouse that in 1158 Henry betrothed Richard to his infant daughter, just as ten years later, the alliance having served its purpose, he betrothed him to Louis VII's daughter Alais, in order to secure the Vexin—the borderland area between Normandy and the royal domain of France, while to secure the Spanish alliance he married his daughter Eleanor to Alfonso III of Castile. He had already got the frontier fortress of Gisors by marrying his eldest son, Henry, to Louis's daughter Margaret. Meanwhile Richard was formally recognized as the future Duke of Aquitaine, Queen Eleanor governing there in his name, and in January 1169 he did homage to Louis for his vast possessions.

The king's quarrel with Becket was brought to a head when he had his eldest son Prince Henry crowned future king of England by Roger Archbishop of York. As the Archbishop of Canterbury alone had the right to crown the king of England or his heir, this was naturally regarded as an outrage, and on his return to Canterbury in December 1170 Becket excommunicated everyone concerned in the coronation.

When the news of Becket's actions reached Henry at his hunting-lodge at Bures, where he was spending Christmas, he cried: "By God's eyes, if all who shared in the coronation of my son are to be excommunicated, I will be counted one of their number. A curse, a curse on the false varlets I have nursed in my household, who leave me thus exposed to the insolence of a fellow that came to my Court on a lame sumpter mule, and now sits without hindrance on the throne itself! Is there none that can be found to avenge me on this upstart clerk?"[11]

[11] Walter of Coventry in *Historical Collections*, ed. by William Stubbs.

"The only way to deal with such a traitor," remarked one of the excommunicated bishops in no very Christian spirit, "is to plait a few withies into a rope and hoist him therewith upon a gallows."

Four knights took the hint. Mounting their horses, they rode post-haste to the coast and though, as soon as their absence was discovered, Henry sent after them, he was too late to stop them crossing over to England, where they appeared before Becket at Saltwood and demanded in the King's name that he absolve the bishops. When Becket replied that it was not for him to raise the ban of excommunication, but the Pope, they abused him as a traitor, went out and armed themselves and shortly afterwards broke noisily into the cathedral during vespers. Laying hold of the archbishop, they tried to drag him outside the church into the cloisters, for at first they shrunk from killing him on his altar steps. But Becket, who had been a soldier himself and was a tall, strong man of commanding presence, flung them off, crying out, "Touch me not, Reginald, thou vile pander!" For reply, Fitz Urse sliced off part of his scalp, almost severing the arm of Edward Grim, the archbishop's future biographer, who tried to ward off the blow with his bare hands. The ruffian de Tracey then struck him, but Becket still stood, wiping the blood from his face, till Richard the Breton struck at his head with such fury that his sword snapped on the pavement. Only then did Becket sink slowly to his knees, murmuring that in the name of Jesus and for the defence of the Church he was willing to die. "And the blood white with brain and the brain no less red with blood, dyed the floor of the cathedral with the white of the lily and the red of the rose, the colours of the Virgin and Mother." Then the subdeacon, Hugh Mauclerk, who had entered the cathedral with the knights, set his foot on the archbishop's neck and, with a sword point, scattered the blood and the brains about the pavement, crying, "Let us away, knights, this fellow will rise no more."

When the terrified monks crept back into the church and turned the archbishop's body over onto its face, they saw a gentle smile on his lips and the eyes closed as if in sleep. Under the body they found Fitz Urse's axe and a small hammer. Beneath the rich vestments they came upon a monk's habit and beneath that a hair shirt and hair drawers, penitential garments that swarmed with lice.

Thomas was dead, but more powerful than he had ever been in his lifetime, for as saint and martyr he now "ruled from the tomb". The townsfolk of Canterbury came and smeared their eyes with his most precious blood and carried away as much of it as they could in little bottles and tore fragments from his clothing. Soon miracles were reported to be taking place near the spot where the archbishop had been butchered. The whole tragedy in its brutality and its idealism, is typical of the twelfth century.[12]

Henry wailed aloud when the news reached Normandy, as well he might do, for he had lost in his struggle with the Church. Dressing himself in sackcloth and scattering ashes on his head, he shut himself up in a room for three days and when not weeping he appeared completely stupified. Sometimes he could be heard screaming, as if possessed by devils. Then he fled to Wales and hid himself among the forests and the hills from the impending excommunication. From Wales he went to Ireland, to sate his madness by further slaughter. He saved himself from excommunication by promising to make compurgation and to submit to penance. But when the papal legate arrived in Normandy to enforce these decrees, Henry was out of reach, for before leaving for England he had given orders that the ports should be closed to papal envoys. For five months a persistent contrary wind made any communication with Ireland impossible.

When Henry returned to Normandy in May 1172 he brought the news that he had extended the boundaries of the Church by his conquest of Ireland for Rome. On Sunday, May 21st he swore publicly in the cathedral of Avranches that he neither commanded nor willed Becket's death, adding that he was nevertheless the unwilling cause of it by his angry words. For penance he was to go on a crusade to the Holy Land within three years, unless absolved by the Pope. But he refused to harm Becket's murderers, pointing out, surely not without irony, that they were the prisoners of the Church and therefore outside his jurisdiction.

At the time of this tragedy, which rocked the whole Christian world, Richard was thirteen. He may have been a spectator of at least part of it and witnessed both his father's terrifying rage and no less terrifying remorse, which must have quite ruined the Christmas party at Bures. Two years later, in June 1172, he was installed at the age of fifteen as Duke of Aquitaine in the abbey church of St Hilary at Poitiers. The sacred lance and banner were given to him by the Archbishop of Bordeaux and the Bishop of Poitiers. After the ceremony, he entered Limoges with great pomp and the ring of St Valeria was placed on his finger—a symbol that he was invested in

[12] Edward Grim, The Murder of Thomas Becket, *Engl. Hist. Documents, 1142–1189,* ed. by David Douglas and George W. Greenaway.

the dukedom not by the king of France but by the saints of the land represented by the local clergy.

II

REBELLION

In apportioning his domains among his sons during his lifetime, Henry II, Lear-like, was the architect of his own ruin. But, unlike Lear, he only gave them titles without either the control of the lands or their revenues. No arrangement could have been more calculated to create jealousy and bad feeling, especially as when all the available land had been divided up among the elder brothers there was nothing left for the old king's favourite, John, who, therefore, came to be known as John Lackland. But when Henry assigned to John, as his marriage portion, some castles in Anjou which already belonged to his eldest brother, Henry the Young King fled to Paris, and Eleanor, who had come to hate her second husband as she had hated her first, incited her sons to open warfare. France, Scotland, and a few Anglo-Norman barons joined the revolt, but in the main both barons and clergy remained loyal to the king. For when Eleanor was found making her way from Poitou to Paris in man's attire, she was arrested by the loyal Poitevins and sent under escort to Henry at Rouen.

What he lacked in faithfulness as a husband, Henry made up for by an almost pathetic attachment to his sons, though Gerald of Wales tells us that he was jealous of them as they grew older, for he could not bear to think of any of them as his successor. At the coronation banquet of his eldest son, Henry served him like an esquire. But the Young King observed: "It is but right, for my father is a king while his was only a count!" At the time this was evidently regarded as a witticism. Eleanor, however, resented the fact that Henry took the same sort of freedom that she had always allowed herself within the marriage bond, and revenged herself not only by inciting his sons to revolt, but by intriguing against him with her first husband! Unfortunately for her, Henry was no Louis and, on his return to England, shut her up at Old Sarum for the rest of the reign, except for brief periods when her presence was required at such family reunions as Christmas.

Henry had already been warned at Limoges by Raymond Count of Toulouse, that his wife and sons had formed a conspiracy against him, but he had made light of it and left Richard and Geoffrey in Aquitaine with their mother. Early in the summer of 1173 they joined their eldest brother in France and there pledged them "not to forsake the king of France, nor to make any peace with their father save through him (Louis) and the French barons". In return Louis swore "to help the Young King and his brothers to the utmost of his power to gain possession of the kingdom of England". Since he was already crowned, Louis told the younger Henry, he should by rights be king of England in place of his father. At the same time, Louis added his voice to Eleanor's and aided and abetted Richard and Geoffrey in their grievances. But Henry's vassals in France did not follow their example and revolt, though for a short time early in 1173 it looked as if the whole Angevin empire was about to disintegrate.

In England those barons who remembered the good old days of anarchy under Stephen still objected to submitting to the law. They objected especially to the garrisoning of their castles with royal troops, still more to the taxes they were required to pay. In France Henry the Young King was already acting the part of king of England and making grants of territories and pensions to his supporters on both sides of the Channel, grants which he sealed with a new seal made for him by Louis' orders.

Meanwhile Henry II, with his headquarters at Rouen, appeared quite indifferent to the plots that were hatching out their cockatrices all round him and gave himself up to his passion for hunting, relying upon his 20,000 Brabantine mercenaries to deal with the trouble when it came. But when Louis laid siege to Verneuil in July, Henry suddenly bestirred himself, crossed over to England, collected his treasure and his adherents, issued instructions for the defence of the realm against the rebels and the menace of Scotland, and was back at Rouen before his enemies had discovered his absence. Towns and castles surrendered to him as soon as he appeared in the field. After the siege of Arques and the death of the Count of Boulogne in July, Philip of Flanders withdrew his forces. Henry went to the relief of Verneuil, which Louis, having asked for a twenty-four-hour truce, burnt down. Then, not daring to face Henry at the proposed conference, turned tail and fled.

Henry returned to Rouen at the end of August and sent his mercenaries to deal with the discontented Breton gentry, who were busy burning and wasting the border districts of Fougères and Avranches. Marching from Rouen and covering a distance of at least a hundred and seventy miles in two days, he took the castle of Dol on August 23rd, and the rebellion in the north came to an end.

✗ After spending September at Le Mans, Henry returned to Gisors to meet Louis in the hope of reaching some agreement with his sons, offering them half his realms in wealth and honours, saving only the actual government of them. The Young King might have half the revenues of England with four castles, if he chose to live there, or half the revenues of Normandy, with the whole of those of Anjou and three castles, if he preferred to live abroad; Richard might have half the revenues of Aquitaine, with three castles; and Geoffrey could have the inheritance of his bride, Constance of Brittany, as soon as the marriage was celebrated. A sufficiently generous offer, one would have thought. But Louis advised the king's sons not to accept it and the meeting broke up in an uproar when the Earl of Leicester not only abused the king, but drew his sword against him. The earl then hurried off through Flanders, collecting troops as he went, and sailed for England. Landing in Suffolk, he made for Hugh Bigod's castle at Framlingham. The king's men, under Humphrey de Bohun and Richard de Lucy, were at that time in the north, chasing the Scottish king back over the border. De Bohun then turned south and intercepted the Earl of Leicester at Fornham and, in spite of overwhelming odds, defeated him utterly, assisted by the local population of Suffolk who, armed with flails and pitchforks, were only too glad of an opportunity to set about the Norman, French and Flemish knights. The Early of Leicester, captured with his wife, was sent over to Henry, who imprisoned them at Falaise, to keep the rebel Earl of Chester company.

Young Henry and Count Geoffrey were still at the French Court, however. Before the end of 1173 Richard, knighted by Louis, had returned to Aquitaine, which in his absence had been left as a prey to the mercenaries. Though not yet sixteen, he at once took control of the situation and soon had a considerable force of knights at his command. In May 1174 his men occupied Saintes. But his father, who was at Poitiers at the time, after a triumphal progress through Maine and Anjou, drove them out again. After storming several other rebel fortresses, Henry returned to Normandy, leaving Richard at large. In Normandy he heard that the French fleet under the

Count of Flanders aided by his eldest son, had assembled at Gravelines to invade England, while an advance guard of Flemings had already landed in Essex and, led by Hugh Bigod, had given up Norwich to fire and sword.

The centre of the rebellion had now shifted from Normandy to England. So, on 7 July 1174, with Eleanor and Margaret of France, and Alais and Constance, the fiancées of Richard and Geoffrey—all now virtually prisoners and to be used at his pleasure—his son John and his daughter Joan, with the Earls of Leicester and Chester, the king crossed over to England from Barfleur and landed at Southampton after a very rough and perilous passage. Having seen his prisoners and hostages safely secured, Henry at once set out on a pilgrimage to Canterbury. Riding hard and only taking bread and water, he reached Canterbury on July 12th and, dismounting before the church of St Dunstan outside the west gate, exchanged his royal robes for a pilgrim's woollen weeds. He then walked barefoot to the cathedral church, where he flung himself in an agony of prayer and repentance before the tomb of his old friend and enemy in the crypt. Having received absolution, he knelt down with his head and shoulders inside one of the apertures of the tomb, the sarcophagus being left partly open so that pilgrims could see the coffin, and baring his back, submitted himself to be scourged by the assembled bishops and monks. Each bishop gave him five formal stripes and each monk three, the number of monks present being about eighty. He spent all that day and half the night in prayer before the tomb, neither taking food nor going out to relieve nature. After lauds at midnight, he visited the altars and saints' tombs in the choir of the church and then returned to the crypt. At dawn he heard Mass and was given some holy water to drink in which relics of St Thomas had been dipped, and a little more to carry away with him in a phial, and then he rode on his way rejoicing to London.

Four days later, news was brought to him that the king of Scots, William the Lion, his most dangerous enemy, had been taken, after a ravaging tour of Northumberland and Westmorland, and was in chains at Richmond Castle. By the end of July all the other distempered lords had made their submission. In three weeks Henry had restored England to peace. Louis, however, with the Young King and the Count of Flanders, had taken advantage of his absence to besiege Rouen. Unable to take the town, Louis fell back upon the underhand expedient of attacking it under cover of a truce. But the citizens manned the walls and repulsed him.

While Henry was busy in England, Richard was equally busy in Aquitaine, killing those who remained loyal to his father, and besieging and sacking their castles. At one time he was as far south as Bordeaux. He tried to win the town of La Rochelle to his cause, but the townsfolk shut the gates in his face. On his seventeenth birthday, 8 September 1174, Henry and Louis met once more beneath the great elm at Gisors. But, we read, "they would not come to the settlement because of the absence of Count Richard, who, at that time, was in Poitou making war on the castles and men of his father". Nevertheless a truce was arranged on the understanding that Henry should now subdue his unruly son by force. But "when king Henry was come into Poitou, his son Richard dared not await him, but fled from every place at his approach, abandoning all the fortresses that he had taken, not daring to hold them against his father". And when he heard the terms of the truce and learnt that he was deserted by his brother and Louis, "he came weeping, and fell with his face on the ground at the feet of the king his father, beseeching his forgiveness".

It was never difficult for Henry to forgive his sons. He told Richard to rise and embraced him, and together father and son entered Poitiers. Richard then went to his elder brother and Louis and assured them that he was no longer an obstacle to peace. So peace was signed at Montlouis in Touraine, and Henry's three sons placed themselves at his mercy "and returned to him and to his service as their lord". They also pledged themselves to accept the provision he had made for them and nevermore to require anything from him, save at his pleasure, nor to withdraw themselves from his service. Richard and Geoffrey then did homage to their father "for what he granted and gave them". The treaty was executed at Falaise in October. Early next year, both Richard and Geoffrey did homage to their father again at Le Mans and in April Henry the Young King did homage at Bures.

The king's provision for Richard, however, did not include his reinstatement either as duke of Aquitaine or Count of Poitou. Richard was merely assigned "two fitting dwelling places, where no damage could come to the king in Poitou", together with half the revenues of Poitou. The Treaty of Falaise thus reinstated Henry as the sole ruler of the Angevin empire.

Richard was now commissioned by his father to return to Aquitaine and to see the provisions of the treaty carried out, which ordained the restitution of their lands and castles to those barons who remained loyal to the king, as well as the restitution of their lands to the rebels, though their castles were to be destroyed. But those Aquitainian nobles who had sided with Richard on the promise of large rewards, naturally felt themselves ill-requited when the youth whose cause they had supported set about dismantling their castles.

After spending Easter 1175 in England with his family, Richard returned to France to subdue the rebellious nobles of Aquitaine. He was still only eighteen. He returned to find that Vulgrin of Angoulême had marched into Poitou with a troop of Brabantines, but that the warlike Bishop of Poitiers, exchanging mitre, stole and chausable for chain mail and *chapeau de fer*, and his crozier for a battle-axe, had utterly routed them. Then Richard called out the feudal levies, "and a great multitude of knights from the regions round about flocked to him for the wages that he gave them".

In May 1176 he began marching against Vulgrin's Brabantines and defeated them between St Maigrin and Bouteville, near Cognac. From there he led his victorious troops into the Limousin to settle accounts with Aimar of Limoges, first taking Aimar's castle of Aixe and then Limoges itself after a few days' siege. In June he fell back on Poitiers to meet his elder brother; and then, with Henry, advanced southwards and laid siege to Châteauneuf, which surrendered within a fortnight. After that the Young King, by no means pleased at the spectacle of his brother's military prowess, left him to carry on the war alone.

> And the young king departed and went into Lombardy, and gave his days to tourneys and vain pleasures, leaving all the barons at war with Lord Richard. And Lord Richard laid siege to castles and to towns, and destroyed them, and took lands and burnt and laid them waste; and the young king held tourneys and lived at ease, and slept and disported himself.....[1]

A ten days' siege sufficed for the capture of Moulineuf, and Richard advanced upon Angoulême, within whose walls were Vulgrin and his father, Count William Taillefer IV, Aimar of Limoges and the Viscounts of Ventadour and Chabanais. After a six days' siege, Count William was forced to surrender to young Richard not only his city but his person and to give hostages for his submission. Richard sent his prisoners over to Winchester, where they fell

[1] Farnell, *The Lives of the Troubadours.*

at the king's feet "and obtained mercy from him", being temporarily reinstated in their possessions. Meanwhile at Poitiers, Henry
the Young King was busy gathering round him those very elements
that had already sided with him against his father in the Great
Rebellion. His chancellor Adam, discovered preparing a confidential
report of these activities for the king, was flogged and imprisoned.

Richard, having reduced northern Aquitaine, turned south to
spend Christmas at Bordeaux. In the new year he marched through
Gascony, taking Dax and Bayonne, and down to St Pierre de Cize
at the foot of the Pyrenees. Taking the castle of St Pierre he was
back at Poitiers by Candlemas. He had made the Basques and
Navarrese swear to keep the peace and not to rob pilgrims on their
way to the shrine of St James of Compostella.

It was, however, by his capture of the fortress of Taillebourg,
hitherto considered impregnable, in May 1179, that Richard first
impressed his contemporaries with his military genius. Never before
had a hostile force so much as looked upon the castle. Taillebourg,
in fact, like Chinon and Loches, was not so much a castle as a small
town perched on the summit of a rock. On three sides it was made
impregnable by Nature. It was girt with a triple ditch, beyond that
was a triple wall, "amply secured with weapons, bolts and bars;
crowned with towers placed at regular intervals, furnished with
handy stone ready for casting from every loophole; well-stocked
with victuals, filled with a thousand men ready to fight, and held
by Geoffrey of Rancogne, one of the most obstinate of the Aquitanian
rebels."[2]

Richard's strategy did not include a direct attack. Instead, in the
implacable manner of William the Conqueror, he began devastating
the surrounding country in order to cut off supplies, carrying off and
burning farm-produce and burning down villages. After he had
done his worst, he pitched his tents on the outskirts of the town, to
the great alarm of the townsfolk. At the end of a week, the defenders were provoked into making a sortie, which was just what
Richard had been waiting for. He fell upon them at the very gates,
and, as they dispersed and retired, he made a sudden dash into the
town itself, giving it up to fire and sword. After helplessly watching
these ravages for two days, the defenders of the castle surrendered and
Richard levelled its walls to the ground. The result of this was the
complete submission of Geoffrey of Rancogne and Vulgrin of
Angoulême. Richard then demolished the walls and defences of their

[2] Kate Norgate, *Richard the Lion Heart*.

cities and sailed for England, where he was received with great honour by his father.

Christmas 1182 was celebrated at Caen with the old king surrounded by his family. Richard brought the troubadour Bertran de Born. The good cheer, however, seems to have been accompanied with little enough good will. Afterwards Bertran complained that it was a very dull party indeed. Henry's Court, he said, was not worthy to be called a Court at all—"no gab and laughter, no giving of presents". As a matter of fact, Bertran had been given the cold shoulder by Richard's sister Matilda of Saxony. "*La fille d'Henri II n'avait pas l'humeur facile des dames de l'Aquitaine,*" says Alfred Richard, "*et elle accuellit avec froideur les avances du troubadour, qui ne craignait pas de déshabiller la belle duchesse dans ses vers, ainsi qu'il avait coutume de la faire à l'égard des dames dont il soupçonnait les charmes par avance.*"[3] The ruffled troubadour therefore, revenged himself by making as much trouble as he could in the Plantaganet family, playing upon the Young King's resentment that he was only king in name and inflaming his jealousy of Richard. Calling young Henry a mockery king, he pointed out that Richard was, after all, effective ruler in Aquitaine, where, he hinted, the barons were only waiting the chance to be revenged upon him for his iron rule. By rights, said Bertran, it was the Young King who should be ruling in Aquitaine, not Richard, his younger brother, who, on the old king's death, might cut adrift from England altogether.

So Prince Henry went to his father at Le Mans and demanded that Richard and Geoffrey should do him homage, as heir apparent, for their continental domains. Geoffrey made no objection and did homage for Brittany. But when it came to Richard, young Henry refused to endorse his possession of Aquitaine, saying that he himself was the rightful representative of the Aquitaine barons. The king overruled this claim, however, and told Richard to swear fealty to his brother. At this point Richard lost his temper and declared that as children of the same parents he and his brother were equals and that if his brother had a right to his father's lands, then he had as good a right to his mother's, and that he would be damned if he would kneel down to him for Aquitaine. "Leaving nought but insults and threats behind him, he then left the court and hurried to his own duchy and began to strengthen its defences." But this was

[3] *Histoire des ducs et des comtes de Poitou*, II, 210.

too much for the old king, and he gave young Henry a full commission to "rise up and subdue Richard's pride."

In the meantime there was news of a fresh revolt among the Poitevin barons, and Henry, however angry he might be with Richard, could hardly allow his brothers to fight against him at such a juncture. Accordingly early in 1183, he sent young Henry and Geoffrey to reason with the rebels at Limoges. Instead of reasoning with them they joined them. Aimar of Limoges tried to terrorize the citizens into joining the league against Richard and, at a signal from Geoffrey, a large body of mercenaries from Brittany began plundering and burning Richard's lands. Richard retaliated by making similar raids into Brittany and by executing all prisoners.

Then another band of mercenaries, employed by Aimar, came up from Gascony in February and were besieging a church at Gorre, near Limoges, when Richard suddenly fell upon them. He had ridden for days without stopping from a castle somewhere beyond Poitiers and such was the suddenness of his attack that his enemies scattered. Many were taken prisoner and Richard struck down the nephew of the commander of the mercenaries, Raymond, with his own hand. Aimar and the rest escaped only because the horses of Richard's troop were too exhausted to pursue them. But the prisoners were dragged to Aixe, where some were cut down with the sword, some drowned and some blinded. Richard was determined to make an example of them.

Such methods did not make him any more popular. The revolt spread and many castles were given up to the Young King. Richard sent an urgent message to his father, but as Henry approached Limoges he was greeted with a flight of arrows, the townsfolk rushed out and a fierce struggle took place until the king's banner was recognized. Henry withdrew to Aixe and that night the Young King came to him and tried to explain the peculiar greeting he had given to him at Limoges. Young Henry then returned to Limoges and the townsfolk swore fealty to him and began to erect walls and ramparts, turrets and battlements round the city with the wood from hastily demolished churches. More mercenaries swept across the country and engaged King Henry's men while the troops of Philip II the new king of France poured in from the north.[4]

[4] Louis VII had died in 1180, leaving Philip with a royal domain hemmed in by the Angevin Empire in the west and by the Kingdom of Arles in the south-east. Philip was also overshadowed by the power of his uncles. William Archbishop of Reims, Henry Count of Champagne and Theobald Count of Blois and Chartres.

Fortunately for Richard and his father there was no concerted plan of attack and all these forces, overrunning Perigord, the Angoumois and Saintonge, wasted their energy in plunder and rapine, desecrating shrines and sending the monks flying in all directions with the relics of their patron saints, as in the time of the Visigoths and Vandals.

While all this was going on the Young King kept up a pretence of negotiating with his father in order to give Geoffrey time to raise more troops, at one moment saying that he had taken the Cross and was going on a crusade, the next moment sueing for peace on his knees and promising hostages. But when the king sent for the hostages his men were shot at. Then Geoffrey asked his father for a twenty-four hour truce so that he might visit his brother in the citadel of Limoges and bring him to reason. But when the truce was granted he went to Limoges and plundered the shrine of St Martial's Abbey, carrying off a large quantity of gold and silver.

At last King Henry lost patience. Calling up the feudal levies of his other domains, he marched to Limoges, broke down the bridge behind him and began a regular siege. The siege dragged on from early March to midsummer. Shortly before Easter, however, the Young King occupied Angoulême with mercenaries hired on the proceeds of the plundered shrine of St Martial. But when he returned to Limoges he was greeted by the townsfolk with showers of stones.

In contrast to the duplicity of his brothers, Richard's conduct appears honest and straightforward. After joining his father in the siege of Limoges, he marched against his brother's mercenaries, who were still at large in the Saintonge and the Angoumois, and chased them pell mell across western Poitou into Brittany. "When the game is played out," said Bertran de Born, who was still writing *sirventes* in support of the Young King and his league against Richard, "we shall know which of the king's sons is to have the land. The young king would have soon conquered if the Count were not so well practised at the game; but he shuts them in so fast and presses them so hard that he has recovered Saintonge by force, and delivered the Angoumois as far as the border of Finisterre. . . . Hunted and wounded wild boar saw we never more furious than he is, yet he never swerves from his course."

Among those pledged to the league against Richard were the immensely powerful Duke of Burgundy and the Count of Toulouse. Bertran cried out in delight that the war begun in Limousin would soon spread all over France, Normandy and Flanders, till not a pack-horse would be seen on the roads.

We shall see battle axes and swords a-battering coloured haumes and a-hacking through shields at entering melee; and many vassels smiting together, whence there run free the horses of the dead and wrecked. And when each man of prowess shall be come into the fray he thinks no more of (merely) breaking heads and arms, for a dead man is worth more than one taken alive.

I tell you I find no such savour in eating butter or sleeping, as when I hear cried "On them!" and from both sides hear horses neighing through their head-guards, and hear shouted "To aid! To aid" and see the dead with lance truncheons, the pennants still on them, piercing their sides.

Barons! put in pawn castles, and towns and cities before anyone makes war on us;

Papiol, be glad to go speedily to "Yea and Nay", and tell him there's too much peace about.[5]

"Yea and Nay" was Bertran's nickname for Richard and could apparently be made to signify either infirmity of purpose or the inflexible purpose of a man of few words, according to how Bertran felt about him at the moment. Alternatively, the name could be taken as having a much deeper significance and as indicating what we now call a split personality. After all, Bertran was widely feared for his tongue and his ability to tell people unpalatable home-truths in his *sirventes*. His names for Henry the Young King and Geoffrey of Brittany were respectively "Sailor" and "Rassa,", but these do not give us much enlightenment about their characters.

Early in June 1183, after doing as much damage as he could, capturing Aixe and plundering Grammont (where his father had planned to be buried), sacking the monastery of La Couronne near Angoulême and pillaging Rocamadour, the most famous holy place of Aquitaine, "Sailor" suddenly fell ill and was carried to a blacksmith's cottage at Martel. Weakened by dysentery, he begged his father to come to him; but Henry had had enough and refused to come, suspecting a trap.

[5] Ezra Pound, *The Spirit of Romance*, pp. 47–8. This poem is recreated in Pound's *Personae* as *Sestina: Altaforte*.

The younger Henry was preparing a proper Plantagenet repentance. He asked to have his cloak, with its Crusader's badge laid across his shoulders. Then he gave it to William Marshall to be carried to the Holy Land and told those about him to take off his soft raiment, clothe him in a hair shirt and put a rope round his neck, with which he bade the assembled clergy drag him out of bed and lay him on a bed of ashes. Lying there, with a stone at his head, as if already in his grave, he received the last sacraments, kissed his father's ring, and died. He had requested to be buried at Rouen.

✱When King Henry heard of his death he was overwhelmed with grief, and told the clergy of Caen to excommunicate all those who were making trouble between him and his sons.

✱The Young King's death, which made Richard heir to the throne of England, was lamented on all hands by the poets to whom he had been especially generous, and Bertran de Born wrote his noble *Planh for the Young English King*, translated by Ida Farnell and also by Ezra Pound in *Personae*:

> If all the pain, and misery, and woe,
>   The tears, the losses with misfortune fraught
> That in this dark life man can ever know,
>   Were heaped together—all would seem as naught
> Against the death of the young English king;
>   For by it youth and worth are sunk in gloom,
>   And the world dark and dreary as a tomb,
> Reft of all joy, and full of grief and sadness . . .
>
> Bloodthirsty Death, that bring'st us bitter woe!
> Well may'st thou boast, since that earth's noblest peer
> To thy dark realm a prisoner must go.[6]

✱The Young King, who died at the age of twenty-eight, was reputed to be the most fascinating of Henry's sons and Walter Map wrote that in spite of his treason against a most lenient father, chivalry, which had almost perished from the world before the Prince's time, was elevated to a higher level of perfection by his example. It is certainly difficult for us, with our different standards, to see quite where his great merit lay, if we are to judge him by his recorded deeds.

✱His death was, however, the end of the league against Richard, who continued implacably to hunt down its other adherents in Perigord. By the end of June Richard was besieging Bertran de Born at

[6] Farnell, *The Lives of the Troubadours*, p. 110-11.

Hautefort. Bertran surrendered after a week and Richard deprived him of his castle and sent him to the king as a prisoner.

"You were wont to boast of possessing more wits than you ever needed to use," Henry said to him. "What has become of them now?"

"Seigneur," replied Bertran, weeping, "*Le jour où le vaillant jeune roi votre fils mourût, je perdis le savoir, le sens et la connaissance.*"

The king burst into tears and said that for the love of his dead son he would grant Bertran his liberty and restore to him his château and all his goods. He also gave him five hundred marks in gold to repair the damage he had sustained in the siege. When Bertran returned to Hautefort, Richard gave him the kiss of peace and Bertran promised that for the future he would find him "as true as any silver". He was as good as his word, for he now knew which of the king's sons was to have the land.[7]

III

FATHER AND SON

In September 1183 Richard received a summons from his father to come to Normandy. On his arrival Henry demanded that he give up Aquitaine in favour of his younger brother John. It was as though the old king wanted to create the very situation between Richard and John as had been the cause of so much trouble between Richard and the Young King. Shocking as this proposal appeared to Richard, it was evidently based on the idea that the head of the family—and Richard was now heir to the crown—should always have direct control of the territories Henry had inherited from his parents—Anjou, Normandy and England, Brittany and Aquitaine devolving upon the junior branches of the house. In any case, Henry seems to have argued, Richard was only acting as his lieutenant in Aquitaine—conveniently forgetting that Richard had already been formally invested as duke and had done homage for his duchy to the king of France, as his feudal overlord. He could hardly have

[7] L. Clédat, *Du rôle historique de Bertran de Born.*

planned to put John, who was not yet seventeen, as ruler over the quarrelsome barons of the south. The request was therefore probably only part of a long term policy to come into effect after his death, when Richard should be ruling in his stead. Nevertheless, though he had tacitly recognized Richard as his heir, he had not yet openly acknowledged him.

It is natural that Richard should have been outraged by such a proposal. Aquitaine came to him through his mother, and for the last eight years he had been fighting to hold it. It was too much to ask him now to give it up to John, even though John was to hold it from him as a feudal fief. Richard doubtless saw this as the first move on his father's part to oust him in favour of his younger brother—for there could be no question which of his sons Henry preferred, just as there was no doubt which of her sons Eleanor had always favoured most.

Diplomatically, Richard asked for time to think the matter over. But that evening, as he rode back to Poitou, he sent word to his father that as long as he lived no one but himself should ever hold the duchy of Aquitaine. So Henry, after alternately threatening and beseeching him all the winter—saying that if he would not give up all Aquitaine, then perhaps he would let John have at least part of it—he gave John permission to lead an army into Poitou to carve out an inheritance for himself. At the same time he substituted John for Richard as the betrothed of Alais of France, Philip having promised to renounce his claims to the Vexin (the disputed territory between the domains of Normandy and the Île de France) if his sister's marriage was celebrated without delay.

As might have been foreseen, Geoffrey of Brittany joined John in the invasion of Poitou. So Richard retalliated with an attack on Brittany. To the feudal barons it was so much more exciting to hunt their own kind than boars and stags, especially when it was accompanied by pillage and rapine. But there does not seem to have been any actual encounter between the brothers in the field.

Towards the end of the year, Henry, thinking that this sort of thing had gone on long enough, summoned his three sons to England, and, on St Andrew's Day 1184, staged a family reunion at Westminster. Even Eleanor was let out of prison for Christmas, and the festival was held at Windsor, with all the family including Henry and Matilda of Saxony and their children. After Christmas Richard went back to Aquitaine and Eleanor was sent back to prison.

Early in the new year Henry knighted John, now nineteen years old, and sent him over to Ireland as Governor. But there John and his young friends laughed at the unfamiliar clothes of the Irish lords and pulled their beards. He also replaced old and experienced settlers by his favourites, robbed Irish allies of their land and spent his soldier's pay on feasting and other amusements, till the Irish lords rebelled and his men grew mutinous. After nine months John was recalled. Nevertheless his father, far from being angry with him, applied to the Pope for authority to crown his darling king of Ireland, and Urban II sent him a crown of peacock's feathers.

At the end of January 1185, Heraclius, the Patriarch of Jerusalem, accompanied by the Grand Master of the Hospital, the Grand Master of the Temple having died on the way, landed at Dover to make a last despairing appeal to Henry for help against the attacks of Saladin, and to offer him the crown of Jerusalem in succession to his second cousin Baldwin IV, a childless leper. They brought with them the Banner of the Holy Cross, the keys of the Sepulchre, and letters from the Pope gently reminding Henry of his pledge to take the Cross within three years of his absolution for the murder of Becket. The Pope also laid stress on the family connexion of the Counts of Anjou with Palestine. Henry received the deputation at Reading, where Heraclius gave such an account of the tottering Kingdom of Jerusalem as moved his audience to tears.

The Latin kingdom of Jerusalem had stood for a century guarded by the military Orders of fighting monks, the Templars and Hospitallers, but since the fall of Edessa in 1147 its history had been one of disruption and decay. For the Counts of Edessa, Antioch, Tripoli and the other great fiefs into which the Holy Land had been divided after the first and second crusade were jealous of each other and pursued their own interests regardless of their feudal overlord, the king of Jerusalem, and the unity of the kingdom. They made separate treaties with the Moslems and lived in the state of oriental princes, only too delighted to have shaken off the semi-barbarism of Christendom. But unfortunately, what with the climate and the eastern diseases to which they were especially prone, they were always dying off, so that the chief offices were frequently in the hands of women and minors. During the twelfth century Jerusalem had had eleven kings. That the kingdom held together at all was mainly due to the military Orders, who were inflamed by a fanatical hatred of the paynim and prided themselves on scarcely having time to wash in their zeal for Christ.

Baldwin VI, whose disease was symptomatic of the state of his kingdom, had two daughters, one of whom, Sibylla, was married to William Longaspata, Marquis of Montferrat, the regent. When William died, Sibyl married Guy of Lusignan, who had been turned out of his lands in Poitou by Henry II after trying to kidnap Queen Eleanor. But the other nobles complained that Hugh, while a good soldier, was no good at dealing with such subtle and cultivated enemies as the Moslems and the Byzantine Greeks. So Baldwin was forced to remove him in favour of Raymond of Tripoli. It was at this point that Baldwin, as a last desperate expedient, offered the crown of Jerusalem to Henry II of England. And now that Saladin had united the Moslem world in a holy war against the Christian colonists, only Henry, said Heraclius, as the most powerful prince in Christendom could save the situation.

In March Henry called a grand council of bishops and barons at Clerkenwell and put the question to them whether a journey to the Holy Land would be consistent with his coronation oath binding him to keep church and people in peace. The barons unanimously replied that his domains were in too disturbed a condition for him to leave them. Henry therefore refused the crown of Jerusalem, but promised to send men and money. Heraclius then asked if he would not at least send Prince John in his stead. Henry would not hear of that, but promised to discuss the question of a crusade with the king of France.

What followed is related by Ralph Higden, monk of Chester, in his *Polychronicon*, translated by John Trevisa in the fourteenth century. " 'King', quoth the patriarch, 'it is nought that thou dost: we seek and ask a prince, and not money: nigh every land in the world sendeth us money, but no land sendeth us a prince ... Hitherto thou hast reigned gloriously, but hereafter He will forsake thee That thou hast forsaken. Think and have mind what Our Lord hath given thee, and what thou hast given Him again: how thou wert false to the king of France, and slewest St Thomas and now thou forsakest the defence and protection of Christendom.' " The king grew angry and Heraclius offered him his neck, saying, " 'Do by me right as thou didst by Thomas, for me it is as lief to be slain by the king of England as of Saracens in Syria, for thou art worse than any Saracen.' " Henry objected that he dared not leave his lands for fear that his sons would rise against him. "No wonder", rejoined the ungracious patriarch, "for of the Devil they came and to the Devil they shall". And with that he stormed out of the court.

But before leaving England he consecrated the recently built Templar's church in Fleet Street.

When Henry met Philip of Normandy in April, the French king agreed with him that the most they could do for the present was to send money to the Holy Land. He then had Eleanor brought over and reinstated her as Duchess of Aquitaine, at the same time sending word to Richard that he must stop making war on his brother Geoffrey and surrender Poitou and its appurtenances to his mother. Further, he was to come to court and make his submission, otherwise his mother would herself ravage his lands with a great host.

Richard had no alternative but to comply and we are told, "remained with his father, an obedient son". Henry then made a progress through his southern domains, which lasted till November, appointing new castelans to the principal fortresses of Aquitaine, in place of Richard's nominees. But Richard's surrender of Poitou was only nominal and designed as a curb for his too-proud spirit, for such was the new understanding between father and son that when Henry went back to England with Eleanor in April 1186, he left Richard with "an infinite sum of money" and bade him go, together with Alphonso II of Aragon, and subdue the Count of Toulouse. So Richard, "straightway departing from Normandy, collected a great multitude of knights and foot soldiers, with which he invaded the lands of the Count of S. Gilles and not only ravaged, but conquered the greater part of them".

Raymond V, flying from place to place in the face of this savage onslaught, sent messengers to Philip of France imploring his aid. But Philip, who was busy plotting with Geoffrey of Brittany, did not want to quarrel openly with Richard or his father. Besides, Henry had just given his word for the fifth time to hasten the nuptials between Richard and Alais. But when, in August, Geoffrey suddenly died and was buried with royal honours at Notre Dame, Philip—who seems to have had a weakness for all Henry's handsome sons—could scarcely be restrained from leaping alive into the vault, such was the love he bore this unpleasant intriguer, whom he had made Seneschal of France and who was already preparing to throw off all allegiance to his father. Geoffrey left an heir Eleanor, whose wardship Philip now claimed—wardships being a most profitable form of medieval investment. Henry's ambassadors, sent to Paris to discuss this claim, were rudely received and told that their king could expect no security from attack in Normandy as long as Richard continued his war against the Count of St Gilles.

When Henry arrived in Normandy next year, 1187, Richard was there to receive him. At a conference at Aumale in April Philip demanded the return of his sister Alais together with her dowry—that is to say, Gisors and the Vexin—and that Richard should do him homage for Poitou—demands not unreasonable in themselves—since Richard still showed no sign of marrying the unfortunate Alais—but felt to be intolerable by the Plantagenets. Talks were therefore broken off, with bad feeling on both sides.

Mustering his forces at Bourges, Philip marched from the French part of Berry into Aquitaine. Whereupon Henry put four armies in the field under Richard, John, Geoffrey (his bastard son by Rosamond Clifford) and William de Mandeville. When he joined them himself, Philip evacuated Chateauroux and for a fortnight both armies camped facing each other on opposite sides of the Indre. Each side expected the other to cross the river. Instead both armies remained where they were and there was a great deal of obscure scheming and parleying, during which the Count of Flanders privately urged upon Richard the importance, for his future interest, of making a friend of Philip. So Richard followed the Count back into the French lines, where he had a long conference with the French king.

Richard had approached Philip without his father's knowledge, and when Henry heard of it he scented treachery. He therefore sent to Philip himself proposing a two years' truce during which both kings might fulfil their vows and go to the Holy Land. But as soon as the truce was granted, Henry would have none of it. On hearing this, Philip ordered the attack on the English lines to begin at daybreak. News of this only reached Henry an hour or so before the attack was due. He sent for Richard and said, "What shall we do? What councel dost thou give me?" "What councel can I give?" answered Richard. "When thou hast refused the truce which yesterday thou desirest? We cannot ask for it again without great shame." But when he saw his father's distress, he offered to renew the request for a truce, though it meant humiliation.

In the French camp he found Philip already armed for battle. Nobly, he knelt down bareheaded before him and offered him his sword and begged for a truce, promising that should his father break it in any way he would submit his own person for judgement in Paris. Philip reluctantly consented.

Such is the account given by Gervaise of Canterbury and one or two others. Gerald of Wales, however, who was most likely present, says that Henry had in the first place written to Philip proposing that Alais should be given in marriage to John with the counties of Poitou and Anjou and all the other territories held by the English crown, except Normandy, which should remain a part of England as Richard's heritage. Philip sent this letter to Richard, who, instead of facing his father with it—for even he seems to have feared the inflamed bloodshot eyes of the terrible old man—went over to the French lines and arranged a truce on his own terms. The next thing Henry saw was his eldest son riding away with the French king.

The family pattern had, in fact, repeated itself, and Richard had now taken the place occupied successively by the Young King and Geoffrey of Brittany as Philip's ally against his father. For when peace was signed, he went to Paris and became so attached to Philip that the two men even slept together at night, till Henry "marveled what this might be" and sent messenger after messenger to Richard begging him to return. Instead, Richard went to Chinon and seized upon the Angevin treasure, with which he at once began to revictual and fortify his castles in Poitou. Then, as suddenly, he returned impulsively to his father and submitted to him as a penitent "for having listened to evil councels that strove to sew discord between them", and swore fealty to him on the Gospels at Angers, on condition of his being reinstated in Aquitaine.

Early in November 1187, when Richard was at Tours, came the terrible news of the fall of the kingdom of Jerusalem. In the decisive battle of Hattin, on the barren thirsty tableland above Lake Tiberias, Saladin had cut the Christian chivalry to pieces, taken Guy de Lusignan prisoner and put to death all the Knights Templars and Hospitallers who had fallen into his hands. The Franks had now been driven out of all Syria and Palestine, except for Antioch, Tripoli and Tyre where Conrad of Montferrat still held out.

For this state of affairs the Christian colonists had only themselves to blame. A three-year truce had been broken when Reginald de Chatillon, Lord of Hebron and Kerak, unable to repress his piratical instincts, pillaged the caravan of Moslem pilgrims on its way to Egypt. Outraged by such treachery, the sultan called all his emirs together for a final assault on the kingdom of Jerusalem. After Hattin he spared the life of Guy de Lusignan and released him on his word as a knight that he would never take up arms against him again—a pledge which Guy promptly broke. But Reginald Saladin beheaded with his own hand in his tent, finally put out of all patience by his truculent bearing. After that, the coastal cities, Acre, Haifa, Caesarea, Sidon, Beyrout, Ascalon and Gaza, fell in quick succession, and Jerusalem was taken in October 1187.

Meanwhile, in the west, Gregory III sent out an appeal for another crusade. The first prince to respond was Count Richard of Poitou. Richard took the Cross at Tours in November from the hands of the archbishop, without waiting to consult his father. From that moment the whole direction of his life was changed. Relieved at one blow from the endless intrigue and bickering and politics, for which he possessed neither the inclination nor the capacity, he now had one dominating purpose to give direction to all his energies. At last he had something worth while fighting for. It was an event celebrated by the troubadours. "He to whom God gave understanding and strength, and who is honoured with all noble qualities, who is count and will be called king, "sang Aimerie de Belenoi, "he is the first to help and succour the sepulchre in which God was laid. And may God in His great mercy, as He is the true Trinity, guide him and give him protection against the false unbaptized Turks."[8]

What motives impelled the men of the Middle Ages to go on crusade? At best, their motives were mixed. "Behold, without renouncing our rich garments, our station in life, courtesy, and all that pleases and charms, we can obtain honour down here and joy in Paradise," sang Aimerie de Pegulhan. "To conquer glory by fine deeds and escape hell, what count or king could ask more? No more is there need to be tonsured or shaved and lead a hard life in the most strict order if we can revenge the shame which the Turks have done us. Is this not truly to conquer at once land and sky, reputation in the world and with God?"[9] For the Pope had proclaimed a special indulgence for the sins of those who fought as soldiers of Christ. "Now they will go, the valient bachelors who love God and the glory of this world," wrote Count Thibaut of Champagne, "those who wisely wish to go to God, and the rest, the cowards, will remain. Blind indeed is he who does not make once in his life an expedition to succour God and who for so little loses the praise of this world."[10] And they grew lyrical on the subject of the number of Moslem girls in the Holy Land waiting to be baptized—a cere-

[8] H. J. Chaytor, *The Troubadours and England*, p. 53.
[9] Alfred Jeanroy, *La poésie lyrique des troubadours*, II, 208.
[10] *Les Chansons de Croisade*, ed. Joseph Bedier, pp. 171–3.

mony which involved total immersion! There were also tales of Moslem damsels who rescued handsome Christian captives from their father's dungeons and entertained them sumptuously in their own apartments—a situation which provided an admirable opportunity for a little propaganda for the true faith.

When King Henry heard that Richard had taken the Cross he was more than annoyed and for several days would not speak to anyone. But when Richard rejoined him in Normandy, he said, "Thou shouldst by no means have undertaken so weighty a business without consulting me. Nevertheless I will not oppose thy pious design, but will so further it that thou mayest fulfil it right well."

In January 1188 the wrangling of the two kings, Henry and Philip, over the eternal question of the marriage of Alais to Richard, or the return of Gisors and the Vexin to France, was interrupted by the arrival of the Archbishop of Tyre, whose account of the fall of Jerusalem had the effect of temporarily uniting them against the common foe. Both Henry, Philip and the Count of Flanders were so moved by the story that they all took the Cross there and then and agreed to set out for the Holy Land together at the next Easter twelvemonth—that is, Easter 1189. The French were to wear red crosses, the English white and the Flemings green. Carried away by the emotion of the moment, many others also took the Cross and vowed to go to the Holy Land to rescue the Sepulchre.

After sending a request for a safe-conduct for himself and his men through the dominions of the king of Hungary and those of the Western and Eastern Emperors, Henry summoned a Grand Council at Le Mans, at which Richard was present, for the levying of the tax known as the Saladin Tithe—that is, the tenth part of all rents, movables and personal property for one year. On January 29th he sailed from Dieppe and, immediately upon landing in England, called another Council at Geddington, Northamptonshire, for the same purpose. Then Baldwin, Archbishop of Canterbury, went off to preach the crusade in Wales, where there seems to have been an unaccountable lack of enthusiasm.

Though Henry never really intended to go to Palestine himself, he compelled many in England to take the Cross. "For the most part they were of the nobility," says Gerald of Wales, "not only friends, but even those of his own family who were obnoxious to him." In fact, Henry congratulated himself on a diplomatic *coup* of the first order. He had got the French king to pledge himself to go to Palestine—"deceived him and intentionally led him on to bind himself to such a great labour and so perilous an undertaking, whilst, as he said, 'as far as I am concerned, I am free to undertake or to avoid the expedition'." Indeed, he hoped to avoid it by getting absolution from the Pope, as, Gerald remarks, "he had frequently done in many unlawful proceedings". All the same, having privately determined not to go to the Holy Land, Henry began to envy all those who were able to go—"even were it his own son". It was this jealousy of Richard, Gerald tells us, which prevented Henry from naming him as his successor and "caused him unjustly to prefer the younger to the proper heirs to his throne."

There were many obstacles in the way of Richard's departure for the Holy Land. Chief of these was the necessity to secure the succession, for he suspected, quite rightly, that as soon as his back was turned he would be dispossessed in favour of John. Nor could he set out without money. He, therefore, asked his father either to lend him the money on the security of Poitou or to give him leave to raise it himself by pawning Poitou with some safe and trustworthy man. He also asked that he might receive the fealty of the English barons, and of his father's continental lands, as his father's heir, before setting out on his long and perilous journey—"saving in all things the fealty due to his father".

Henry answered that Richard should go to Palestine with him, that they should have in common all things needful for the journey and "that nought should separate them but death". This had a fine sound but actually meant nothing, for Richard knew very well that his father had no intention of going to Palestine. He thereupon began preparations for his own departure and wrote to his brother-in-law William the Good of Sicily (who had married his sister Joan) to ask for his aid in the voyage, saying that he was determined to set out as soon as summer arrived.

His plans were upset by a fresh rebellion in Poitou fomented by his father in order to detain him, and headed by his old enemies Aimar of Angoulême, Geoffrey of Rancogne and Geoffrey of Lusignan, elder brother of King Guy of Jerusalem. It was this Geoffrey who now ambushed and killed one of Richard's dearest friends and gave his lands to Aimar and Geoffrey of Rancogne. Richard retaliated by destroying their castles, burning and wasting their farms and vineyards, and finally besieging them at Taillebourg. He promised to spare their lives on condition that they joined him on the crusade.

But no sooner had he reduced these rebels to submission than Raymond of Toulouse—also incited by Henry—seized upon and mutilated some merchants who were passing through his territory. This had the desired effect of delaying Richard still longer by forcing him to launch a full-scale invasion of Gascony with his Brabantine mercenaries. After capturing seventeen castles and laying waste the entire countryside, he reached the outskirts of Tolouse itself, which so much alarmed Raymond that he offered to give Richard satisfaction in the courts of France. Meanwhile, in support of Raymond, Philip, the other crusader, had invaded Aquitaine, though he beat a hasty retreat on the approach of Richard from the south and Henry from the north in a pincer movement.

Futile as the new war was, feelings were rapidly becoming embittered on both sides. During his campaign in the country of Toulouse, Richard had captured Raymond's lover Peter Seilun and imprisoned him under the most harsh conditions. Raymond retaliated by capturing two knights attached to Henry's household, who were on their way back from a pilgrimage to St James of Compostella, and refused to give them up except in exchange for Peter Seilun. Then he began a treacherous war, laying ambushes for Richard and his men.

While attempting to cut off the return of a foraging party to Chateauroux, which was being held against him by William de Barres, Richard was surprised in the rear by a sudden sortie from the town. Thrown from his horse, he only just managed to escape capture or death through the help of a friendly butcher and eventually rejoined his father with the remnant of his army. When Philip, who had meanwhile invaded Maine, failed to overtake them, he burned down Trou in a rage, though the approaching vintage season compelled him to disband a large part of his army in Berry. The Bishop of Beauvais then began ravaging the Norman borders. When Henry protested, Philip replied that he would not cease from warfare till all Berry and the Vexin were in his hands. An abortive meeting between the kings between Trie and Gisors in October ended by Philip significantly cutting down the great elm under which conferences between the rulers of Normandy and France had traditionally been held, though it was proposed that differences should be settled by a combat of four champions, two from each side. This had to be abandoned because of Richard's anger with William the Marshal for not selecting him as one of the champions. "You are our lord the king's most direct heir," protested William, "it would be an outrage and a crime to risk your life in such a business." "It is true, Richard," his father added, "what he has said is right."

Richard and his father now attacked Mantes, held by William de Barres, and Richard was able to avenge his humiliation at Chateauroux by taking de Barres prisoner. But de Barres broke his parole and escaped—a dishonourable act that was to have consequences later on.

Next day Richard left his father and went into Berry, where Philip followed him in October, after another abortive conference with Henry at Chatillon, on the border of Touraine and Berry. Richard now opened negotiations on his own account, offering to submit his quarrel with Raymond to the judgement of the French Court and in order that peace might be made between his father and the king of France. His proposal, however, displeased his father and Philip sought to impose on him conditions so unpalatable that Richard was driven to call him "a vile recreant".

All the money that had been collected for the crusade had already been spent and Henry was compelled to disband his mercenaries. The rest mysteriously melted away. When Philip also disbanded his armies, the Counts of Flanders and Blois began to have scruples about fighting brother crusaders. From Richard's point of view the war was doubly futile, for he needed Philip's help to secure his right to the succession against John, and without Philip's friendship he could hardly leave Europe. He therefore got the two kings to meet once more on 8 November 1188 at Bonmoulins. Before the conference he had a private interview with Philip, and in fact, arrived at the meeting-place in his company. Philip had made it clear that his help depended upon Richard marrying his sister Alais, who was still kept by Henry at the English court, though, of course, it was in his interest to keep father and son at loggerheads.

The Conference of Bonmoulins lasted three days, and the longer it lasted the further the prospect of peace receded. There were the usual recriminations and threats, demands and counter-demands. Philip opened the proceedings by proposing that each side should renounce the conquests they had made at each other's expense since they had both taken the Cross at Gisors two years earlier. But Richard opposed this, objecting that if he gave up Cahors and many other places forming a part of his domains in exchange for Châteauroux, Issoudun and Gracay—that is, the overlordship of a few castles in Berry—he would stand to lose a thousand marks a year. Then Philip, developing the plan he and Richard had worked out together beforehand, offered to restore all his conquests if Henry would cause his subjects to do homage to Richard as his heir and would allow his marriage to Alais to take place immediately. Henry replied, "that he would on no account do this in existing circumstances, since he would appear to be acting under constraint rather than of his own free will." Nevertheless, enfeebled by illness, and premature old age as he was, Henry must have seen that the game was nearly up.

Once more Richard repeated the demand that he should be acknowledged his father's heir there and then and that his marriage with Alais should be celebrated forthwith. Once more Henry refused. The two kings were standing, with Richard and the Archbishop of Reims, in a ring of spectators, when Richard exclaimed, "Now I believe what hitherto seemed to me impossible"—that is, the rumour that the old king was keeping Alais as his mistress and that he intended to supplant Richard in favour of John—rumours which Philip was only too eager to relay to him to keep the fire of his resentment smouldering. That smouldering fire now broke into flame. Drawing his sword, Richard knelt down before Philip and did him homage for all the continental possessions of the Angevin house, saving his father's right to tenure during his lifetime. In return Philip promised him Chateauroux and all the other castles he had taken from Henry in former wars.

The old king remained speechless. At first his heavy round face went deadly pale, then purple. He seemed unable to say or to do anything except to agree to a truce until St Hilary's day, 13 January 1189, when they were all to meet again. The conference then broke up and Richard rode off in company with the French king, whereat once more, "all men marvelled". But by this decisive action, unfilial as it appeared, Richard had cut his way out of the web of shifty diplomacy in which he had been entangled by those two subtle men Henry and Philip.

He now went south to Poitou, ignoring his father's messages. On his way he stopped at Amboise to send out two hundred letters calling up all the king's vassals, Normans, Angevins, Poitevins. So William the Marshal, whom his father had sent after him, reported.

Henry sent Geoffrey the Bastard to secure the fortresses of Anjou and himself went to Saumur for Christmas. It must have been a desolate festival at Fulk Nerra's castle on the Loire. Most of the old king's Court had deserted him to follow the rising star of Richard, who was celebrating Christmas with great good cheer at Paris.

IV

THE KILL

JANUARY 13th, 1189, arrived and with it the expiration of the truce. But Henry postponed his meeting with Philip till February 2nd, and then to April 18th. He was suffering acutely from a fistula, and was tired and depressed in body and mind. He looked so ill that the prelates attending him induced him to make his confession. From Chinon and Le Mans he sent unheeded messages to Richard, who now watched his every move with suspicion, and joined with Philip in a raid across the Norman borders. Then the tired old king sent Baldwin, Archbishop of Canterbury. But Richard curtly refused to see him. At length he consented to meet his father after Easter on the borders of Anjou and Maine. But the meeting came to nothing, as by now neither could trust the other, and Richard went south again to prepare for war. Henry followed him as far as Le Dorat (Haute Vienne) and then returned wearily to Chinon.

The Pope, fearing that the war in France would put a stop to the crusade, sent a succession of legates to make peace. One of these, John de'Conti, reaching Le Mans in May, excommunicated all trouble-makers, except the two kings who were the source of all the trouble. But he made them promise to submit their quarrel to his arbitration and to that of the archbishops of Reims, Bourges, Canterbury and Rouen. On June 4th, accordingly, another conference was held at La Ferté-Bernard, when Philip again demanded the marriage of Richard and Alais, that Richard should have security for his succession to his father's dominions and that John should accompany him on the crusade. These demands were then repeated by Richard. Once more Henry refused and proposed instead that Alais should marry John—thus virtually disinheriting Richard. Upon Philip's indignant rejection of this proposal, the papal legate threatened him with an interdict unless he agreed. Philip retorted that the Church had no right to interfere between the king of France and his vassal and that evidently the legate had "smelt English gold". Richard jostled the cardinal rudely and the meeting broke up in an uproar.

Henry now returned to Le Mans with John and Geoffrey while Philip and Richard, following at his heels, overran Maine. Castle after castle surrendered to them. On June 9th Ballon, only fifteen miles from Le Mans, fell. But Henry refused to leave his birthplace and the townsfolk stood by him. His illegitimate son Geoffrey and his beloved John were still at his side, with some half dozen faithful barons, a large company of knights and a force of mercenaries.

On June 11th a thick fog shrouded the valleys of the Sarthe and its tributary the Huisne, and under cover of this Richard and the French moved steadily nearer to invest the capital of Maine. William the Marshal, reconnoitring up the Huisne had seen them, but on his return to Le Mans he did not tell the king. Next morning, however, as the fog lifted, Henry himself saw from the walls the French pavilions pitched along the edge of the wood on the other side of the river. It came to him as a profound shock and William the Marshal led him back into the town quite dazed. Henry knew that Richard was familiar with all the fords over the Huisne and the weakest points in the city defences, and all day they waited for the attack and all the next night. Early next morning Henry heard Mass, disarmed his bodyguard and went forth in his "cotte de linge", evidently unable to believe that either Richard or Philip would attack his person.

But already Richard's men were sounding the Huisne with their lances and crossing to the southern gate. Here William the Marshal greeted them and slew many Poitevin barons. Then Stephen de Turnham, the Seneschal of Anjou, fired the suburbs on the eastern slope of the mount in order to clear his front, but the wind blew the flames over the walls and the city itself was soon ablaze. Henry's knights made a gallant last stand on the partly destroyed bridge over the Huisne, but they were out-numbered and had to retire and some of the enemy followed them into the city. When the rest of the French tried to cross, however, the bridge collapsed, and this allowed Henry time to escape by the north gate on the road to Fresnay, with John and Geoffrey.

But Richard was across the river, too, and rode furiously after his father. Some of his men outstripped him in the chase and came into conflict with Henry's rearguard. William des Roches had just unhorsed one of the king's knights when Richard dashed up shouting:

"William, you waste your time in folly! Mend your speed: ride on!" At the sound of that voice, William the Marshal, the most accomplished chevalier of his time, turned his horse and spurred straight for Richard. But Richard caught his lance and turned its point aside with his hand, crying in alarm:

"God's feet, Marshal! Slay me not! I wear no hauberk."

"Nay," answered William contemptuously, "may the Devil slay you, so will not I!"

Instead, he thrust his lance into Richard's horse, bringing both horse and rider to the ground—a gesture which saved Henry from the humiliation of capture by his own son. Then he turned and rode after the king.

As he struggled to his feet, Richard shouted angrily at his men through tears of rage, "You have spoilt everything! You are a lot of distracted fools!"

Two miles from Le Mans, Henry paused on the brow of a hill to look back on the burning city and to curse God. "For that Thou, God," he cried, "hast taken from me this day the city which I loved most on earth, in which I was born and bred, where lies the body of my father and that of St Julian, I will requite Thee as I can. I will take from Thee that thing Thou lovest most in me."

At first he fled northward, with a small escort towards the Norman border, where his strength lay. Riding without pause for twenty miles in the overpowering heat, to which many had already succumbed, he reached Fresnay by nightfall. Here he spent the night with his kinsman the Vicomte de Beaumont. Worn out with fatigue and chagrin, he refused to undress, but threw himself down just as he was with Geoffrey the Chancellor's cloak over him.

Next day his friends urged him to rally his forces in Normandy and to summon aid from England to renew the struggle. But the old king had lost heart and felt that his end was near. His one desire now was to get back to Touraine and die in peace. He made his commanders William de Mandeville and William Fitz Ralph swear that should anything happen to him they would surrender his castles to John, and to John alone. He gave Geoffrey the command of his troops and bade him escort the faithful barons as far as Alençon in Normandy, and then come back and rejoin him in Anjou.

Then, almost alone, the king made his way through the Angevin woodlands which he knew so well as a huntsman, though the journey south from Fresnay to the Loire was through country thick with hostile troops. Keeping well to the west of Le Mans in the area of Saint Suzanne, he met Geoffrey again at Savigny with a hundred picked knights and got through safely to the great castle of Chinon on its hill overlooking the tranquil valley of the Vienne in the last days of June.

"In token of the approaching decease of the king, one Friday night before the festival of the Nativity, at the hour of the night when all was quiet, and when all were in their first sleep, a comet appeared in England—which is wont to be considered as a precursor of the death or birth of princes—far lower than the common stars, and also the planets, in this nebulous air, flying along like a globe of fire, with a noise like thunder, but longer and more equal, and emitting a splendid light, but greater and more lasting than a continued sunbeam." So wrote Gerald of Wales of one of the signs foretelling the king's death. About the same time he had a horrible dream in Chinon castle. "It seemed to me (for I was at that time following the Court) as if the body of the king, then apparently dead, being carried by night into the left transept of a certain church, all the lamps which were hanging on high were suddenly extinguished, and broken in pieces, and dashed on the pavement by a sudden flight of crows, ravens and jackdaws ... also the wax candles, two of which stood by the feet of the body, were thrown down by the birds and extinguished. But two which were standing upright at the head, before they could be taken hold of by those who were standing around, fell of themselves from the candlesticks upon the ground, and were broken in pieces. Thus all the lights being extinguished, we, who seemed to be present at the nocturnal obsequies, immediately went forth (not, indeed, in an orderly manner, but flying out from the church very hastily and in fear) and left the body alone, filled equally with fear and horror, besieged, as it seemed to me, with unclean birds, and altogether destitute of all human comfort."

At about the same time, as it turned out later, Baldwin, Archbishop of Canterbury, had an even worse dream. "It seemed to him that when he was entering a certain church he found the body of a dead man lying on a bier, which on a sudden, to the dread of the bystanders, raised itself on its elbow, and with a shrill voice uttered these words, 'Where am I, where am I lying?' And when the reply was given, 'that it was in the church', it added, 'The church is not the place for me; carry me forth quickly from hence.' And having thrown off the garment with which the corpse was covered, it appeared to be that of King Henry. But when the body was carried out, and the archbishop had now entered with the priest to hear Mass, he beheld the altar stripped of everything, and having a large fissure through the middle; and when he had come nearer he saw, as it were, human excrement in it and a great quantity of filth around the altar on all sides. And when the archbishop angrily asked the priest of the church why he allowed the altar of the Lord to be so defiled, the priest answered, 'O my lord, that man whom you have seen carried forth just now, he it was who thus dishonoured my church'."

Worse still, Saint Godric, a hermit of the north of England, had a vision of the king and his four sons first of all cleaning and wiping the altar and the feet of the crucifix, and then climbing via the altar up onto the crucifix itself "and there sitting for some time, they began to defile the altar on every side with their urine and excrement."

Meanwhile, as Henry lay ill at Chinon, Philip and Richard were making a triumphal progress along the Loire valley by Chaumont and Amboise. On June 30th they established themselves on the south bank of the Loire outside Tours. The river, half-dried up with the heat, was easily crossed, and on July 3rd the famous city was stormed.

"Maréchal," said Henry, when William the Marshal joined him at Chinon, "did you hear, as you passed over the road, that the king of France has taken my city of Tours?"

"Sire," replied William, "the bold Capetian does you much injury. It is even so."

No sooner had the king received confirmation of this news than Philip Augustus sent Philip of Flanders and the Archbishop of Reims to summon him to a conference at Colombières, half-way between Tours and Azay. Henry's barons, seeing no hope of anything now but surrender, advised him to go. But his son Geoffrey, who could not bear to witness his humiliation, begged to be allowed to remain behind.

The king found lodging at a small commandery of Knights Templars at Ballan, near Colombières, but no sooner had he reached it than he was seized with racking pain in every nerve and limb of his body. "Maréchal," he cried, "a cruel pain, beginning in my heel, has spread through my feet and legs. My whole body is on fire." William persuaded him to go to bed.

Next day Philip August summoned him, as his vassal, to appear

before him. But Henry could neither sit nor stand. Richard assured
the French king that his father was malingering. Stung by this
taunt, Henry struggled up from his bed, got somehow onto his
horse and rode, supported on both sides, to the meeting-place. When
Philip saw his ashen face, he offered to spread a cloak on the ground
for him. Henry refused it. He had not come there, he said, to sit
down with them, but to hear what the French king demanded of
him and why he had taken away his lands. As was his custom at a
parley, he would keep his horse.

Philip Augustus replied bluntly that he required, first of all, unconditional surrender. He had not been sent for to discuss terms, but
to accede to demands. As Henry was deliberating what to reply, a
tremendous clap of thunder broke upon the stifling air directly over-
head. Both kings started back in terror as lightening struck the
ground between them. Then, as they rode forward again, there
came a second peal, louder than the first. Henry nearly fell from
his horse and, completely unnerved, placed himself wholly at
Philip's mercy. The terms of his surrender were then read to him.
First he was required to do homage to Philip, to wipe out his opposition to his feudal overlord. Then Alais was to be surrendered and
placed under guardians chosen by Richard, who was to marry her
on his return from the Holy Land. Richard was to receive fealty of
all the barons of the Angevin dominions on both sides of the
Channel—that is to say, Henry was virtually required to abdicate,
though he should hold himself ready to meet Philip and Richard at
Vézelay at mid-Lent next to set out on the crusade. Finally he must
renounce all claims to Auvergne and pay an indemnity of 20,000
marks. The allegiance of his barons would depend on his fulfilment
of the provisions. And last humiliation of all—he must give Richard
the kiss of peace. Henry murmured acceptance of the terms, but
begged that at least he should be given the names of all those who
had sided with Richard against him. But when Richard went to
Ballan to receive the kiss of peace, as Henry gave it to him, as he
was bound to do, he murmured:

"God grant I may not die, before I have had my revenge on you!"

This was looked upon as a good joke at the French Court. When
Richard, says Gerald of Wales, "carried back these words as a
measure of the concord established between himself and his father
(he) aroused thereby the great mirth and astonishment of the French
king and the whole court".

Henry was carried back to Chinon on a litter. As his fever and delirium grew upon him, he lay muttering, "Shame, shame on a conquered king." Roger Malchet, the vice-chancellor, went to Tours to get the list of the names of all the rebels. But as he unfolded the parchment and prepared to read, sitting by the king's bed, he could only say, "Sire, may Jesu Christ help me, for the first name that is written here is the name of Count John, your son."

"Say no more," said the king, turning his face away.

But still he could not believe it and started up again.

"Can it be? John, my darling child, my very heart, for love of whom I have incurred all this misery? Has he indeed forsaken me?"

Roger gently confirmed it, and the king turned his face to the wall. "Let all things go now as they will," he murmured. "I care no more for myself or for the world."

All that day and the next he lay trembling from head to foot, muttering incoherently. Suddenly he would start up and curse himself and his sons. Only Geoffrey the Chancellor could calm him, and with his head on his son's shoulder and his feet on the knees of a faithful knight, the dying king at last fell asleep.

When he awoke he saw Geoffrey standing over him and brushing away the flies that settled on his face. "My dearest son," he said, "thou, indeed, hast always been a true son to me. So help me God, if I recover of this sickness, I will be to thee the best of fathers, and will set thee among the chiefest men of my realm. But if I may not live to reward thee, may God give thee thy reward for thy unchanging dutifulness to me." And he whispered in Geoffrey's ear that he hoped to see him bishop of Winchester or York. Then he took off his gold leopard ring and asked that it should be sent to the king of Castille, the husband of his daughter Eleanor, and to Geoffrey himself he gave a precious sapphire ring.

He was then carried into the chapel of the castle and laid before the altar. Here he made his last confession, was absolved and, after taking the sacrament, died in his fifty-sixth year on 6 July 1189, worn out with fever and grief and the violence of his passions.

Gerald of Wales, who attributes Henry's miserable death to his indifference to and contempt for the church and her ministers, relates what happened next. "When his body was exposed to view in the courtyard all, without exception, as they are wont to do at such time, indulged their rapacity to such an extent that the body was left for some time without any garment whatever to cover it; until a certain youth, with his own small and thin cloak, such as young men usually wear in the summer, ran up and covered the naked parts of the body as far as he could, although it scarcely reached down to the knees. Thus was fulfilled the surname which had been given him in his early years, when he was only a duke that is, Henri Curt Mantel. For in truth he introduced the fashion of short cloaks from Anjou into England. . . . In addition to this when his body was conveyed from Chinon to Fontevraud, scarcely any persons could be found who would sew up the corpse in the shroud of fine linen."

Indeed, during the three days in which the king's body had lain at Chinon, his servants had rifled everything they could lay their hands upon. It was even difficult to find anyone to follow in the funeral procession, they had all been in such a hurry to run and make their peace with the dreaded Count Richard. William the Marshal, Geoffrey and a few knights remained, however, and these saw that everything fitting was done. They carried the body of the king on their shoulders down from the rock above Chinon, across the bridge that he had built over the Vienne and along the side of the shallow tranquil river through Candes to Montsoreau, where the little procession turned off over the low hills to the great Abbey of Fontevrault.

And as Henry lay in state, in his borrowed relics of royalty, before the high altar, the veiled sisters kneeling at his side murmuring psalms and prayers for his soul, in the evening came Count Richard and stood looking down at his dead father. Some say that he showed no emotion whatever. But, according to Gerald of Wales, "when the face of his father became visible by the napkin being taken off, wherewith it was covered; and as it appeared to all as if tinted with colour, and not deprived of its usual fierce aspect, when the count beheld it not without loud weeping and horror which belong to the flesh, and perhaps some natural grief, he knelt down before the altar, and remained a short space in prayer; but scarcely sufficient to recite the Lord's prayer. But as soon as he had entered the church (as they relate who were present and saw it) both nostrils of the king began to flow with blood, and did not cease to do so as long as his son remained in the church, so that they who were sitting near and attending to the funeral were scarcely able to wipe and cleanse the mouth and face with a napkin." To all present this appeared as a manifest sign that Richard was the murderer of his father.

Next day when the body was delivered for burial "scarcely was a decent ring to be found for his finger, or a sceptre for his hand, or a crown for his head, except such as was made from an old head-dress which was found." And so, concludes Gerald, "he who with the most ample kingdoms heaped up riches in the heights of towers and in the parts beneath the earth, not knowing for whom he gathered them, and left them filled with silver and gold for a man whom he had bitterly hated more than any in the world. And thus, as if by a peculiar punishment from Heaven, like another Tantalus, he did not escape the miseries of want amidst plenty, caused by his own violence, and by the author of his death succeeding him in everything."

Henry still lies at Fontevrault beside his enigmatically smiling wife and his lion-hearted son, his nose knocked off, but a crown on his head, a sceptre in his hands, and gold sandals to his feet.

After Richard had finished his hurried *pater noster*, he rose and, speaking for the first time, bade William the Marshal follow him. He had not seen the Marshal since he had been unhorsed by him near Le Mans and many feared for William's safety now. But outside the church, Richard turned to him and said:

"Fair Sir Marshal, you had like to have slain me; had I received your spear-thrust, it would have been a bad day for both of us."

"My lord," answered William, "I had it in my power to slay you; I only slew your horse. And of that I do not repent me yet."

"Marshal," said Richard, "I bear you no malice, you are forgiven."

So the Marshal reminded him of the dead king's promise to give him the hand of Isobel, Countess of Pembroke and Striguil, as a reward for his faithful service of the Plantagenets. Richard now confirmed this and sent him, with Gilbert Pipard, an officer of the Exchequer, over to England to release the queen and to authorize her to act as regent until he could himself cross the sea.

John hastened to join the brother he would have supplanted and Richard received him with honour. Indeed Richard looked with favour on all who had remained faithful to his father, but somewhat ungraciously confiscated the estates of those who had deserted his father to follow him. These, he said now, were traitors and must be expected to be treated as such. But only one who had held high office under Henry did Richard treat harshly. This was Stephen of Turnham, who had set fire to Le Mans and who now refused to surrender the treasure at Chinon. He was loaded with chains and cast into prison, though even his disgrace was only temporary.

After that Richard and John went to Saumur. Richard spent three weeks putting the affairs of Aquitaine, Anjou, Touraine and Maine in order and then turned back to Normandy. At Séez on the way to Rouen, the Archbishops of Canterbury and Rouen absolved him from the excommunication pronounced upon him by the papal legate for taking up arms against a fellow crusader, his father, and he was girded with the ducal sword and invested with the standard of Normandy.

At Rouen Richard held his first Court as Duke of Normandy and king elect of England. In honour of the occasion he made a series of royal grants, as though he were already king. To John he confirmed his father's grant of the County of Mortain and £4,000 worth of land in England. Geoffrey was nominated to the see of York, in accordance with his father's last wishes; William the Marshal was granted the hand of Isobel de Clare, and the hand of his niece Matilda was bestowed upon Geoffrey of Perche, thus securing the frontiers of Normandy and Maine. At first, therefore, Richard showed himself judicious and only too willing to do all that was right.

As soon as he met Philip Augustus between Trie and Chaumont-en-Vexin, the French king, his primary purpose achieved in the ruin and death of Henry Plantagenet, dropped all pretence of friendship towards his old ally and abruptly demanded the return of Gisors and Vexin. On this occasion Richard was able to put him off by a bribe of four thousand marks, over and above the twenty thousand demanded of Henry at Colombières, and a promise to marry Alais. In return Philip left him in possession of all his father's dominions, except Berry and Auvergne. Both princes then pledged themselves to start for the Holy Land not later than Lent the following year.

For three weeks longer Richard lingered in Normandy, winning all hearts by his gracious and affable demeanour. Meanwhile, in England, his mother made a progress through the realm, taking oaths of fealty in her son's name from all the freemen of the land, releasing prisoners, pardoning criminals, relaxing forest laws and making sure that the coming of Richard to his kingdom would seem to all like a deliverance. This indiscriminate clemency, however, appeared far from prudent to William of Newburgh. "At that time," records William, "the gaols were crowded with criminals awaiting trial or punishment, but through Richard's clemency these pests came forth from prison, perhaps to become bolder thieves in the future." Among these were many who had transgressed the barbarous forest laws, which prescribed blinding and castration for anyone lower in rank than a knight or a clerk who poached in the royal forests, which then covered the larger part of England.

On August 12th Richard and John sailed from Barfleur. Richard landed at Southampton and next day at Winchester took possession of the royal treasure. He was met by Queen Eleanor, Glanville the Justiciar and a great train of bishops and barons. From Winchester he went to Salisbury, where William the Marshal's marriage to Isobel de Clare was celebrated, as well as the marriages of several other distinguished personages. On his leisurely progress through southern England—unlike his predecessors Richard was in no hurry to be crowned—news came of a Welsh raid across the border and he was for turning back to punish the invaders, when his mother, who was in London making preparations for the Coronation, sent an urgent message for him to proceed. At Marlborough, John's wedding to the heiress of Gloucester was celebrated and Richard made him further grants amounting to about £1,000 a year. At the same time he confiscated the treasure and effects of the Bishop of Ely, who had just died—three thousand odd marks to defray the cost of the coronation. By August 30th he had reached Windsor, where his mother rejoined him.

Richard entered London on 1 September 1189, and the English welcomed him rapturously, roaring themselves hoarse as he progressed splendidly down the Strand to St Paul's. The gaols had been emptied to swell the enthusiasm, and both Queen Eleanor and Richard himself well understood how to make a fine show.

PART TWO

SOLDIER OF THE CROSS

Our kyng among the Sarezynes ryt,
And some to the sadyl he slyt:
A knyght he hyt above the scheeld,
That hed and helm fleygh into the feeld ...
Blythe was the Crystene felawrede
Off Kyng Richard, and off hys dede,
Fore none armure withstood his ax,
No more than a knyf dos in the wax.

KYNGE RICHARD CUER DU LYON

I

RICARDUS REX

Among the noble and celebrated cities of the world that of London, the capital of the kingdom of the English, is one which extends its glory farther than all the others and sends its wealth and merchandise more widely into distant lands," writes William Fitz Stephen.[1] "Higher than all the rest does it lift its head. It is happy in the healthiness of its air; in its observance of Christian practice; in the strength of its fortifications; in its natural situation; in the honour of its citizens; and in the modesty of its matrons. It is cheerful in its sports, and the fruitful mother of noble men. . . .

"It has on the east the Palatine Castle [the Tower], very great and strong . . . on the west there are two castles [Baynard Castle and the Tower of Montfichet] very strongly fortified, and from these runs a high and massive wall with seven double gates and with towers along the north at regular intervals. London was once also walled and turreted on the south, but the mighty Thames, so full of fish, has with the sea's ebb and flow washed against, loosened, and thrown down those walls in the course of time. Upstream to the west there is the royal palace [Westminster] which is conspicuous above the river, a building incomparable in its ramparts and bulwarks. It is about two miles from the city and joined thereto by a populous suburb. . . . Everywhere outside the houses of those living in the suburbs, and adjacent to them, are the spacious and beautiful gardens of the citizens, and these are planted with trees. Also there are on the north side pastures and pleasant meadow lands through which flow streams wherein the turning windmill makes a cheerful sound. Very near lies a great forest with woodland pastures which are the lairs of wild animals: stags, fallow deer, wild boars and bulls. The tilled lands of the city are not of barren gravel, but fat Asian plains that yield luxuriant crops and fill the tiller's barns with the sheaves of Ceres.

[1] The *descriptio Londoniae* appears as a preamble to Fitz Stephen's Life of Thomas Becket. From *English Historical Documents*, 1142–1189, ed. by David C. Douglas and George K. Greenaway (1953).

"There are also outside London on the north side excellent suburban wells with sweet wholesome and clear water that flows rippling over the bright stones. Among these are Holywell, Clerkenwell and St Clement's Well. These are all frequented by great numbers and much visited by the students from the schools [St Paul's, Holy Trinity, St Martin, and others] and by the young men of the city, when they go out for fresh air on summer evenings. Good indeed is this city when it has a good lord."

That good lord, they liked to think, had now come to them. For London, by the twelfth century, was famous for its prosperity and the civilized living of its citizens—a terminal point on the trade route from Constantinople by the Danube and Regentsburg to the Rhine and the narrow seas.[2] This trade was controlled by the men of Lower Lorraine, who brought to London goldsmiths' work, precious stones, cloth from Constantinople and Regentsburg, fine linen and coats of mail from Mainz, also wine. Furs came from Russia, purple silk from China. The king had first choice of all these things, then the men of London might buy what they wished. One should be careful when speaking about barbarous living conditions in medieval London. . . .

The coronation of Richard I at Westminster on 3 September 1189 was the most splendid and elaborate ceremony of its kind Londoners had ever seen and set the pattern for all those which followed, right up to the present day. Richard revelled in regal pomp as much as his father had hated it. Tall and straightly fashioned, with his amber hair, his "vision lift upward and divine", he might—except for his white Crusader's cross—have been a model for Marlowe's Tamburlaine, the most impressive figure who had been crowned since the Conqueror.

Early on this September morning Richard was met at his chamber door at Westminster Palace by the Archbishops of Canterbury, Rouen, Dublin and Trèves, with a company of other bishops, abbots and clergy in rich copes and bearing the Cross, the holy water, thuribles and burning tapers. There followed a solemn procession to Westminster Abbey. Led by the lesser clergy, after whom came abbots and bishops, Geoffrey de Lucy, walked bearing the cap of maintainance, and next to him John Marshall, elder brother of William, with the spurs. In the third rank was William Longsword, Earl of Salisbury (another of Henry II's illegitimate children),

---

[2] F. M. Stenton, *Norman London*. Hist. Assn., 1934.

carrying the rod topped by a dove; John, Earl of Mortain and Gloucester, with the sword of state; and William Marshal, Earl of Pembroke, with the sceptre. In the middle of the procession the chequer board with regalia and robes was borne by six barons. Afterwards came William de Mandeville, Earl of Essex, with the crown, and immediately behind him Richard, Duke of Normandy, walking under a silk canopy supported on lances and carried by four barons of the Cinque Ports. On his right hand walked Hugh de Puiset, Bishop of Durham, and on his left Reginald Fitz Jocelin, Bishop of Bath.

On reaching the abbey, Duke Richard took his seat on a chair, the *sedes in pulpito*, in front of the throne in the middle of the crossing, and was formally elected king by the acclamation of both clergy and people. The antiphon *Firmetur Manus Tua* was then sung while the king brought his offering of a cloak and a pound weight of gold to the altar. The Litany followed, the king kneeling. After listening to a short sermon, the king elect took the coronation oath, swearing on the Gospels and the relics of the saints to maintain Church and people in good peace to the best of his ability, to put down all wrong-doers and to temper justice with mercy. The prayers of consecration followed—*Omnipotens Semptiterne Deus*, *Benedic Domine*, *Deus Ineffabilis*, while the king was being undressed behind a curtain for the hallowing. First of all, his head was anointed by the Archbishop of Canterbury with chrism—holy oil mixed with balsam—then his chest and shoulders were annointed through slits cut in his shirt. After that his head was bound in a chrism cloth, not to be removed until the eighth day. He was then clothed with tunic and dalmatic, the cap of maintainance placed on his head, and his feet shod with gold-laced sandals by two earls. Investiture with spurs, sword, stole and mantle came next. The king was then led up to the high altar and, taking the crown, gave it to the archbishop. But before crowning him, Baldwin adjured him in God's name not to presume to take on this dignity unless he meant to keep his oaths, and Richard answered that with God's help he would. Baldwin then placed the crown on his head and gave him the sceptre to hold in his right hand and the rod royal in his left.

After the crowning the *Te Deum* was sung and the crowned and anointed king was brought back by the bishops and the barons, with the cross and candlesticks and three swords carried before him to his throne on the central platform. At the end of the *Te Deum* the archbishop pronounced the *Sta et Retine*. Mass followed, the king communicating.[3]

The king was then led back in solemn procession to his apartment, where he took off his heavy coronation robes and put on another crown and garments "more light and easy". At the coronation banquet which followed at Westminster Palace, Richard sat with none but the clergy, the earls and barons being accommodated at a table apart.

The banquet was interrupted, however, by an unseemly disturbance at the doors of the palace. Richard had given orders that no women or Jews were to be admitted, either to his coronation or to the banquet. But the Jews had been much favoured as moneylenders by his father and a deputation of them now arrived at Westminster with gifts for the new king. "While the king sat at meat," says Higden, "some of the Jews pressed among other and came within the palace gate, and one of them was y-smitten with a man's fist. Then the rabbish people weened that the king had so bidden, and up with staves, bats, and stones, and laid on the Jews and made them to flee." Worse followed in the City. "And the people, raving and crying, brake up the house where the Jews were y-flowen for dread, and burned and spoiled and took what they might." This was the signal for a general pogrom. Synagogues were desecrated, whole Jewish families were burned inside their houses and those who tried to escape the flames were cut down or lynched in the streets. When Glanville, the Justicar and some of the nobles arrived with a small force to restore order, the mob had got quite out of hand and the city remained in the hands of the people all night. Richard was indignant at this disorderly breach of the peace on his coronation day, and afterwards some of those who had taken part in the rioting were punished, but only for the damage done to Christian property. "The other cities and towns of the kingdom emulated the faith of the Londoners," says Richard of Devizes, "and with a like devotion dispatched their bloodsuckers with blood to hell. . . . Winchester alone spared the vermin." Unfortunately, the Jews, who owned about a third of the movable wealth of the kingdom, had chosen this very moment, when noblemen and knights were pawning their estates to go on crusade, to raise their rates of interest. Doubtless they regarded this move as good business.

Meanwhile coronation festivities continued for three days. "And I saw such abundance of meats set forth that none might keep

[3] Sir James Ramsay, *Angevin Empire*, pp. 266–9.

account or tally thereof," sings Richard's *jongleur* Ambroise, "nor ever in my life have I seen a Court served in courtlier fashion. And I saw vessels of great price in that hall that is so fair, and tables saw I so close pressed together that they could in no wise be numbered. Bounteous was the feast, stately and magnificent."

Once crowned, Richard lost no time in making his preparations to leave the country. His one idea was to get out of England as soon as possible, and start for the East. For this he needed all the money he could collect.

His first act on landing had been to have an exact account taken of the contents of the royal treasury at Winchester. Of the Saladin Tithe, what had not already been spent on wars in France had been given into the keeping of the Templars. Fortunately there were several bishoprics vacant and various other appointments to be made, and those who filled these positions should, Richard determined, pay dearly for the privilege. The Bishop of Ely had just died and one of the king's first acts was to seize upon all his goods and chattels.

On September 15th Richard summoned a Grand Council at Pipewell, Northamptonshire, when the question of the regency came up. First of all Glanville, the chief justiciar, an old and trusted minister of Henry II, was thrown into prison and relieved of the greater part of his possessions. Then, broken with grief and utterly bewildered, the poor old fellow was pushed off to the Holy Land. His son-in-law, Ralph de Ardenne, was also "utterly lost by reason of his careless talk", and, unable to pay the enormous fine demanded of him, packed off to Palestine also. The reason for his brutal treatment of a man who had grown old in the service of his country, says William of Newburgh, was that "he saw that the new king, being a novice, was wont to do many things without due deliberation and forethought". In fact, Glanville was thoroughly disgusted both by the king's methods of raising money and by his vices, and his mind, it is said, became enfeebled with vexation and shame. To Richard he was probably a father-figure, and therefore someone to be done to death.

In Glanville's place, Richard appointed William de Mandeville, who, though he had been brought up in Glanville's household, was evidently more pliable and knew how to keep his mouth shut. He now shared the regency with the king's cousin, Hugh de Puiset (Pudsey to the English), Bishop of Durham, and a consultative committee of five justices. These appointments were reasonably good and probably made on the advice of Queen Eleanor. At the second day's sitting Richard made his chancellor William de Longchamp, a lame, stammering dwarf, Bishop of Ely and his half-brother Geoffrey Bishop of York.

The king, remarks Richard of Devizes, "readily unburdened all whose money was a burden to them." A fruitful source of revenue was a tax levied from all those who had originally taken the Cross and now repented of their earlier enthusiasm, Richard having got leave from Clement III to absolve from the crusade men needed in the government of the country during his absence. Those, therefore, who now wanted reserved occupations had to pay for them. How much they paid was a personal matter between themselves and the king. The sale of other public offices followed. Every sheriff throughout the country was deposed and told to bid for his reinstatement. Those who refused, or who did not bid high enough, were put in prison. Their counties and castles were then put up for auction. Hugh de Puiset, being a great Prince Bishop, was required to pay an enormous sum for his share in the regency and still more for the earldom and county of Northumberland. "See," said the king flippantly, "how of an old bishop I have made a new earl!" Puiset, at least, must have laughed a little uncomfortably at this not very good joke. Even Richard's friend Longchamp had to pay £3,000[4] for the chancellorship, while Hugh Nonant, Bishop of Coventry, had the priory of Coventry for 300 marks and the sheriff-doms of Warwickshire, Leicestershire and Staffordshire knocked down to him for a further 200. Gerard de Camville got Leicester-shire and Lincoln Castle for 700. And so the money "rolled like nuts in the Exchequer". To one who ventured to remonstrate at this remarkable auction, the king snapped: "I would sell London itself if I could find a buyer for it!"

No wonder de Glanville's mind gave way! Longchamp, the chancellor, and soon to be chief justiciar and papal legate, was a very different sort of man. The son of a Norman labourer and a member of the master race who made no secret of his contempt for the English, he was a type who appeared again in the Wolseys: utterly unscrupulous, but wholly devoted to the king's interest, he was the sort of man who got things done and is said to have used both hands as though they had been right hands and to have moved from one

[4] To reach something approaching the present value of the £ one might multiply by three then by fifteen. The mark was worth two-thirds of the £.

end of the country to the other like a flash of lightning. The king returned his devotion and even stood by him after he had been hounded out of the country. He is said, too, to have had a particular aversion to women.

Meanwhile the troubadours were beginning to taunt both Richard and Philip Augustus with their tardiness in starting on the crusade. Bertran de Born wrote a sly *sirvente* addressed to Conrad of Montferrat, who had saved the situation in the Holy Land by occupying Tyre after the general débâcle and holding it as the only port open to the crusading armies. "I know two kings who are slow to help you," wrote Bertran, "now hear who they are. King Philip is one, for he doubts King Richard and the latter doubts him likewise: now would they were both in the chains of Sir Saladin, for they keep deceiving God since they have taken the cross and speak no word of going." Others seem to have had similar doubts, in view of what H. J. Chaytor calls "the notorious instability of Richard's character". Gaucelm Faidit wrote that Richard could not have the credit of a crusader by staying at home and Peirol complained that the crusade was delayed by the quarrels between Richard and Philip.

Accordingly early in November envoys arrived from France, with letters from Philip saying that he and his barons had sworn on the Gospels to be at Vézelay ready to start on the crusade at the close of Easter next (1 April 1190) and asking for a similar oath in return from Richard. For reply Richard exacted from the envoys an oath on the king of France's soul that he would indeed fulfil his pledge, and at a great council at Westminster caused William the Marshal to take an oath on his behalf.

After a diplomatic pilgrimage to St Edmund's, the king set out for Dover, reaching Canterbury on November 25th. Here, during a stay of twelve days, he got through a surprising amount of business. He settled the long-standing quarrel between Archbishop Baldwin and the monks of Canterbury over the archbishop's attempt to establish a college for secular canons at Hackington, near Cambridge, out of the revenues claimed by the Canterbury monks. Matters had come to such a pass that Baldwin had blockaded the monks in their own conventual buildings in order to starve them into submission. Richard then granted the virtual independence of Scotland to William the Lion, and restored to him his English estates, in consideration for a lump sum down. This, unlike the other methods of raising money, was a wise move, for it ensured the immunity of the north of England from invasion during the king's absence on crusade.[5]

His half-brother Geoffrey's quarrelsome nature was then turned to account. Although Geoffrey's appointment to the See of York had originated in Richard himself, Geoffrey had been making trouble about his brother's other appointments to the Deanery and Treasurership of York. To bring him to heel, Richard got Hugh de Puiset and Hubert Walter to renew their original objections to Geoffrey's appointment to the archbishopric, till Geoffrey offered Richard a large sum for it. Richard then gave him the kiss of peace, but, on second thoughts, raised the price of his forgiveness to £2,000.

To John he now imprudently granted the counties of Cornwall, Devon and Somerset, though John already held Nottinghamshire, Derby and Dorset and a long chain of castles stretching the length of the kingdom. Except that his mother was still there to protect his interests, it appeared to many at the time as though Richard were content to abandon England to his young brother and that he was going on a pilgrimage to the Holy Land to redeem his crime of patricide. Others prophesied that, his health being what it was, he would never return. This, at any rate, seems to have been what John hoped.

Richard had assembled at Dover and other southern ports all the seaworthy craft to be found from Hull to Bristol, and it was from there that he set sail for Normandy on 12 December 1189. With him went the Archbishop of Rouen, the Bishops of Bayeux and Evreux, and his chancellor. His English fleet comprised about forty-five ships, with crews of twenty to twenty-five each. His own great wargalley, with its red sails emblazoned with the leopards of Anjou, which became the golden lions of England, and its crew of sixty-one men, piloted by Alan Trenchemer, was to meet the king at Marseille.

Christmas was held at Lyons-la-Foret, in Normandy, in great state, though we learn that "there was little singing of gestes". On December 30 the two kings, Richard and Philip, met to make regulations for the Crusade and for the protection of the property of

[5] More typical of his methods was the sale of the title and estates of William Mandeville, Earl of Essex, who died at Rouen in December, for £4,666 to Geoffrey de Say, followed by their resale next year by Longchamp—the instalments not having been paid regularly—to another claimant, Geoffrey Fitz Peter. Richard, of course, sanctioned the last transaction. Ramsay, *Angevin Empire* (pp. 280–1).

each other's subjects. They promised to observe good faith towards one another and decreed that all those who had taken the Cross should set out from Vézelay not later than the octave of Easter (April 1st). They met again on March 16th to confirm the peace terms proposed on December 30th and to swear to serve each other faithfully and to defend each other's possessions.[6] All barons present swore that they would not make war on either king's territories as long as they were on crusade, and the bishops undertook to excommunicate any who broke the terms of the covenant. The kings then agreed to meet at Vézelay to start on the crusade on July 1st.

Somewhat earlier, in March, Richard had summoned a great council in Normandy to settle the disturbances that had arisen in England as a result of the death of William de Mandeville and the rapid rise to power of Longchamp. For as soon as Longchamp became Bishop of Ely and joint justiciar with du Puiset, he forbade du Puiset to appear at the council table at all. Then he deprived him of his sheriffdom of Northumberland. The Bishop of Winchester was next to suffer and lost the county he had just bought and two castles. Complaints soon began to reach the king and a great concourse of bishops and barons, including Queen Eleanor, John, Geoffrey and Richard's unfortunate betrothed Alais, now a virtual prisoner, converged upon Nonancourt.

First to arrive was the little monkeyish Longchamp, who was thus able to put his case to the king unapposed. As a result not only were all his actions confirmed, but, to the disgust of everybody, he was appointed Justiciar in Chief, given control of the Tower of London, and de Puiset's authority was curtailed to the region north of the Humber. Not content with that, Richard asked the pope for a legatine commission for his favourite, and by June Longchamp was supreme in both Church and State, *ipso facto* dictator. Had he been trying to do so, Richard could hardly have created a situation more calculated to play straight into the hands of John, though it is true that his brothers were required to take an oath not to enter England for the next three years. But, at his mother's request, John was released from his pledge. So much for the political foresight of Coeur de Lion, who could put the supreme power into the hands of a man both hated by and hating the English. Perhaps it was an

---

[6] This agreement was signed: "Moi Philippe, roi des Francais, envers Richard, mon ami et mon fidèle vassal. Moi Richard, roi des Anglais, envers Philippe, mon seigneur et mon ami." The feudal relationship is here quite explicit.

indication of his own feelings towards England, for there is no doubt that his heart was in Poitou.

Longchamp hurried back to England with a commission to prepare all things necessary for the king's journey. First of all, horses had to be requisitioned. The justiciar collected 10,000. As for ships, Richard had been gradually assembling them from all the seaports of England, Normandy, Poitou and Aquitaine ever since his accession, till a fleet of about a hundred vessels had been assembled. On an average each ship carried, besides the crew, forty men-at-arms with their horses and forty foot-soldiers. The whole fleet would, therefore, carry about 8,000 men, though there were fourteen large busses, or cargo ships. "Richard's fleet," we read in L'Histoire de Guillaume le Maréchal, "comprised great ships with broadsides well protected, manned with stout crews well able to defend them. On board he put abundance of gold and silver, rich furs, precious vestments, arms of all sorts, supplies of bacon, wine, cheese, flour, biscuit, pepper, cumin, wax, electuaries, various drinks, spiced meat, and syrup." Richard was indeed going to rescue the Holy Sepulchre, but he was going to do it as comfortably as possible. For the majority, of course, victuals meant beans and bacon. The Anglo-Norman fleet set out from Dartmouth soon after Easter 1190, and the arms at Dartmouth still commemorate this event.

Richard held his summer Court at Chinon, presumably with his mother and Alais, soon to be committed to the tower of Rouen under a close guard. In June he issued an ordinance for the conduct of his fleet.

Richard, by the grace of God, King of England, Duke of Normandy and Aquitaine, and Count of Anjou, to all his men—Health. Know that with the common counsel of approved men we have had the following regulations drawn up.

Whoever on board ship shall slay another is himself to be cast into the sea lashed to the dead man; if he has slain him ashore he is to be buried in the same way. If anyone be proved by worthy witnesses to have drawn a knife for the purpose of striking another, or to have wounded another so as to draw blood, let him lose his fist; but if he strike another with his hand and draw no blood, let him be dipped three times in the sea. If anyone cast any reproach or bad word against another or invoke God's malison on him, let him for every offence pay an ounce of silver. Let a convicted thief be shorn like a prize-fighter; after which let boiling pitch be poured on his head and a feather pillow be shaken over it so as to make him a laughing-stock. Then let him be put ashore on the first land where the ships touch. Witness myself at Chinon.

A brutal ordinance, no doubt. But then the pilgrims were a rough lot. All vessels had been chartered for a year and the sailors got their pay in advance at a rate of 2d a day, or about £3 a year, and double that for the captains. The orders to the fleet were to sail round the coast of Spain and await the king at Marseille.

Many bequests to abbeys both in France and England are recorded for June and, visiting Fontevrault, Richard asked the aristocratic nuns there to pray for his success. He then made an expedition into the county of Bigorre, Haut Pyrenees, and hanged William de Chis for plundering pilgrims on their way to the shrine of St James of Compostella in Spain.

From Chinon Richard went to Tours, where he received the pilgrim's staff and scrip from Archbishop Bartholomew, from whose hands he had received the cross two years before. The king prostrated himself before the shrine of St Martin, then took down from over the relics of the saint, where it hung, the banner emblazoned with the golden cross, to carry in the wars against the enemies of Christ. But, says Roger de Hoveden, "when the king leant on the staff it broke"—an ill omen for the success of the third crusade.

Richard set out from Touraine on 27 June 1190 with his army 8,000 strong, to meet Philip at Vézelay in Burgundy. In fact the streets of Tours became completely blocked with pilgrims and the townsfolk were terrified at such a vast concourse of men "with their heavy martial tread". But their yet unsullied armour glittered in the sun. "Many good knights were there and many crossbowmen of high repute," sings the *jongleur* Ambroise in his *Estoire de la guerre sainte*. "Had ye but seen the host when it came forth! The earth trembled with their coming, but all the folk were sorrowful because of their lord so full of prowess. There was weeping of ladies and damozels, of young and old, of ugly and fair. Grief and pity oppressed their hearts because of their friends that were departing. . . . A more piteous convoy had ye never seen."

On the second day in July they saw Vézelay the shrine of St Mary Magdalene, the towers of the great basilica rising above the clustering grey houses at the top of its hill, the white dusty road snaking upwards.[7] At the entrance to the basilica, Christ in majesty spread enormous hands in an awful half-threatening, half-welcoming gesture. Inside all was light and arches of tigerish striped stone, the capital of each column abounding with wild, flame-like carvings, blazing with azure and vermilion and gold. On one capital the pilgrims may have noticed *jongleurs* piping to the demon of lust, seen caressing the breasts of a naked girl. On others, beasts and chimaeras chased and tore each other in fantastic orgies. It was such capitals, prevalent in the Romanesque churches of Aquitaine as well, that St Bernard had condemned as unseemly. But, says Ambroise, "God had stolen all that great assembly from the Devil, for 'twas on His behalf that they were come together. At Vézelay, on the mountain, there did God lodge His company.... There He had brought together the goodliest company of youth that ever was gathered in this world." There Philip and Richard swore that whatever might befall, they two should stand together, and that whatever spoils might fall to their share they would divide them equally. Had they forgotten that their mission was to restore the kingdom of Jerusalem —a project which involved the reconquest of the whole of Syria and Palestine from the united forces of Egypt and Mesopotamia? But with God all things were possible.

The kings left Vézelay on July 4th, riding together at the head of their armies, and came to Corbigny, where they held a court at which a decision was reached on certain matters in dispute touching the rights of the counts of Poitou and the Chapter of St Martin of Tours. Their next stop was Moulins-Engilbert on July 5th. From there the route lay through Taluns (Toulon), Le Bois Ste Marie, Belleville-sur-Saône, Villefranche (Villa Franca) to Lyon, which was reached on July 10th after a march of six days. And as they passed through the villages, the people came out with gifts and jugs

---

[7] The reputed remains of St Mary Magdalen, who is said to have landed with the two other Marys in the south of France after the Crucifixion, had been stolen from St Maximin in Provence, whose monks watched with mortification the growing wealth of Vezelay brought by the pilgrim traffic. In 1279, however, a Gallo-Roman sarcophagus was unearthed in the crypt of St Maximin and it was at once claimed that the Magdalen's actual body had been discovered. This report once more diverted pilgrim traffic from Burgundy to Provence, and Vezelay sank into unimportance till restored by Viollet-le-Duc. The Magdalen's blackened skull may still be seen in an illuminated niche in the crypt of St Maximin.

of water, while the women held up their babies to be touched by those whose destination was the Holy Sepulchre. At Lyon the kings had agreed to divide their forces, Richard marching down the left bank of the Rhône to Marseille, the French crossing the Alps to Genoa, where the famous Genoese sailors would take them to the next meeting-place at Messina.

The two kings reached the Rhône before the main force, crossed at once by the narrow wooden bridge and set up their *pavillons* on the high ground. When the army, estimated at about 100,000, began to cross, the bridge gave way. But God so ordered the matter, says Ambroise, that, "so far as could be discovered", not more than two were drowned, in spite of the fact that the Rhône was in flood. In this emergency, Richard collected all the "little skiffs, narrow and shallow" that could be found—they sound just like the boats still in use by Rhône fishermen—and lashing them together, made a pontoon bridge by which the remainder of the host crossed "with exceeding difficulty—but so fareth he who laboureth on God's behalf", an operation which occupied three days.

After courteously seeing the French king on his way for a few miles, Richard rode back and led his host southward. By July 16th they had reached Valence, and then went on by Loriol on the Drome. But passing through Montelimar, the inhabitants, probably Albigenses, reviled the crusaders and Richard, in a rage, assaulted the town and took its lord prisoner, though, afterwards, at the entreaty of some of his nobles, he let him go. He then continued his march through Orange, Sorgues, Bompas near Avignon to Martigues.

It was a tired and very thirsty band of Christian soldiers that reached Marseille at the end of July, after covering 221 miles from Lyon at the hottest time of the year. Possibly the knights divested themselves of their heavy suits of chain mail, with their mail stockings, and great barrel-shaped helms like steel sweat-boxes; but the foot-soldiers had no one else to carry their arms and thick padded coats, and one hopes that they reached the seaport still glorifying the name of the Lord.

"And if anyone blamed the good King Richard, who wishes me to sing, because he did not at once make the passage [to the Holy Land], now I give him the lie, as each one sees, for he withdrew the better to leap forward," wrote Folquet of Marseille, "he was indeed a count, now he is a wealthy absolute king, for God gives good support to good will, and as I spoke well of him at his taking the Cross, I spoke the truth, and now we see it, because then I did not lie."[8]

Peire Vidal went on the crusade, too, but he only got as far as Cyprus for there, as we read in *The Lives of the Troubadours*, "a knight of Saint Gilles caused his tongue to be cut out, because he made believe that he was his wife's lover." Nevertheless, he married a Greek and returned to Languedoc. Like all poets, he was poor. But before starting out he had written to Richard: "Count of Poitou, I complain of you to God and God likewise complains to me, He of His Cross and I of my money. Count of Poitou, you and I are praised by the rest of men, you for your good deeds and I for good words."[9] But Bertran de Born merely complained that lack of funds kept him at home, and contented himself with encouraging the others.

Richard was very angry when he found that his fleet had not yet reached Marseille. So, after waiting there a week, bitten by the mosquitoes of that region, he hired two large busses and twenty well-armed galleys and put to sea on August 7th, with a "small household and the chief men of his army". While Baldwin Archbishop of Canterbury, Hubert Bishop of Salisbury and Ranulf de Glanville, who embarked from Marseille at the same time, sailed direct to Tyre, Richard began coasting slowly along in sight of the shore, putting in at Nice, Ventemiglia and other pleasant places each night. "It should be known," says Hoveden, "that from Marseilles to Acre it is only fifteen days' and nights' sailing with a fair wind and that is by the great sea route by which, after losing sight of the hills behind Marseille, land is not seen, either on the right hand or the left, till Sicily is sighted: and if any land should be sighted on the right hand, it is the land of the pagans (Spain and her islands) and if on the left hand it is land of the christians." But galleys, he adds, dare not put so far out to sea, "because if a storm should arise they would easily be sunk: they must always navigate near the land." The distance from Marseille to Acre via the Straits of Messina, is about 1694 nautical miles. Under very favourable conditions, ships at this date travelled at not more than five knots an hour.[10]

Richard reached Genoa on August 13th to find Philip ill and to

[8] Chaytor, *The Troubadours and England*, p. 53.
[9] *Ibid.* p. 56.
[10] Lionel Landon, *The Itinerary of King Richard I.*

hear that Frederick Barbarossa, Red Beard, the emperor of Germany, who had started out before either of them on the overland route, had died as a result of bathing too soon after lunch in the river Calycadmus in Cilicia, while the bulk of his great army had either succumbed to the plague or melted away and found its way home again. So next day, Richard sailed for Portofino, where he remained resting for five days, probably with an attack of fever. He then resumed his journey in pleasant yachting style, putting in at Pisa, where the Bishop of Rouen joined him. Then, evidently feeling the need for exercise or tired of the motion of the ship, he landed with a small escort at Baratti and rode to the castle of Piombino, rejoining his ship on August 23rd. On the 25th he entered the Tiber at the Faros di Roma, where he was met by Octavian, Cardinal Bishop of Ostia, who invited him to Rome. Far from accepting the invitation, Richard soundly rated the cardinal for the exactions of the curia, and the amount of money he had had to pay out for Longchamp's legateship and other matters.

He reached Naples on August 28th and remained at the Abbey of St Januarius for ten days. Leaving Naples on September 8th, he rode to Salerno and stayed there five days to consult the doctors of the university about his health. While at Salerno he heard that the main body of his fleet had overtaken him and was approaching Messina. But he does not seem to have been in any hurry to join it and continued his leisurely cruise past Amalfi and Couza, every now and then putting into shore for the night.

But as he rode over to La Bagnara on the Strait of Messina he had a disagreeable adventure which very nearly put an end to his crusade altogether. Passing through a certain village with only one attendant, he noticed a magnificent falcon in the window of a peasant's hut and as, with Richard, to want was to have, he dismounted and pushed his way in and took the bird. He was just about to remount and ride off with it under his arm when he was stopped by the owner of the falcon and an argument arose. The man drew a knife and Richard began beating him with the flat of his sword. Soon the king was surrounded by a crowd of angry villagers, who began to stone him, and the next moment the leader of the crusade for the rescue of the Holy Sepulchre was in the midst of a most undignified battle. Stones flew thick and fast, but Richard with his long reach, got the better of them and, "narrowly escaping from their hands", rode on to the Priory of Bagnara.

Probably not in the best of tempers—for he did not stop at the priory—Richard rode on to the straits and crossed at once to Messina, camping outside the town by the great lighthouse. The next day, 23 September 1190, mustering his fleet he made a more suitable entry into the harbour. "So great was the splendour of the approaching armament, such the clashing and brilliancy of their arms, so noble the sound of the trumpets and clarions," writes Richard of Devizes, "that the city quaked and was greatly astonished, and there came to meet the king a multitude of all ages, people without number, wondering and proclaiming with what exceeding glory and magnificence that king had arrived, surpassing the King of France, who with his forces had arrived seven days before." Indeed, all the way along Philip Augustus felt himself put into the shade by Richard, as the original Augustus had felt himself rebuked by the glory of Antony. Ten years younger, Philip had none of Richard's renown as a warrior. His methods were more politic; but it was he who won in the end.

Meanwhile, the English fleet had had an eventful voyage. Ten ships from Dartmouth, sailing towards Lisbon, "having St Matthew of Finisterre, or of Finis Posternae, on their left, and the great sea by which men go to Ireland on their right..." and "leaving all Poitou, Gascony and Biscay on their left... on the day of the Lord's Ascension (May 3rd) about the third hour, a fierce and terrible tempest swept down upon them; in a moment, in the twinkling of an eye, the ships were parted one from the other. While the tempest yet raged, and all were calling upon the Lord in their distress, the blessed Thomas the martyr, Archbishop of Canterbury, appeared thrice very clearly to three persons, who were in a vessel of London. On board this vessel were William Fitz Osbert and Geoffrey the Goldsmith, citizens of London. To these three St Thomas spoke as follows: 'Be not afraid. I, Thomas Archbishop of Canterbury, the blessèd martyr Edmund, and the blessèd confessor Nicholas have been appointed by the Lord guardians of the fleet of the king of England. If the men of this fleet keep themselves from evil deeds and do penance for their past offences the Lord will grant them a prosperous voyage and direct their steps in His paths.' After repeating these words three times the blessed Thomas faded from their sight; the tempest subsided at once, and there was a great calm on the sea."[11]

[11] Roger of Hovedon, quoted by T. A. Archer, *The Crusade of Richard I, 1189–92.*

Putting into Silves in Portugal, the farthest outpost of Christendom—the town had only been captured from the Emperor of Morocco the year before—the Portuguese were so delighted to welcome the hundred young warriors on board that they broke up their ships and would not let them go. And when the other ships of the English fleet arrived at Silves, Sancho I of Portugal was so heartened that he refused the favourable terms proposed by the Moors. But the English behaved very badly at Silves and several of them were punished according to the ordinance of Chinon by Robert de Sablun. On July 24th the main fleet arrived at Silves, making up the total of 106 great ships laden with men, victuals and arms. Setting out again, they crept round the coast of Spain till they came to the Straits of Africa, which they passed on August 1st, and coasting slowly along by Tarragona and Barcelona, they at last reached Marseille on August 22nd.

Of the English contingent the first to arrive in the Holy Land were Baldwin Archbishop of Canterbury, Hubert Bishop of Salisbury and Ranulf de Glanville. Having sailed directly from Marseille, they reached Tyre on September 16th and then, as there was no sign of Richard or Philip, went on to the camp outside the walls of Acre. "There we found our army (I say it with grief and groaning) giving up to shameful practices, and yielding to ease and lust rather than encouraging virtue," wrote Archbishop Baldwin to his convent at Canterbury on 21 October 1190. "The Lord is not in the camp; there is none that doeth good. The chiefs envy one another and strive for privilege. The lesser folk are in want and find no one to help them. In the camp there is neither chastity, sobriety, faith, nor charity—a state of things which, I call God to witness, I would not have believed had I not seen it... On the feast of St James (July 25th) more than 4,000 of our choicest foot-soldiers were slain by the Turks; and on the same day many of the chiefs perished... The Queen of Jerusalem, the earl of Ferrers, and the earl of Clare's brother... Ranulf de Glanville, and innumerable others are dead, but the kings have not arrived, nor is Acre taken."

Poor old Ranulf de Glanville, weakened by the fatigue of the journey, had succumbed to the epidemic that now raged in the camp as a result of the dirt, the flies, the vermin and the frightful stench from the unburied dead, who lay rotting under the burning sun—that is to say, the foot-soldiers mentioned in the archbishop's letter. Ten thousand of these men, the sergeants as they were called, disgusted at the continual bickering and inactivity of their feudal overlords, had taken matters into their own hands and attacked the Moslem camp, which surrounded them on the land side. Saladin saw what was happening, withdrew and allowed the foot-soldiers unsupported by cavalry to enter the camp. Then when they were busy with loot, the Saracen light horsemen swept down from the hills and massacred the lot. Guy de Lusignan and his knights contemptuously left the lower orders to their fate and soon the terrain between the Christian camp and the tents of Saladin's brother, Malik el Adil, was littered with corpses. Many French women who had also taken part in the expedition—presumably prostitutes—lay dead among the others. After that the river Belus ran for more than a week with blood and lumps of decomposing flesh. Meanwhile the siege of Acre dragged on, the kings did not come, Archbishop Baldwin died; and the camp gave itself up to debauchery.

II

SICILIAN ADVENTURE

On his arrival in Sicily, Richard leapt ashore and Philip came to meet him. The two kings fell upon each other's necks and "all the great men of the City of Messina, and the clergy and people, stood on the shore marvelling because of all they saw and what they had heard concerning the king of England and his power". Destriers were brought and Richard and his household mounted and rode to the house of Reginald de Muhec in the vineyards outside the city, the royal palace being already occupied by Philip.

The rest of the English force that had arrived before the king, having been denied access to the city, were encamped along the shore. In fact the temper of the Messinese—"a parcel of Griffons and low fellows of Saracen extraction", as the English chroniclers describe them—was hostile in the extreme. They had already had bitter experience of other crusaders, and as Ambroise admits, "they distrusted their women folk with whom the pilgrims conversed". So the Lombards broke up the tents of the pilgrims and killed many of them and outraged their corpses. The situation was made all the more dangerous by the fact that Tancred, who had usurped the throne of Sicily after the death of William the Good, now posed as the champion of the people of Sicily against the unwelcome crusaders. He was also preparing to turn to his own account any differences that might arise between the two kings. William the Good, the husband of Richard's sister Joanna, had, it is true, been enthusiastic about the crusade; but apart from that he had lived in his pleasure-palace surrounded by oriental slave-girls. These pleasures were not productive of an heir, though they brought on his death at an early age. Unfortunately, in order to appease the German emperor, he had given his aunt Constance in marriage to Henry of Swabia, with the promise that if he died without children, she should inherit the kingdom of the Two Sicilies—that is, Sicily and Apulia. But on his death his bastard cousin Tancred drove the Germans out of the country. Otherwise, Tancred, the last of the Norman kings of Sicily, appears to have had different tastes from his cousin in amorous affairs and is described by his chronicler as "*semi-vir, embryo infelix et detestabile monstrum.*"[1] As for Joanna, Tancred kept her in virtual custody as a bargaining piece.

On his arrival, Richard set up a gigantic gallows outside the crusaders' camp and at once began to make use of it. "His judges delegate spared neither sex nor age," we are told, "and there was one punishment for a stranger and for one born in the land." Philip, on the other hand, left the evil-doing of his own men unpunished, which the Sicilians seemed to have preferred to the stern even-handed justice of the English king, whose punitive measures only inflamed local feeling still more. Soon the people of Messina refused to allow the long-tailed Englishmen, as they called them, to buy food in the city, and whenever they came upon them singly or in small parties, they killed them.

Meanwhile, Tancred not only held Joanna as a prisoner, but what was worse he withheld her dowry and a large bequest that William the Good was known to have made to Henry II in his will. This included a golden table twelve feet long, a silk pavilion big enough for 200 knights to banquet in, a hundred galleys "fitted out for two years", 60,000 seams (a mule's or ass's burden) of corn, and the same number of barley, wine, and twenty-four golden cups and plates. This bequest had evidently been intended as William's contribution to the crusade. Richard now claimed it as Henry's heir and demanded the return of Joanna and her dowry, as well as the golden chair that was the customary seat of the queens of Sicily.

[1] Vincent Cronin, *The Golden Honeycomb*, p. 154.

On receiving these demands, Tancred, who was at Palermo, sent Joanna off at once with her "bed gear" and a million *tersini* in lieu of her dowry. Richard lodged her temporarily at the Hospital in Messina. Then, crossing over to Calabria, he seized the Castle of La Bagnara, turned out the Griffons and established her there. On the way back to Messina, on October 2nd, he seized a fortified monastery on an island in the straits, dispatched by various tortures the monks who resisted, and adds Richard of Devizes, "caused them to be exhibited as a gazing-stock to their friends". Presumably they were the wrong sort of Christians—that is, of the Greek Orthodox Church. The monastery Richard converted into a storehouse and arsenal.

The spectacle of these brutal and aggressive acts naturally led the Messinese to expect worse to come and they renewed their attacks on the "long-tailed Englishmen", killing them by forties and fifties. "Now it chanced on a certain day (October 3rd) that one of our men was bargaining with a woman over some fresh-baked bread she had exposed for sale. And as they were talking together and he was disputing over the price, the woman suddenly flew into a passion because he offered her less for the loaf than she wanted. And she began to call him names, and could scarcely refrain from smiting him with her fists or tearing out his hair. And lo! suddenly there gathered together a crowd of citizens who had heard the woman's wrangling. These seized the pilgrim, beat him pitilessly, tore out his hair, and, when they trod him underfoot, left him almost lifeless. But King Richard, as soon as the uproar arose, came forth and begged for peace and friendship, declaring that he had come on a peaceful mission and merely to fulfil his pilgrimage, nor did he cease from his efforts till everyone had departed without anger to his own house. And yet, thanks to the industry of that old enemy of the human race, the contention was renewed on the morrow in a more deadly way."[2]

Next day Richard called a conference to discuss the situation. But even as the conference was sitting "there rose up a shout of men crying that the natives were openly slaying the king of England's followers. As the king paid no attention to this—chiefly because the Lombards declared it was not true—there came up a second messenger with the news that the natives had set upon the pilgrims. The Lombards, though they had themselves just come from the contest, were dissuading the king from believing this information, when there

[2] *Itinerarium Regis Ricardi.*

appeared a third messenger running up in haste and declaring that peace was not to be thought of while their very lives were in danger."

So Richard left the council and rode to the scene of the disturbance, where he found Admiral Margarit and Jordan del Pin, the wardens of Messina, stirring up the townsfolk against the English. As soon as they saw Richard they greeted him with jeers about his tail, which the crowd of Greeks and Lombards outside the walls eagerly took up.

When Richard returned to his quarters his fury astounded even his nearest friends, who, we are told, scarcely dared to look him in the face. "O my soldiers!" he cried, as he strove to master his choking anger, "my kingdom's strength and crown! who have endured with me a thousand perils, do you now see how a cowardly rabble insults us? Shall we vanquish Turks and Arabs? Shall we be a terror to nations the most invincible? Shall our right hand make us a way even to the ends of the world for the Cross of Christ? Shall we restore the Kingdom of Israel when we have turned our backs before vile and effeminate Griffons?"

The knights roared with one voice that they were ready to conquer all Sicily at his command. Richard replied that he was glad to hear it and that if Tancred did not speedily satisfy him for his sister's dowry and King William's legacy he was prepared to depopulate the country and sell the Messinese into slavery. So saying, he then caused the trumpets to be blown for a general assault on Messina, put on his armour and rode back to the city with a small party of knights.

At his approach the townsfolk scattered like sheep. It is said that the king had not twenty of his men when he first set upon them. At the entrance to a postern gate he laid low several of them, disabling others. He then gave the command for a general assault upon the city. "Then might you have seen his people going up, scaling the embankments, and cutting the bars of the gates assunder; and there were many taken and slain. Into the midst of the streets rushed certain ones but soon repented thereof ... And whosoever may have been the last the king himself was one of the first that durst enter the town. Thereafter entered full ten thousand men."[3] The *Itinerarium* gives further details. "As the enemy's darts and stones were flying thickly we lost three knights of special repute, to wit, Peter Torpreie, Matthew de Sauley, and Ralf de Roverei. ... The number of

[3] Ambroise, *Estoire de la guerre sainte*.

citizens and others defending the walls was reckoned at more than
50,000. There might you see our galleys attempting to besiege the
city from the harbour near the palace. But the king of France kept
them out of the main harbour, and hence it came to pass that some
of them who were already within and would not depart perished by
arrows.... But why say more? King Richard got possession of
Messina in one attack quicker than any priest could chant matins.
Aye and many more of the citizens would have perished had not the
king in his compassion ordered their lives to be spared."

Their goods and their wives, however, were another matter.
"Whatever precious thing was found, whether gold or silver, became the possession of the conquerors. Moreover fire reduced the
galleys of the citizens to dust." Hostages were taken and Richard
set up his banners along the fortifications. But he gave instructions
that in the general plunder of the city the French within the royal
palace were to be respected. Nevertheless, Philip as Richard's feudal
superior, was most indignant when he saw the English standards
waving on the city walls and demanded that they should be taken
down and his own set up. And, though he had hindered rather than
helped the operation, he did not forget to claim half the loot, according to the Vézelay agreement and altogether became so unpleasant
that Richard, at one point, determined to strike camp, load up his
ships and start for the Holy Land without him. But two days later
he agreed that the French *fleur de lys* should be set up on the walls
beside the golden lions of England, and gave the fortifications of the
city over to the Templars and Hospitallers as a hostage till Tancred
should fulfil his demands.[4]

During the negotiations with Tancred, Margarit and Jordan du
Pin, the wardens of Messina, decamped one night with all their gold
and silver. Richard at once seized upon their houses, their galleys
and whatever other movables they had left behind. He then
strengthened his own arsenal and storehouse by digging a wide and
deep trench across the island on which it was situated, and began
building a high wooden tower on a hill overlooking the city, which

---

[4] The Hospitallers, or Knights of St John, originated in a foundation
for destitute pilgrims in Jerusalem made by the citizens of Amalfi before
the first crusade. The Templars, a sovereign order of fighting monks,
existed to protect pilgrims to the Holy City. They derived their name
from the Temple of Solomon made over to them by Baldwin II, whose
palace it had been. Geoffrey de Vinsauf describes them as "devoted to
slaughter".

he called Mategriffon, or Kill Greek. To speed negotiations he announced his readiness to take all Sicily as he had taken Messina. He was not prepared, he said, to wait indefinitely, but would get what he wanted in his own way.

Once again, this hectoring attitude did not improve relations with the Messinese, who now refused to sell any food at all to the English camp, and "but for God and the navy" says one chronicler, "many would have had a poor life". Fortunately the fleet was well stocked.

Up to now Tancred had been playing a waiting game, watching to see which of the two kings would prove most useful to him. Having failed in his attempts to bring about a marriage between one of his daughters and either Philip himself or Philip's infant son Louis, and since Richard had shown his prowess in the capture of Messina, it was with him that Tancred decided to ally himself. He agreed to pay 20,000 ounces of gold (about £15,000) in settlement of Joanna's dower, with another 20,000 ounces in settlement of all other claims and as an advance on the contract of marriage between young Arthur of Brittany aged three, whom Richard had designated as his heir, should he die without issue, and one of Tancred's daughters. In return Richard agreed to give Tancred his aid against anyone who should attack him or invade his lands. The most likely person to attack him was the German emperor, who claimed Sicily and the duchy of Apulia in the right of his wife Constance. By this treaty, therefore, Richard was supporting a usurper and giving Henry VI a legitimate grievance against him.

Regulations were then drawn up by the three kings, Richard, Philip and Tancred, for the conduct of the armies in Sicily, for the disposal of the property of those who died on crusade and the treatment of deserters. The price of bread and wine was fixed, gambling restricted, the rates of exchange settled, and Richard and Philip once again swore on the relics of the saints to keep faith with one another. This renewal of the pact was necessary, because Philip had only recently offered Tancred his help against his sworn ally. But, says Ambroise, "the knights who had been waiting about in Sicily all the summer lamented and complained because of the expense to which they were put." Richard therefore promised to recompense them all for the unavoidable delay, distributing goblets of silver and gold among them, according to their respective stations. The foot-soldiers got at least 2d each and to the ladies who had been driven out of Syria he gave rich gifts. "So all the host was of good cheer because of his honour and his largesse and because of the peace that was come." But as by this time it had grown too late in the year to risk a sea-journey to Palestine, it was agreed to remain at Messina for the winter—a strange decision considering the desperate plight of the camp at Acre. Nevertheless, the risk of losing everything in a stormy passage was too great.

Something—perhaps the approach of Christmas—now put Richard into a repentant mood. "He called to mind the foulness of his past life," says Roger of Hovedon, "and after contrition of heart gathered the bishops and archbishops who were with him at Messina together in Reginald de Muhec's chapel. Then, falling naked at their feet he did not blush to confess the foulness of his life to God in their presence. For the thorns of his evil lusts had grown higher than his head and there was no hand to root them up." And Hoveden adds cryptically: "Happy is he who after repentance has not slipped back into sin."

Richard celebrated Christmas at Mategriffon with a great feast to which he invited King Philip and his nobles. "I was eating in the hall," says Ambroise, "but never did I see there a dirty cloth nor a cup or spoon of wood, but rich plate with carving and figures, and adorned with precious stones; there was nothing cheap or common, and the feast was so nobly served that everyone was satisfied. Nor ever did I see anyone give such rich gifts as King Richard gave on this occasion. For he gave the king of France and his folk vessels of gold and silver."

Among the attributes of chivalry largesse is understandably ranked very high by medieval writers, and in Richard largesse was only equalled by prowess.

Unfortunately the good humour of the feast was somewhat marred by civil broils, when the Pisans and the Genoese, jealous of their monopoly, attacked the English oarsmen. The noise came to the king's ears as he sat at meat in Mategriffon. But the disturbance was not quelled until several people had been killed. Next day, too, when they were all gathered at divine service celebrating the birth of the Prince of Peace at the Church of St John of the Hospital, "a certain Pisan drew his knife and wounded one of the king's oarsmen in the church; upon which the Pisans and the galley-men fell to again, and many were slain on either side."

Early in February Richard was involved in another rather childish and discreditable incident, on a par with his scuffle with the Calabrian peasants in the matter of the falcon. He was out riding

with a company of French and English knights when they met a
countryman with a load of rushes or long canes. They stopped him
and bought (or took) some of his rushes with the idea of tilting at
each other with them. Richard challenged William de Barres, who
had once unhorsed him and whom he had subsequently taken
prisoner and let out on parole on his honour as a knight, but de
Barres had dishonourably broken his parole and escaped—an offence
not easily forgiven. And now as they rode at each other with bull-
rushes, de Barres's bullrush broke off the head of Richard's bullrush. For some reason this infuriated the king and he charged
wildly at de Barres, who just managed to keep his seat, though
Richard himself "came down quicker than he liked". Mounting
another horse he rode at de Barres again, and again failed to unseat
him, "for William stuck fast to his horse's neck". At this the king
became almost beside himself and went on charging senselessly at
the harassed knight.

The assembled nobles could hardly believe their eyes. What had
begun as a game, now looked like ending in disaster, and when the
young Earl of Leicester, de Barres's brother-in-law tried to intervene, Richard shouted furiously: "Leave me to deal with him
alone." After that the king charged repeatedly at his opponent, but
being quite unable to unseat him, finally burst out, "Get thee
hence, and take heed that I see thee no more, for henceforth I will
be an enemy to thee and thine for ever." De Barres complained to
Philip, his feudal overlord, and next day the Bishop of Chartres, the
Duke of Burgundy, the Count of Nevers and many other nobles
went down on their knees to Richard begging his forgiveness. But
it was all no use. Three days later de Barres had to leave Messina
"because the king of France would no longer keep him in his service against the will of the king of England". Yet de Barres was
one of the most puissant knights of France and was married to the
daughter of the great Earl of Leicester.

Queen Eleanor now seems to have decided that it was time for
Richard to get married. She did not want either John or little Arthur
(with the troublesome necessity of a regent) to succeed to the throne.
So taking the bull by the horns, she set out for Sicily with Beren-
garia, the daughter of Sancho VI of Navarre, and in February
Richard dispatched ships to Naples to meet them and their escort,
Philip Count of Flanders. But on account of the multitude of men
who accompanied them, Tancred refused them leave to go on to
Messina—very overcrowded with pilgrims already—and they had

to spend a month at Brindisi, where they were honourably received by Admiral Margarit.

Berengaria was the sister of the famous jouster, Richard's companion Sancho the Bold. Ambroise, who perhaps saw her on her arrival in Sicily, says that she was "a prudent maid, a gentle lady, virtuous and fair, neither false nor double-tongued". Walter of Hemmingburg describes her as "a renowned, beautiful and prudent virgin" whom Queen Eleanor now produced as "a salubrious remedy against the great perils of fornication". Not that Eleanor minded the fornication. She wanted Richard to marry Berengaria for the sake of the Navarrese alliance against Toulouse, not because she thought he would be happy with her. The contemporary chroniclers all stress Berengaria's "prudence" and seem to be agreed that she was more accomplished than beautiful. But whatever she was like, it was Richard's duty to produce an heir to secure the succession. If, however, he was to marry Berengaria it was evident that he could not now marry Alais of France.

Early in February Richard heard for the first time of the disturbances that had arisen in England between his brother John and the chancellor Longchamp, and he wrote to William Marshal—who had not accompanied him on the crusade—telling him that he was sending Walter of Coutances, Archbishop of Rouen over to England and that Walter was to be admitted to the council of the justiciars, who should act upon his advice. He also wrote to the chancellor and the justiciars ordering them to give the manor of Kirton in Linsey to his half-brother William Longsword.

In March he went to meet Tancred at Catania. Tancred gave him a splendid reception and entertained him for three days at the palace. "As the two kings went in company to visit the blessed Agatha's tomb the clergy and people met them before the entrance to the temple praising and blessing God, who had made them such close friends." On the fourth day Tancred loaded his guest with presents, gold, silver, horses and silk, but Richard would not accept any of them, giving to Tancred instead King Arthur's sword Excalibur, which had recently been dug up at Glastonbury. Then Tancred gave him four large ships called *ursers*—round sailing vessels for carrying horses—and fifteen galleys and accompanied him on his way as far as Taormina, where Philip was to meet them.

But at Taormina, Tancred produced a letter which he said he had received from Philip in which it was stated that Richard was a traitor who would not keep faith with anyone and promising that if Tancred felt inclined "to set upon him suddenly by night", Philip and his men would help to destroy him and his army. Richard could hardly believe his eyes, "for," said he, "the king of France is my lord and my sworn comrade in this pilgrimage." Tancred replied that he had indeed received the letter from Philip by the Duke of Burgundy and that if the duke denied having brought it, he, Tancred, was ready to prove his words against him by one of his lords—that is, by a judicial combat or ordeal.

This seems to have convinced Richard of Philip's perfidy and he went back to Messina by a different route so as to avoid meeting him. Next day, when Philip returned to Messina, Richard would not speak to him, and when he asked why Richard treated him in this way Richard produced the incriminating letter. At first, says Hoveden, "the king of France was struck speechless by his evil conscience". Then he said that the letter was a forgery and that Richard had invented the whole thing as an excuse for not marrying Alais. Richard replied bluntly that as for that, nothing would induce him to marry his father's whore. He then produced witnesses who "were ready to maintain this by every method that Alais succeeded Rosamond as the king's concubine" and that his father "had begotten a daughter on her". At this point the Count of Flanders stepped between the angry kings as mediator, and Philip released Richard from his obligation to marry his sister if he would compensate her and send her back to her people as soon as he returned from crusade. At the same time he urged Richard to make the March passage with him to the Holy Land. Richard readily agreed to compensate Alais, but said that he could not now possibly leave Sicily before August and that he was, in any case, thinking of returning to England to settle matters there. After a talk with his mother a few days later, however, he evidently changed his mind and decided to go through with the crusade. So Philip issued a proclamation:

> In the name of the Holy and undivided Trinity, Amen. . . . Know all men present and to come that a firm peace hath been made between us and our friend and faithful liege Richard, the illustrious king of England—of a good heart and will we grant the aforesaid king to marry whomsoever he will, notwithstanding the covenant made between ourselves and him regarding our sister Alais whom he ought to have married.

As soon as the new treaty of friendship was made and sealed

Richard was anxious to get rid of his feudal overlord. He gave him ships and began scattering largesse among his knights and sergeants, "till many said that none of his predecessors had given away in a year so much as he gave away in a month". He also promised to keep the peace towards de Barres.

Philip set sail for Acre on March 30th. Richard accompanied him a few miles out of the harbour and then, when he was safely on his way, turned aside to Reggio to pick up his mother and Berengaria, whom he lodged with his sister at La Bagnara. Four days later, the formidable old queen, her mission completed, left again for England, with the Archbishop of Rouen, to keep watch upon her other son.

III

THE CONQUEST OF CYPRUS

THERE was now nothing to keep Richard in Sicily. On 10 April 1191, after a delay of six months, he at last continued his pilgrimage to Jerusalem. His fleet sailed from Messina in the following order: in the first line went three ships, one with Joanna and Berengaria, the other two carried part of the king's treasure and armaments. The second line consisted of thirteen vessels, the third of fourteen, the fourth of twenty, the fifth of thirty, the sixth of forty and the seventh of sixty. Lastly came the king himself in his war galley Trenchemer. It had two banks of oars and the prow was furnished with an iron beak to transfix the enemy.

A fair wind carried this armada out of the strait and into the open sea, and the king's galley sped forward to overtake the slower vessels, the busses and the great dromonds in the front rank. Then the wind dropped and the ships anchored between Calabria and Mount Etna. Next morning the wind rose again, but feebly, and by nightfall the fleet was becalmed again. But on Good Friday, April 12th, about the time of the Crucifixion, a great wind scattered the fleet and the pilgrims "suffered sore distress and much misease in mouth and heart and head," which, however, they gladly endured for the sake of Him Who on that day had suffered so much for them. All Good Friday the wind buffeted them about, and when night fell they saw the king's ship still leading and showing the way by a great candle burning in a lantern. For upon Richard, we are told, no tempest had any effect: he remained perfectly calm, healthy and hearty, brave and strong, on sea as on land.

For three days the fleet sailed on, till on Wednesday in Easter week, April 17th, they came to Crete. There they dropped anchor and rested. But twenty-five transport ships were found to be missing, "whereat the king was sore displeased and very wroth". Next day they sailed on to Rhodes in a high wind, and lofty were the waves, and it seemed to the pilgrims that God was pleased by the course they were following. At Rhodes they stayed ten days while Richard made inquiries about Isaac Comnenus, the self-styled emperor of Cyprus. He was told that Isaac did everything to hold up supplies to the Holy Land and was in close alliance with Saladin.

At one time Cyprus had been an important supply-base for the crusaders. In 1156 Reynaud de Chatillon, whose headquarters was Antioch, had invaded the island and captured the Greek governor, many leading churchmen and prominent citizens. Some of these he mutilated in his pleasant fashion, and sent as a present to the emperor at Byzantium. Now, however, Isaac Comnenus ruled Cyprus as an independent Greek tyrant. Richard suspected that his missing ships had been driven south by the great storm on Good Friday and had probably put in at Cyprus. If so, they would be in need of assistance. Among those missing were the three dromonds which carried his wife and sister, the greater part of his treasure and the Great Seal.

As it turned out, these ships had been wrecked trying to put in at Limassol and Roger Malcael, the vice-chancellor had been drowned with the Seal hanging round his neck. Those who managed to struggle ashore were disarmed and imprisoned by Isaac Comnenus, who, with the experiences of his predecessors in mind, had given orders that no crusaders should be allowed to land. The boat carrying Berengaria and Joan had managed to keep clear of the rocks and had put out to sea again for fear of Isaac.

At the end of a week the starving knights shut up in the castle of Limassol, managed to fight their way out and, though they had only three bows between them, put the fear of God into "the base Grecian rabble". At the same time the ship with Richard's frailer treasure on board was brought into harbour and Isaac invited the ladies to land, but this they were loth to do, in spite of gifts of meat, bread and wine. Meanwhile more and more of Isaac's troops had assembled on the shore and just as Berengaria and Joanna were about to land after all, Richard's fleet hove in sight.

It was Sunday the sixth of May. The king had had a bad passage and was in a bad temper. Nevertheless he sent a courteous message to Isaac, requesting him to make amends for the evil his people had done to the shipwrecked pilgrims. Isaac was on shore, surrounded by his troops, and he cut the king's messenger short with an insulting exclamation "Phrut"—for when he lost his temper he would froth at the mouth and emit noises like a boiling kettle. The messenger went back and repeated this to Richard, whose reply was equally brief—"Aux Armes!".

Between the fleet and the shore lay five of Isaac's armed galleys and on the shore were Isaac's troops drawn up behind a barricade of doors, window-frames, shutters, barrels, benches, boxes and planks. Behind them lay the fortified town of Limassol.

Boats were lowered from the transports and the knights and crossbowmen got into them, while the Griffons on the shore "like dogs they howled at us", says Ambroise.

First the crossbowmen sent a deadly volley whistling into the enemy's galleys, killing many of the oarsmen, who were soon tumbling into the water, four by four. Then the galleys were captured by the knights and under a rain of arrows and crossbow-bolts the Greeks on the shore began to waver and give ground. "And then might ye hear our men howl at them as they had howled at us, ere we began to advance, but our rowers moved ever onward, albeit withersoever they came bolts and darts rained down upon them."

When Richard saw his men about to land, he sprang from his galley into the sea and, wading ashore, led the attack on the beaches. Most of the Greeks who lined the shore were, according to Roger of Hovedon, more or less unarmed and quite unskilled in battle; but they made a stand against the terrible iron-clad knights, pathetically holding stakes, bits of wood, seats and boxes before them for a wall. But the knights cut them down right and left, till the sea-waves ran red, and Richard wielding his axe, chased some of them right into the town, and out into the fields beyond. He then saw Isaac and, running after him, caught a sumpter horse that had a sack for saddle and stirrups of cord, and, mounting, called out, "Emperor, come and joust!" But the emperor had no mind to joust and rode off into the mountains on his fleet Arab courser Fauvel. So Richard gave chase up the mountain paths.

When he returned to Limassol, he found it "forsaken of the
Griffons" but stocked with enormous supplies of corn, wine, oil, and
flesh. Joanna, Berengaria and the whole fleet then sailed into the
harbour, and the horses were landed and exercised. The poor beasts,
we learn, were "all stiff and benumbed and dizzy, having been for
a whole month on the sea, standing ever."

Next morning, before it was light, Richard set off with about fifty
knights for a surprise attack on Isaac's camp. His scouts had told
him of its whereabouts five miles away in the mountains. "Marching
along without any noise, they came to the emperor's host and found
it sleeping. Then with a great and terrible cry the king entered their
tents, whilst the enemy, being roused from sleep, became as dead
men ... because the king of England's army was setting on them
like ravening wolves."[5] Ambroise says that the king was riding some
way in advance of his main force, with a small body of knights, and
that when they saw the vast Greek camp spread out before them, a
clerk came to Richard and asked him whether it would not be better
to wait for the army to come up before attacking. "Sir clerk," said
the king, "get you to your writing, and leave matters of chivalry to
us, in the name of God and of St Mary." With these words, he set
his steel helmet on his head and charged the foe "more swiftly than
the falling thunderbolt", driving full tilt through the camp and
throwing everything into confusion. After that the main body of his
troops came up and butchered the Greeks in their tents. "No man
ever knew the number of the dead ... they that had horses fled
away up to the hills or down into the dales.[6]

Among those who fled to the mountains was the Emperor Isaac.
Richard had already struck down his standard-bearer and once more
chased the flying Greeks up the precipitous mountain paths. The
booty that fell into the pilgrims' hands was enormous—gold and
silver plate from the emperor's tent, his bed, "silken stuffs and
stuff of purple dye, horses and mules laden as for a market, hauberks
and helms and swords, oxen and kine, nimble goats, rams, ewes and
lambs, mares with foals sleek and fat, capons and hens and cocks,
plump mules with embroidered cushions on their backs ... and so
many Greeks and Armenians that the road was fair cumbered with
them." Their captured standards Richard sent back to England to
be hung above the shrine of St Edmund of Bury.

At Limassol Richard issued a proclamation that "all people of

[5] Hovedon.   [6] Ambroise.

the land who did not desire war might come and go in safety, but such as did seek war should have no peace or truce with him." Three days later on May 11th the leading crusaders arrived at Limassol to do homage to Richard and to seek his support against Philip Augustus, who was planning to depose Guy de Lusignan, the titular king of Jerusalem, in favour of Conrad of Montferrat, Lord of Tyre. Richard went out to meet their galleys and on board he found Guy de Lusignan himself—a native of Poitou who had been exiled to the Holy Land some time ago for killing the Earl of Salisbury while on a pilgrimage to St James of Compostella— Geoffrey de Lusignan his brother and Humfrey of Toron, Bohemund Prince of Antioch, Raymond Count of Tripoli, and Leo brother of Rupin de la Montaine, prince of Armenia.

Richard gave them a royal welcome and next day, on Sunday, May 12th, celebrated his marriage to the accomplished and prudent Berengaria in the chapel of the castle at Limassol.[7] Indeed he could not have delayed it much longer, for already there were whispers about Berengaria's compromised virginity. Richard of Devizes even refers to her unchivalrously as "presumably still a virgin". But the king, we are told, was glorious on this happy occasion, and showed himself jocose and affable—which, evidently, was not often the case. The ceremony was conducted by Nicholas, the king's chaplain, and the same day Berengaria was crowned Queen of England and Cyprus by the Bishop of Evreaux. Richard made a settlement of dower upon her of lands in Maine.

The marriage over, Richard turned to more important matters. With the aid of the reinforcements brought by Guy it was decided to undertake the conquest of Cyprus. The island lay right across the supply route to the kingdom of Jerusalem and could not very well be left in enemy hands. When news of this was brought to Isaac in Nicosia he suggested holding a conference to discuss peace terms. The conference was held in a garden of fig-trees between the harbour and the road to Limassol. Richard arrived for the talks mounted on a splendid Spanish horse, "having on its hinder part two golden lion cubs rampant and as if snarling at each other". He was dressed in a tunic of rose-coloured samite and a mantle "bedight with small half-moons of solid silver set in rows, interspersed with shining orbs like suns". On his head he had a scarlet cap. Isaac swore fealty to him, agreed to pay an enormous indemnity

[7] That is, the castle which stood before the present fourteenth century one used as a gaol.

and to supply him with 500 horse for the crusades. As a surety, he placed all his castles in the king's hands. The kiss of peace was exchanged and the emperor was led to his own tent, where he shortly realized that he was, to all intents and purposes, Richard's prisoner, although the detention of a vassal, after having received his homage, was a breach of the feudal tie. So, in the night, Isaac mounted his steed Fauvel and fled to Colossi. As soon as his absence was discovered, Richard, treating his flight as a breach of the treaty, gave orders for him to be pursued. Next day Guy de Lusignan marched on Famagusta, while Richard went round by sea.

But at Famagusta the palace was deserted. Instead of Isaac, Richard was met by Philip's envoys who urged him to come to Acre without further delay, Philip himself having already been there for a month. The tone of the messenger was so peremptory that the king, we are told, "raised his eyebrows and words were spoken which it is not meet to write." Not for half the wealth of Russia, said Richard, would he leave Cyprus till he had conquered it and made it his principal supply base. Then, after sending ships to block-ade the other ports, he left Famagusta and marched inland to Nicosia. On the way there, fearing an ambush the king took com-mand of the rearguard. And, sure enough, Isaac, unable to stop the advance of the Frankish knights, confined himself to harassing their column as it moved slowly through the unfamiliar terrain. He got near enough to shoot a couple of poisoned arrows at Richard, who at once dashed after him. "But the emperor was mounted on Fauvel, who bore him away with the swiftness of the stag that fleeth amain, straight to the castle of Kantara."

When Richard entered Nicosia the people came out of their houses and acknowledged him as their lord and father. But he made them shave off their beards, which to a Greek was an unbearable insult and a sign of servitude.[8] When Isaac heard of it, he nearly went mad, and after that, whenever he caught any of the crusaders, he cut off their hands and feet and put out their eyes. One day, as he sat at breakfast, one of his councellors advised him to surrender to Richard before it was too late. Isaac was so angry that he struck the speaker with his knife and cut off his nose. The emperor was not a very pleasant character and was reputed to have murdered his wife—that is, the sister of William II of Sicily—and his son, because the boy admitted to liking the Latins.

[8] Beards had gone out of fashion in the West. The Normans shaved regularly and looked upon any superfluity of hair as effeminate.

· Meanwhile at Nicosia Richard fell ill. So he divided his army into three parts and left the direction of operations to Guy de Lusignan, who besieged and took the castle of Kyrenia and with it Isaac's wife and daughter. The emperor was so upset by this that he lost all further interest in the defence of Cyprus and ordered the immediate surrender of the fortress of Didimus. But by this time, in any case, the greater part of his followers had deserted him, and, seeing that further resistance was useless, at the end of May he came and threw himself at Richard's feet and embraced his knees. Richard played with him, like the great cat he was. At first he received Isaac graciously, seated him at his side and had his daughter brought to him. Then, abruptly changing his aspect, he granted Isaac's request that, being a king, he should not be put in irons, loaded him with silver chains instead and dispatched him to Margat above Tripoli as a prisoner of the Templars.

The people of Cyprus—that is, the foreign trading community—willingly yielded up to Richard half their possessions in gratitude for being freed from Isaac's tyranny. The government of the island was then put in the hands of two Englishmen, Richard de Canville and Stephen de Turnham, who were instructed to send regular supplies of Cyprian wine, barley, wheat, sheep and bullocks to Palestine. Altogether, the booty from Cyprus was vast. Among the horses taken was Isaac's unmatched steed Fauvel, henceforth to bear the Lion Heart.

Richard had delayed so long on the way that news now reached him of the imminent fall of Acre. "Never may such a thing befall," he cried, "as that any should be able to take it without me!" After that nothing could hold him in Cyprus. The two queens, with Isaac's little daughter, had been already sent on to the kingdom of Jerusalem in two busses. The king himself sailed from Famagusta on June 5th with Guy de Lusignan and his peers.

Shortly after his departure, the ungrateful people of Cyprus revolted and set up a new emperor, a kinsman of Isaac's whom Stephen de Turnham, after crushing the revolt, hanged.

In 1196 the Hermit of Neophytus wrote bitterly: "The English king, the wretch, landed in Cyprus and found it as a nursing mother, and had it not been so, he too perchance would have suffered the fate of the German [Frederick Barbarossa] . . . The wicked wretch achieved nought against his fellow wretch Saladin, but achieved this only, that he sold our country to the Latins for 200,000 pounds of gold."[9]

[9] C. D. Cobham, *Excerpta Cypria*, p. 12.

IV

THE WALLS OF ACRE

It was very nearly a hundred years ago since the first crusade and the capture of Jerusalem in 1099. Then a vast international brigade, marching overland via Byzantium and Anatolia and led by Bohemund Prince of Tarento, Robert Duke of Normandy (who pawned his duchy to William Rufus), Raymond of Toulouse and Godfrey de Bouillon, had celebrated their arrival in the Holy City by a great massacre of Jews and Moslems.

"If you had been there," wrote Fulcher of Chartres enthusiastically, "your feet would have been stained up to the ankles with the blood of the slain.... Not one of them was allowed to live. They did not spare the women and children. Those who clamboured up onto the roof were shot to death with arrows." Raymond of Agiles adds further gory details. "Piles of heads and hands were to be seen in the streets of the city. One had to pick one's way over the bodies of men and horses.... In the Temple of Solomon men rode in blood up to their knees and bridle reins. Indeed it was a just and splendid judgement of God that this place should be filled with the blood of the unbelievers."[1] So the word of Christ was brought back to Jerusalem.

The ostensible purpose of the first crusade was to assist the Greek Emperor Alexius against the Seljuk Turks. But the crusaders had other ideas—the conquest of Syria and Palestine with the aid of Venetian, Pisan, Genoese and Scandinavian fleets. Baldwin I became King of Jerusalem, the coastal cities were conquered and the barons from the West were given provinces and became feudal lords of Antioch, Edessa and Tripoli, and carried on wars indiscriminately against both the Greek Christians and the Moslems, temporarily allying themselves with one emir against another and only paying lip-service to the crown of Jerusalem. Raymond of Toulouse carved out for himself the county of Tripoli, while Tancred pushed the boundaries of the state of Antioch as far as Aleppo in northern Syria. The mercantile cities of the Mediterranean were granted special trading privileges and grew rich on the pilgrim traffic to Jerusalem.

[1] Quoted by John L. La Monte, *The World of the Middle Ages*, p. 342.

All this could be done because the Moslems were divided among themselves. There was rivalry between Aleppo, Damascus and Mosul, and the Sultan at Baghdad was more or less indifferent to his westernmost provinces. Moreover the ferocity of the Christians was widely feared. The capture of Edessa by Nurredin in 1147 had precipitated the Second Crusade, which, however, only gave the Moslems a poor opinion of the Franks. For a short time after 1163, Amaury, brother of Baldwin III, held Cairo till routed by Nurredin's general Shirkuh, who got rid of the Fatimid viziers and proclaimed Nurredin's rule over Lower Egypt. In this Egyptian campaign, Shirkuh was accompanied by his nephew Salah-al-Din Jusuf ibn Ayjub, called by the crusaders Saladin. At his uncle's death Saladin became Vizier of Egypt and two years later, in 1171, he quietly liquidated the Fatimid caliph and became ruler of Egypt. At his death, Nurredin left his dominions to his son Salah, "a young man", says Bohardin, "unequal to the cares and responsibilities of sovereignty and to the task of driving the enemies of God from the land". Saladin, therefore, advanced upon Damascus and, as Bohardin charmingly says, "took Salah's education in hand, together with the government and the re-establishment of order". The re-establishment of order involved fighting and defeating several of Nurredin's generals. It was his conquest of Syria that brought Saladin into conflict with the Franks.

Saladin's decision to roll up the map of the kingdom of Jerusalem was taken after Reginald de Chatillon's ill-judged expedition against Mecca in 1182, which accomplished nothing beyond insulting the Moslems and earning the undying hatred of the Sultan. By this time Baldwin IV was a helpless leper and the kingdom of Jerusalem was divided on the issue of the regency between the court party, mostly composed of first generation immigrants, and the old Franco-Syrian barons. The Syrian Franks feared above all things the succession to the throne of Guy de Lusignan, the husband of Baldwin's sister Sibylla, whom they called "soft-headed".[2] To forestall this, they crowned Baldwin V, Sibylla's son by a former husband. But after ruling a few months Baldwin V died, and the throne was

---

[2] The Lusignans were an ancient Poitevin house claiming a descent as picturesque as that of the house of Anjou. Melusine, the wife of Raymondin de Lusignan, was reputed to have become a serpent "from the waist downwards" every Saturday night. Eventually she was turned into a dragon—an allegory which might be paralleled in many marriages. At this time Guy de Lusignan was already sixty-four years old.

seized by Sibylla herself and her husband Guy. The barons then offered the crown to Isabella, Sibylla's younger sister, and her husband Humphrey of Toron. But Humphrey did not want to be embroiled in the dispute, so the barons had to put up with Guy after all—except Raymond of Tripoli, who, utterly furious, allied himself with Saladin.

The fears of Guy de Lusignan were only too well justified, for it was he who led the entire Christian army to destruction at Hattin. It was at this point that Reginald de Chatillon treacherously attacked a Moslem caravan as it passed through his territory and captured Saladin's sister. After the Battle of Hattin, Saladin, as we have seen, beheaded Reginald with his own hand.

Meanwhile Raymond of Tripoli had become reconciled to Guy de Lusignan and had moved south to Jerusalem. As soon as he did so Saladin attacked his castle and city of Tiberias, which was defended by his wife. It was the attempt to relieve Tiberias that led to the disaster of Hattin in July 1187. As the army marched across the desert, they became parched with thirst, Moslem raiders harassed them and they were tortured by the sight of Lake Tiberias below. But between them and the water Saladin had drawn up his cavalry, and just as the Franks reached exhaustion point he attacked. Mad with thirst and the burning sun, many flung away their arms and cried for water and the battle became a rout. King Guy surrendered with the Templars, but the infantry and men-at-arms were all butchered. It was the end of the kingdom of Jerusalem. Only Tyre, seized and held by Conrad of Montferrat, remained as a port open to the West.

Guy remained Saladin's prisoner for a year. Then released on his honour as a knight that he would never bear arms against Islam again, he was given a safe-conduct to the coast, where he at once began the siege of Acre. Indeed, the real goal of the third crusade was not the Holy Sepulchre, but Acre, the commercial centre of the Levant.

And now, leaving the low sandy coast of the Cyprian's isle at Famagusta, with its temples still standing on the shore, Richard set sail for the Levant, "hale and light as a feather". As they approached the Holy Land, they saw Margat, the great fortress of the Knights of St John on its hill overlooking the realm of the Old Man of Musse and his Assassins. Next Tortosa came in view; then the terraced castle of Botron and Tripoli, a white city by the sea, and the lofty towers of Djebait.

Suddenly, between Beirut and Sidon, they sighted in the near distance a ship so enormous that it seemed to them that it must rival Noah's ark. As they drew nearer they saw that she was a three-master, covered with green felt on one side and on the other with yellow, "as if she were some work of faerie". They hailed her and the answer came in French, "We are Genoese for Tyre." But one of Richard's oarsmen recognized the ship, for he had seen her at Beirut being loaded with all manner of arms, barrels of Greek fire, a great supply of victuals, 800 Turks, all picked warriors, and two hundred serpents, "hideous and grey", to be let loose against the Christian camp outside Acre. This oarsman now said to King Richard, "Sire, have me slain or hanged, an this ship be not a Turkish ship". Richard at once sent another galley in pursuit and as it drew near the great ship it was greeted with showers of bolts and arrows. These, coming from above with such speed and force, caused so many casualties in the Christian galley, that the pilgrims began to waver till Richard swore that he would hang them all if they let the ship escape, so the attack was renewed. At last a storming party managed to clamber on board, but were driven back and flung into the sea. Then divers swam under the great ship and secured her rudder with cords, while others clambered on board again, only to have their hands and feet hacked off and their bodies flung back into the sea. An assault by the knights was equally unsuccessful, till Richard gave the order to each of his galleys to ram the Moslem ship with their iron beaks, till it began to heave over and sink. The Turks who jumped overboard were either shot down with arrows or cut to pieces as they struggled in the waves among their own serpents. Richard saved some thirty-five emirs and engineers, but the rest were left to drown.

The sinking of this ship was Richard Coeur de Lion's first great success on the crusade. For had it ever reached Acre with its stores and reinforcements, that city would probably never have been taken. "Thus did God bring disaster upon the infidels." Bohardin, the "infidel" historian, says that when the captain of the ship saw that disaster was imminent, he scuttled her himself and that the Christians rescued only one man that he might bear the news to Saladin, who on hearing it "accepted this also with the hand of resignation for the sake of God, who will not suffer the reward of them that love righteousness to perish". But, as Gibbon observes, "from the vicissitude of success, each side might have learned to suspect that Heaven was neutral in the quarrel". Had they done so, there could hardly have been a crusade on the one side and a holy war on the other. Saladin, it seems, was quite ready to allow pilgrims through to Jerusalem, and after his capture of the city in 1187 he gave those who could pay for it a safe conduct to the seaports of Syria.

The siege of Acre had now been going on for two years, during which time more than a hundred thousand crusaders had been killed and an even greater number lost by disease or shipwreck on the way. Only a small proportion of the survivors could ever hope to return to their native lands. "Never," remarks Gibbon from his serene point of vantage in the eighteenth century, "did the flame of enthusiasm burn with a fiercer or more destructive rage."

At the conclusion of the sea-fight, the wind, which had been against Richard's fleet, suddenly shifted to the north and carried them to Tyre. But here the guards would not open the gates, saying that their lord Conrad had forbidden them to do so. Richard and his men, therefore, pitched their tents on the shore and early next morning, the wind still favouring them, they hoisted sail and after passing the fortress of Scandalion and Casel Imbert, the towers and minarets of Acre rose up in the distance, and then, by degrees all the fortifications of the city.

Around Acre, says Ambroise, were camped "the flower of all the peoples of the world". They were not, however, all crusaders by any means, for the besiegers of Acre were themselves besieged by the forces of almost the entire Moslem world. Saladin occupied the heights behind the city and, although the number of crusaders had been increasing ever since 1189, when Guy de Lusignan rashly began the siege, for a long time there were not enough of them to blockade the city completely, and the Christian camp had to entrench itself both against constant attacks from the hills and sorties from the city. Indeed Saladin could call upon an almost unlimited supply of men, and by the time the two kings arrived outside Acre the morale of the camp, reduced as it was by starvation and disease, was at its lowest ebb.

As he approached, Richard saw from his ship "an innumerable army of Turks swarming on the mountains and valleys, the hills and the plains, and having their tents, bright with coloured devices, pitched everywhere". He reached Acre with his armada on June 8th. "Then had you heard the trumpets sound, honouring Richard, the knight without peer!" sings Ambroise. "I don't think that any mother's son hath seen or could describe such rejoicing as was made in the host over the king. The night passed in feasting, drinking and singing to the sound of trumpets, clarions and flutes, and the whole camp blazed with the light of innumerable tapers." To the Turks the coming of Richard and his galleys meant that all approaches to Acre were now blocked and that unless Saladin could draw off the Christian force, the garrison was faced with starvation.

Acre lies on a triangular spit of land, whose apex points to the west. "The port which is not so convenient as it should be," says Richard of Aldgate, "often deceives and proves fatal to the vessels which winter there: for the rock which lies over against the shore, to which it runs parallel, is too short to protect them from the fury of the storm. And because this rock appeared a suitable place for washing away the entrails, the ancients used it as a place for offering sacrifices, and on account of the flies which followed the sacrificial flesh, the tower which stands above it was called the Tower of Flies. There is also a tower called the Cursed situated on the wall which surrounds the city: and if we are to credit common report, it received its name because it was said that the pieces of silver for which Judas betrayed his Lord, were made there. . . . ."

Since his arrival in April, Philip had been the acknowledged leader of the crusaders, and though there had been no actual progress in the siege he had brought fresh hope. He pitched his camp in front of the Cursed Tower, the largest tower in the fortifications, in the middle of the eastern wall and had been bombarding it night and day with enormous blocks of stone. Ironically, the walls the crusaders were besieging were their own, the gigantic fortifications reared by the Knights Templars. In spite of Saladin's attempts to engage them in the plain, the bulk of the Christian camp, including the women, had been busy filling up the great ditch in front of the walls with stones, the bodies of animals and the corpses of their comrades—for it was the thing to ask, as you lay dying, that your body should be used to help fill up the fosse. As they worked the Turks shot at them with arrows and threw down immense stones and burning pitch—"rivers of abominable stench and livid flame that consumed both flint and steel".

Any large-scale attack upon the city was made impossible by Saladin's counter-attacks. At Philip's first assault the defenders "raised a tumultuous clamour, and shouted to the skies, so that it resembled the crash in the air caused by thunder and lightening, for some had this sole duty—to beat basins and platters, and by other means, to make signal to Saladin and the army without . . ." And then the Moslem hordes would come pouring down from the hills and throw themselves upon the barricades in the most desperate hand to hand fighting. But though they might be driven off again, their continual attacks prevented any progress in the siege, "whence the king of France, overcome by fury and anger, sank into a state of languid sickness, from sorrow, it is said . . ."

Another obstacle was the jealous rivalry between the various Christian leaders. As soon as he arrived, Richard did everything to undermine Philip's position and to make it clear that he was to be regarded as the leader of the crusade. When he learned that Philip was paying his men three gold bezants apiece each month, he offered four to any knight who would enter his service. The Pisans and Genoese flocked to his standard, but he declined the homage of the Genoese as they were already pledged to Philip, though he confirmed by a charter "the customs they were wont to have in the land of Jerusalem"—a sublime assumption of royal authority which the French king must have found very galling. Then, Henry of Champagne, Richard's nephew, having come to the end of his resources, applied to Philip for a loan. Philip promised to lend him the money if he would pawn Champagne. So Henry approached his uncle, who gave him £4,000 and a supply of food for his men and horses without any political strings attached to it at all—evidence that while Philip's main object throughout was the aggrandisement of France, Richard was concerned with nothing but the success of the crusade—always provided that that was achieved under his leadership.

On June 10th Mategriffon arrived and was set up. Next day Richard's archers were looking down into Acre from the tall wooden tower that had been built to overawe the Greeks and Lombards of Messina. Meanwhile the slings of the Duke of Burgundy and those of the Count of Flanders, the Templars and Hospitallers, hurling their great stones over the fortifications, "never ceased to spread terror among the Turks". In addition to these Richard had constructed improved slings which would carry farther than any of the others and were effectively armoured with layers of rawhide and ropes. A stone from one of these, it is reported, killed twelve men. Of such power and range were these slings, which were plied night and day, that they either shattered in pieces the object they struck or ground it into powder. The camp itself was protected by a turf embankment, with deep ditches from sea to sea. This was built by the pilgrims under difficulties for the Turks continued to annoy them from morn till night. Many died from the stench of the dead bodies which corrupted the air and by the fatigue of constant watchings, while others simply died of their wounds.

Then, quite suddenly, Richard fell ill again. "His face and lips all wasted by a sickness men called leonardie", with peeling of the skin, loss of hair and of the nails of the hands and feet. Another source calls it "arnoldia" and it seems to have been combined with a renewed attack of malarial fever. First his armour became unaccountably heavy, then he found he could not stand. The attack lasted till the first week in July, when Acre surrendered. But between malarial attacks, Richard had himself carried about the camp in a litter, and wrapped in a quilt, continued to supervise the construction of slings and assault towers and to give directions to his sappers. He also exchanged courtesies with Saladin who chivalrously sent him fruit and snow. Richard wanted an interview, but Saladin replied that "kings should not have speech with each other till terms of peace between them have been arranged". However he agreed to a meeting between the king and his brother, Malek el Adil. When the time for it came, Richard was too ill to leave his tent, and Saladin sent him a present of a Negro slave—proceedings which were watched with increasing suspicion by the French. It was observed also that Queen Joanna's Moslem slaves had already deserted to the enemy and that Saladin began to send men into the Christian camp by night, who crept into the tents with long knives in their sleeves and took prisoners. Those who resisted had their throats cut.

Recovering from his illness first, Philip, much to Richard's annoyance, ordered a general assault to be made upon the walls of Acre on June 14th. This broke down as usual under a Moslem counter-attack. Philip then launched a second attack on June 17th. Saladin replied with another counter-attack, when his mamelukes penetrated the camp. But they were driven back again by Geoffrey of Lusignan, who "slew ten of them with an axe in a most glorious manner.... Such was his courage and activity that no one since the time of those famous soldiers Roland and Oliver, could lay claim to such distinction." On June 22nd the crusaders launched an attack on Saladin's camp in the sector north of Acre, only to be repulsed. Next day their attack on Nahr-el-Na'mein's camp to the south was also repulsed. Then Philip placed an enormous mangonel called the Bad Neighbour opposite the Accursed Tower. But the Turks destroyed it with another mounted upon the walls, which was known as the Evil Kinsman. Philip rebuilt the Bad Neighbour and the

Turks destroyed it again, at which the French king fell sick once more with vexation. And whenever the French attacked, the English would not join them, nor would the French or Germans join with the English.

Meanwhile, Philip constructed a special kind of scaling-ladder which he called "the Cat" and also a hurdle, or circleia, "put together firmly with a complication of interweaving most subtly wrought," under cover of which he potted at the Turks on the walls. But a heap of dry wood followed by Greek fire fell upon the Cat and the circleia and burnt them to bits. "Upon which the king of France was enraged beyond measure, and began to curse all who were under his command, and rated them shamefully for not exacting condign vengeance of the Saracens, which had done them such injuries." In his mortification and rage he ordered another assault upon Acre on July 2nd, which Richard, because he could not join it himself, boycotted.

As usual, the attack was the signal for the Moslem counter-attack on the Christian camp. "The Frankish fanatics, posted behind their trenches presented the appearance of a solid wall," writes Bohardin, "several of our men penetrated the camp, only to be met with an unbreakable resistance. An enormous Frank, standing on the parapet, drove back the Musulmans single-handed, launching stones, with which his comrades kept him supplied, at our men. He had more than fifty wounds from arrows and stones, but nothing stopped him. He held up the Musulmans till he was burnt alive by a bottle of naphtha thrown over him by one of our officers." The heroism of this giant in the defence of the camp was paralleled by that of a woman in a green mantle who did not stop shooting at the enemy till she was overwhelmed and trampled to death. "We killed her," says Bohardin, "and took her bow to the Sultan." Nevertheless, the Turks inside Acre offered to surrender, if their lives and property were spared, and when Philip replied that the surrender must be unconditional, many of them threw themselves over the walls in despair. Next day another attack was launched by the French. Aubry Clement, Marshal of France, who had sworn to take Acre or die, climbed into the breach that had been made in the wall near the Accursed Tower with a party of knights, only to find that the breach was too narrow. The ladders collapsed behind him and the Marshal was killed. But the attack of July 3rd was decisive, and if Acre was not taken that day, she was wounded mortally.

Three days later Richard had himself carried out to the walls under cover of a hurdle and shot a Turk who had rashly put on the rich armour of Aubrey Clement. He then offered a high reward to anyone who could pull out a large stone from the wall beneath the Accursed Tower. Many volunteered, but it was a costly operation in life and limb. On that day Richard's men and the Pisans nearly entered the city. But the Turks fought like fiends, winning the unwilling admiration of the crusaders. Again they offered to surrender through their two principal emirs. But Richard replied: "Do you think my power so small that I cannot take by force what you now offer as a favour? Look at your shaken walls and tottering turrets, and then tell me if you require to evacuate before I become master of the town." Their offer was refused and they were told to refer the matter to Saladin. But Saladin was in no hurry to give up the city and hoped to spin out negotiations till all his reinforcements from Egypt arrived. Meanwhile he systematically devastated the surrounding country. On July 8th he burnt Haifa and during the next two days cut down all the vineyards and orchards round Acre.

The Accursed Tower fell with a roar of stones and rubble on July 11th. As the smoke and dust cleared away, revealing a great breach in the wall, "then did our squires put on their armour, like the brave and nimble warriors they were, and swarmed up the ladders and moving towers", says Ambroise. The assault was commanded by the Earl of Leicester, André de Chavigny and Hugh le Brun (Hugh Brown) Bishop of Salisbury, with a troop of Pisans. Hacking their way across the smoking rubble, lopping off heads and hands and arms with the sweep of their long, heavy swords, their battle cry rang out above the shrieks and curses: "Christ and the Sepulchre!" But the starving, desperate Turks put up such a resistance that the attack was repulsed. As the squires mounted up to the top of the walls, they were met with cascades of Greek fire and those behind on the ladder "durst not await the fire, but must perforce get them down again," says Ambroise, "nor do I know how many died there in the course of this undertaking". The fire ran down their armour in blazing streams and wherever it entered a joint or a rivet it burned to the bone. Many knights tore off their armour, screaming with pain, and were at once shot down by Saracen arrows.

While this desperate fighting was going on, the main force of the crusaders were at supper, for Richard was determined to have the credit for taking Acre all to himself and held his men in reserve for the final assault. Negotiations too were in progress—though Saladin

did his best to interrupt them with repeated attacks on the Christian camp—and at one point Philip agreed that the garrison of Acre
should go free, without even laying down their arms. But Richard
would not have that, and it was not till July 12th in a great assembly
at the Templars' headquarters, that agreement was reached. The
terms were that the True Cross should be restored; 1,500 prisoners
in Saladin's hands, including a hundred named prisoners of rank,
were to be released; 200,000 bezants were to be paid over to Philip
and Richard, and 1,400 to Conrad in ransom. One month was to be
allowed for the fulfilment of these conditions. Meanwhile the garrison of Acre and their families should be kept as hostages.

The heralds then made proclamation throughout the camp that
no man was to insult the Turks by word or deed. "When the
famous Turks, of such wonderful valour and warlike excellence,
began strolling about on the city walls in all their splendid apparel
previous to their departure, our men gazed on them with the utmost
curiosity. They were wonder-struck by the cheerful features of men
who were leaving the city almost penniless . . . men whom loss did
not deject, and whose visage betrayed no timidity, but even wore
the look of victory. It was only their superstitious rites and their
pitiful idolatry that had robbed such warriors of their strength."[3]

Saladin was much annoyed when he heard the terms of the truce
and was about to dispatch a swimmer with a letter expressing his
disapproval, when he saw the Christian banners and crosses gleam-
ing in the fires of joy on the walls of Acre. But the prolonged cheers
of the crusaders were echoed by equally loud lamentations from the
Saracen camp, where there were signs of growing mutiny. After
this, says Richard of Devizes, "many of the paynim returned to
their own lands, in great dread of coming into contact with the
Christians, who had resisted so great a multitude so boldly."

Entering the city, Conrad of Montferrat planted one flag on the
citadel, another on the minaret of the Great Mosque, and a third
on the Tower of Battle, in place of the flags of Islam. "Then ought
you to have seen the churches that were left in Acre," cries Ambroise in indignation, "how the Turks had mutilated and defaced
paintings [which they regarded as idolatry], overthrown the altars
and beaten crosses and crucifixes, for to do despight to our beliefs
and to satisfy their own mischief—and had made of them their own
mahomeries—that cursed folk whom may God curse with his
Mouth!"

[3] *Itinerarium.*

Acre surrendered on 12 July 1191, a little more than a month after King Richard's arrival before its walls, without his having struck hardly a blow to take it. For nearly all that time he had lain sick in his tent. Having taken the city, the crusaders at once began quarrelling about its partition. Richard took up his quarters in the palace of the kings, Philip in the Templars' establishment. Leopold of Austria, as head of the German contingent, claimed equality with the kings of England and France and ran up his standard beside Richard's. But one of Richard's partisans hauled down the German standard and threw it into the ditch under the walls, an action for which Leopold lived to be revenged. It was said that Richard could brook no rival to his supremacy. Had not the Templars intervened, writes Otto of St Blaise, the Germans and the Italians would have set upon him openly. There were other causes of dissension, too. Those crusaders who had been at the siege from the beginning and had endured pestilence and famine and borne the brunt of the terrible fighting when Saladin attacked the camp for eight days without intermission, demanded their share of the booty. But the kings put them off with promises.

Established in the royal palace with his wife and his sister, flushed with victory, Richard now proposed to Philip that he and all the other crusaders should bind themselves to stay in the Holy Land for three years, unless Saladin surrendered it before that time. But Philip, who was suffering from dysentery, said that he wanted to go home. He was, as Gibbon puts it, "weary of sacrificing his health and interest on a barren coast". It is said that the ambassadors (among whom were the Bishop of Beauvais and the Duke of Burgundy) who brought this intelligence, could not at first speak for tears of shame and rage, till Richard, divining their purpose exclaimed: "If your king leaves undone the work for which he came hither, he will bring shame and everlasting contempt upon himself and France, so he will not go by my counsel. But if he needs either go or die, let him do what best pleases him and his folk."

In Richard's view, and that of the majority of the nobility, Philip, by deserting the crusade at the very beginning, would disgrace himself to such an extent that the only thing left for him to do was to die. Later, Philip said that he had suspected Richard of trying to poison him. The story goes that as he lay desperately ill, Richard came to him and said that Louis, his only son, was dead, hoping by this additional shock to kill him. Possibly this really was Richard's intention for he could not have known that about this time Louis had also sickened of a dysentery and that on July 15th, according to Rigord, his life was despaired of until he was cured by a touch of a nail from the Cross. "And on the same day and at the same hour," says Rigord, "his father Philip in lands beyond the sea was cured of a like disease".

This act of brutal vindictiveness by a man who had no children of his own—apart from an illegitimate son, begotten by accident—is on a par with the story of his vast amusement when he learned that, having called for pork, his cook had given him a cut from a young Moslem prisoner. Richard thought this such a good joke, we are told by the fourteenth-century romancer, that he called for "the head of the pig" to be served up to him for supper. There was no fear of famine, he told the Moslem ambassadors while with one Saracen he could feed nine or ten of his Christian men. And, he invited the emirs to a feast, the first course of which consisted of the boiled heads of their own relations. But the ambassadors had no appetite and the king exclaimed:

> Frends, be nought squoymous,
> This is the maner of my hous,
> To be served ferst, God it wot,
> With Sarazynes hedes abouten al hot.

The Frankish merchants and nobles who had formerly held property at Acre now pressed their claims, appealing to Philip. Philip wrote to Richard insisting that their claims should be met and adding one of his own for half of Cyprus, according to their Vezelay agreement to divide the spoils of the crusade. Richard replied by claiming half the lands of the Count of Flanders who had died earlier in the siege, lands which adjoined the Norman Vexin.

An epidemic, spread by swarms of flies from the trenches round the city with their noisome mess of festering corpses, put an end to this argument, and while Richard exchanged presents with Saladin, Philip fell a victim to the same dread disease of "arnoldia" that had earlier afflicted his brother crusader, losing his hair and the nails of his hands and feet. More than ever, he felt that it was time to go home, although Richard offered him a half share of everything he had gathered together for the crusade if only he would stay. When Philip refused, saying that he was too ill, Richard made him swear that on his return to France he would not invade the Angevin lands. Philip swore on the relics of the saints, and the Duke of Burgundy, Henry of Champagne and other nobles stood surety for him.

Guy de Lusignan and Conrad of Montferrat—who had meanwhile reconciled himself to Richard—then pleaded their rival claims to the Crown of Jerusalem before a Court presided over by the two kings—both pretty grisly objects by this time, with their bald heads and blotched peeling faces, Richard shivering and chattering with fever. The upshot was that Guy should hold the title for life and that Conrad and Isabella should succeed him to the exclusion of his heirs. Then, after granting his share of Acre to Conrad and making the Duke of Burgundy general of his army in Palestine, Philip sailed on July 31st for Tyre, where he re-embarked in three Genoese ships, "and entrusting himself with sobs and tears to the sea, was carried by God's will to Apulia". He left followed by the curses of the crusaders and loaded with gifts of perfume and rich clothes from Saladin. Conrad was equally anxious to get away from Acre and went off with a large number of Moslem prisoners, whom he hoped to dispose of on his own account. Leopold of Austria left, too, with hatred in his heart.

Their departure cleared the air. Those who were left were told to make themselves ready with their arms and their horses to move south along the coast road to Ascalon. After having the ships loaded with provisions and military engines, Richard paraded the archers and paid them handsomely and also gave large sums in gold and silver to the French "for to hearten them".

On August 2nd Saladin was informed by Richard's envoys that the kings had agreed to the payment of the ransom by three monthly instalments—the first on August 11th to consist of more than two-thirds of the total—the Holy Cross, 600 Christian prisoners and 100,000 dinars. On August 5th a delegation was sent to Tyre, calling upon Conrad to return and to send back all the Moslem prisoners in his possession, since they were needed to exchange for Christians. Conrad replied that he would never again meet Richard, "for he feared him more than any man on earth", neither would he return the prisoners. "This is madness!" Richard exclaimed when he heard this, and he threatened to go to Tyre and fetch the prisoners away himself. But it was pointed out to him that Conrad could, if he were so minded, intercept all supplies to Acre—which he was, in fact beginning to do. So it was decided to send a more conciliatory delegation led by Hugh of Burgundy, Philip's representative, and on August 12th they returned with the Moslem prisoners. Conrad himself, however, still refused to join Richard.

The first instalment of Christian prisoners arrived, together with the ransom money, but neither the True Cross nor the specially named 100 prisoners of rank were returned.[4] Richard therefore refused to release the Acre garrison and called upon Saladin to fulfil his part of the treaty. Saladin replied, that he would do so if the Franks either released all the Moslem prisoners in their hands, in which case he would give other hostages for the missing lords, or if the Franks gave him hostages for the lives of the garrison. This appeared unnecessarily complicated to Richard and he proposed in return for what was now due under the treaty to give a solemn oath to return the Acre garrison. But Saladin, no longer having any belief in the Christians' good faith, refused to agree to this. No exchange of prisoners, therefore, took place, and the "first term" of the treaty was postponed until August 20th.

On August 14th Richard led his troops out of Acre and pitched his tents near the Saracen lines. Two days later Saladin asked for a parley with Richard, and then failed to keep the tryst, declaring: "I did not come because I could not fulfil the agreement which my people had made with him"—meaning, according to Ambroise, that many of the notable Christian prisoners had already died. Skirmishing then broke out between the two camps in which the king took his full share. Saladin then withdrew his advance guard two miles farther south.

August 20th, the day fixed for the fulfilment of the treaty, dawned and Richard advanced to the pits at the foot of the hills which the Saracens had just evacuated. Noon passed without a word or a sign from Saladin, and Richard declared that the Sultan had once more broken his word. About four o'clock he rode out into the centre of the plain lying between Al Ayadijeh and Keisan with his army and ordered all the survivors of the Moslem garrison of Acre, with their wives and children to be brought before him. As they stood there, helpless and in chains, he gave the order that they should be butchered to the last child. Richard himself gives the number of those done to death in this way as about 2,600. Bohardin raises the figure to more than 3,000. The whole thing was done quite methodically. The prisoners were sorted out. The more important ones

[4] The True Cross, when captured at Hattin, was mounted in gold and set with precious stones. Richard's envoys had seen it in Saladin's camp and had, says Bohardin, prostrated themselves before it with cries and lamentations. After that it was sent to Damascus. Another account says that it went to Baghdad where the Kalif buried it under the threshold of a gate to be trodden underfoot.

were spared to be ransomed, the strongest were kept for slave labour. Then, in true crusading spirit, the children were torn from their screaming mothers' arms and butchered. After that the bodies were ripped up and the entrails searched for gold and jewels; even the gall-bladders were cut out for medicinal use.[5]

This cold-blooded massacre of helpless prisoners is, perhaps the ugliest incident in Richard's career—the hounding of his old, sick father to death was ugly enough and so was the treatment of Alais. But his contemporaries, whether Christian or Moslem, do not seem to have been shocked at all. Bohardin is just a little puzzled as to his motive, though he suspects that the real motive was military necessity. The king wanted to move on and thought it unwise to leave so many prisoners in his rear. Ambroise the jongleur, and the chroniclers exulted in the massacre. In the later *Romance of Rychard Cuer de Lyon* we read:

> They were led into the place ful evene,
> Ther they herden aungels of hevene:
> They sayde: 'Seynyors, tuez, tuez!'
> 'Spare hem nought, behedith these!'
> King Richard herde the aungelys voys,
> And thankyd God and the holy croys.
> Then were they behedyd hastelyche,
> And cast into the foule dyche.

Legally prisoners were slaves and could be disposed of accordingly to a conqueror's whim. It would be quite wrong to suppose that because the conqueror was in this case a Christian he was open to even the more elementary feelings of humanity and compassion. The sort of Christianity we have to look for among the crusaders is to be found expressed in the fierce, snarling beasts on the historicated capitals of Burgundian and southern romanesque churches—the griffons, lions and dragons tearing their prey and the Knights Templars "devoted to slaughter".

As soon as they saw what was happening, the Moslem advance guard threw themselves upon the Christian host, even as the slaughter was taking place; but, though fighting went on till nightfall, they could not break through the wall of steel to save their comrades. The Christian army then withdrew, leaving the plain covered with the mutilated corpses of men, women and children. A similar massacre was carried out within the walls of Acre by the Duke of Burgundy.

[5] Hovedon records that it was discovered that the Moslems had swallowed quantities of gold and jewels.

Up till then Saladin had acted chivalrously, liberating the garrisons of the towns and castles he captured and allowing them to return to their own lands. He now took reprisals on all the Christian prisoners, either executing them on the field or sending them to the slave market at Damascus. The True Cross was sent to Damascus, too, and the rest of the ransom money distributed among his troops.

V

"HELP US, O HOLY SEPULCHRE!"

RICHARD was impatient to move on. But the army in Acre was not so enthusiastic about the prospect of a long march through barren country in the burning heat of the Levantine summer. For Acre, as Ambroise writes nostalgically, "was full of delights, good wines and girls, who were often very beautiful. The men abandoned themselves to wine and women and to all manner of follies." It was good while it lasted. But Richard sat grimly in his tent waiting for his orders to be obeyed. All women, he said, except washerwomen, who washed heads and linen and were "as deft as monkeys in removing fleas", but who "would not be an occasion of sin", must be left behind. Left behind also were Joanna and Berengaria and the little Cyprian princess. The walls of Acre had been rebuilt and the city was put under the command of Bertran de Verdun and Stephen de Longchamp, guardians of the king's treasure.

By August 23rd the bulk of the army, totalling some 100,000 men, was encamped by the river of Acre, the Nahr Na'men, waiting for their comrades to tear themselves away from the silken girls and the sherbet. At dawn on the 24th they lit their customary fires before breaking camp. "There had ye seen chivalry!" cries Ambroise, "'Twas the fairest company of bachelors, the most valiant and choicest that ever was seen before or afterward!" But hardly had they begun their march when Saladin launched an attack upon the rear of the column in the southern suburbs of Acre. This was beaten off with difficulty by Jacques d'Avesnes, Hugh de Tiberiade and William de Barres. On the 25th the column marched from the river Belus to the coast and crossed the Kishon, Saladin keeping watch on their movements from the hills. And as they struggled along the rough coastal track, the light Saracen horsemen came down upon them by twenties and thirties. For these horsemen, carrying only a bow, a mace, a sword and a reed lance with an iron tip, could ride much faster than the heavily mailed Frankish knights. As soon as they were driven off they returned again in clouds of dust, crying out in their high-pitched screaming voices: "There is no god but Allah!" Black foot-soldiers came running, too, with scimitars and light shields, "a race of demons".

Richard had disposed the line of march in three columns. On the side nearest to the hills, on the left, were the infantry with bows and crossbows, with which they replied to the Moslem fire, and acted as a shield for the more important inner column of mounted knights. Nearest the sea marched the third column with the baggage wagons and the sick, and every few hours this column changed places with the men in the rank nearest the hills, and these rested in their turn. In this way the crusaders could fight as they marched. And they marched with admirable discipline in a solid impervious mass, withstanding all provocations to break their ranks. Bohardin says that he saw one infantryman marching along quite unconcerned with ten arrows sticking into the back of his mailed surcoat. The engines and other supplies, with the load of specially sharpened Sicilian flints for the mangonels, kept a parallel course by sea. Richard led the vanguard of English and Norman knights, massed like a wall about the dragon standard on its cart, with the royal arms of England floating above it.

The coastal road to Haifa, originally a good Roman one, was by this time little more than a track through the dry brush and burning white sand of the shore. In places the mountains came down to the sea, and as they passed through a defile, the baggage team lagged behind. At once the Saracen horse swooped down from the slopes of Carmel and cut them off from the rearguard. John Fitz Luke spurred forward and told the king; Richard at once galloped back and fell upon the Turks "like a thunderbolt". In this rearguard action a certain Everard, one of the Bishop of Salisbury's men, lost his right hand. But he, "without changing countenance, seized the sword with the left hand and, closing with the Turks, stoutly defended himself against them all". Everard was a stout fellow, but there were many such. William de Barres also distinguished himself by his signal valour and was taken back into Richard's favour. All the prisoners Saladin took in this fight he killed, sparing only the washerwomen.

The army then continued its march. Soon they came to a river

Richard I and Berengaria of Navarre. Drawn from their effigies at Rouen and Le Mans by Albert Way and Thomas Stothard. The effigy of Richard was discovered under the pavement on the north side of the choir at Rouen Cathedral in 1838

Jerusalem from the South.
From an engraving by David Roberts

Jaffa. From an engraving by David Roberts

St. Jean d'Acre.
From an engraving by David Roberts

A Jongleur

A Queen, possibly Eleanor of Aquitaine, from the west portal of
Chartres Cathedral. From *La Cathédrale de Chartres,* by Marcel Aubert

Henry II and Eleanor of Aquitaine. Drawn from their effigies at
Fontevrault, before restoration, by Thomas Stothard

Second Great Seal of Richard I

A Knight Crusader. From the Temple Church, London. Restored by Edward Richardson in 1842, destroyed by a German bomb in 1941

A Knight Templar. Drawn by Thomas Stothard

William Marshal. Plaster cast of an effigy from the Temple Church, London, since destroyed by a German bomb. Early 13th century

King John from the effigy in Worcester Cathedral

and cisterns, and there in a pleasant place they pitched their tents.
From the way in which the ground had been trodden down all
about, they judged that the Saracens had camped there before them.
The next day, being August 25th, after a short march, they reached
Haifa. Between the sea and the deserted town, they rested two days,
for the foot-soldiers were very heavily laden with food and arms,
"on which account they had endured much toil and thirst in the
late battle". The baggage wagons were overhauled and lightened.
Then the army resumed its march, with the Templars in the van
and the Hospitallers in the rear, "both of which Orders bore themselves so manfully as to be a very pattern of virtues". But, as usual,
the foot-soldiers fared worst, scratched and torn by thorns, their
faces cut by stiff reeds, as they broke their way through the scrub
along the shore.

A difficult march of eight miles, during which they caught and
killed many wild animals, brought them to Caphernaum, which
Saladin had levelled with the ground. Here they stopped to dine;
then after another four miles they reached Casel of the Straits, where
later crusaders were to rear the gigantic fortress of Athlit. They
spent two days at Casel of the Straits and unloaded fresh supplies
from the fleet. Each night, before retiring to rest, everyone stretched
their arms to heaven and cried in chorus *Santum Sepulchrum
Adjuva*, Help us, O Holy Sepulchre! the tears streaming down their
cheeks as they prayed to God for mercy and aid. But when they laid
down to sleep tarantulas bit them. The noblemen and knights were
provided against this emergency with ointment and other antidotes.
But each night the clashing of shields, helms, swords and pots and
pans to drive away the insects, effectually drove away sleep also.

Richard now rode on ahead of the army to Merle, where Saladin
had camped only three days before, and passed the night there on
his own. Next day, when the army came up, he again rode ahead,
reconnoitring. "Now the journey along the sea-shore was very
grievous to the army. Many fainting from the heat and out-wearied
by the labour of the long march dropped down dead and were
buried where they fell. . . . But on many others who were exhausted
by the journey the king took compassion, and had them transported
in the galleys and ships to the halting-place."[1] This was Caesarea,
which the Turks were even then busy dismantling, though they fled
at the approach of the crusaders.

The army camped on the banks of the River of Crocodiles—so

[1] *Itinerarium.*

called by them because two knights who bathed in it were eaten alive. At Caesarea, they could not help noticing that the buildings were constructed with wonderful art. Here, too, the ships brought in many stragglers from Acre.

Before dawn on September 1st the army struck camp and resumed its march through the burning desolate sand-dunes. As soon as they began to move, the Saracen horsemen came down upon them again, pouring into the column flights of arrows, to which the crossbow-men in the outer rank replied with their deadly bolts. By midday, after a march of only two miles, they came to a ravine which they called the River of the Dead, being a river which flowed sluggishly beneath a thick covering of matted reeds and rushes. But they crossed it warily and pitched their tents on the other side, when the Turkish horsemen retired once more to the hills. "For whenever they were in camp," writes Bohardin, "there was no hope of doing anything with them." In the afternoon Saladin moved his head-quarters higher up the same river and for two nights the armies camped side by side.

The track along the shore now became so impassable, with lagoons and brushwood and the sword-like papyrus reed that they were forced to make their way inland up the left bank of the Dead River and across the slopes bordering the Plain of Sharon. Saladin was not yet ready for a pitched battle and at the approach of the crusaders moved his camp once more farther south into a forest. But his cavalry still harassed the Christians, and so many horses were lost in the rain of Saracen darts and arrows that the army was "almost in despair", till Richard rode up and down the line shout-ing encouragements.

Marching in closer formation than usual, they moved doggedly on. At last the Saracen attacks became so intolerable that they opened their ranks and let the cavalry through. At one point, indeed, the French, struggling along in the rear under the Duke of Burgundy, were cut off and nearly annihilated. In this encounter the Count of St Pol distinguished himself and Richard, who was always in the thick of any mêlée and fought with a complete disregard of his own safety, was wounded in the side with a javelin. The wound was only a slight one and, we are told, acted as a spur, for he remained charging about for the rest of the day slicing off heads and arms with his long reach to avenge the pain he suffered.

At nightfall the enemy drew off and tents were pitched in a very marshy district near the Salt River, some seven or eight miles from

Caesarea. Many wounded horses had to be killed and eaten by the
starving army, and the knights came to blows in the sale of the flesh,
till Richard proclaimed that he would give a live horse to any man
who made a present of a dead one to the most valiant and needy of
his men at arms.

Meanwhile Saladin was collecting a vast army for the annihilation
of the Christian host in the Forest of Arsûf. On the morning of
September 4th Richard asked for a parley, to which Saladin agreed,
while fresh Turkoman reinforcements came up. So early next day
Richard met Saladin's brother Malek el Adil, with Humphrey of
Toron as interpreter. "What conditions am I to propose to the
Sultan in your name?" asked Saphadin. "One condition only,"
replied Richard proudly, "that you restore the whole land to us, and
go back to your own country." Saphadin at once broke off negotiations.

The battle was now imminent. The Christian army made its way
slowly through the forest. "It was said," writes Ambroise, "that the
heathen pack, the black-faced unbelievers, were within the forest of
Arsûf, and that on that day they would set it on fire and make so
great a burning that the host would be roasted therein." Whoever
said that must have been intent on spreading alarm and despondency, for the army marched steadily through the forest without
mishap and came out to the plain on the other side.

It was evident that Saladin had chosen this plain north of Arsûf
for a decisive battle. It was a place wide enough for the deployment
of cavalry and yet afforded shelter from the woods that came down
to within two miles of the sea. "The circumcised folk" had also
come down from the hills, "thick as the drops of the rain", out-
numbering the crusaders by about three to one.

But the army still marched on. The Templars were in the van;
the Bretons and Angevins next; then the Poitevins under King Guy;
then the Normans and English in charge of the standard under
Richard himself; the Hospitallers brought up the rear with the
Flemish *preux chevalier* Jacques d'Avesnes and William de Barres.
Each of these five battalions was divided into two squadrons, horse
and foot, which marched parallel to each other, while the Duke of
Burgundy and some picked French knights rode up and down the
line regulating the movement, Henry of Champagne acting as a
special guard nearest to the hills. What the army had to do was to
fight its way through to Arsûf, six miles along the sea-shore.

When the Christian vanguard was nearing the outskirts of Arsûf about nine in the morning of September 7th, waves of Negro and Bedouin foot-soldiers swarmed down upon them from the hills, howling and yelling and pouring in arrows and darts. Then came the light horsemen, with their fluttering pennants, with lines of trumpeters riding before them; they came in clouds of dust, in an encircling movement, with wailing cries and the shrill music of timbrels and tambourines and pipes.

But the main Saracen attack was destined for the rear, forcing the Christian rearguard to march backwards. After the Negro and Bedouin archers had discharged their arrows and darts, came the Turkish cavalry whirling maces and scimitars. "On steeds swifter than eagles they thundered down upon us, till the whirling dust raised by their rapid flight blackened the very air." They threw the foot-soldiers of the Hospital into confusion. But the knights held their ground in face of successive attacks, though there was not one man among them, says Ambroise, who did not wish his pilgrimage over. To the accompaniment of an infernal din of brass drums, gongs, rattles, timbrels, pipes and screams of "There is no god but Allah and Mahomet is his prophet!" the attacks went on for hours under the burning sun of the morning, the Turks hammering at the iron-clad knights with their maces, the air darkened with their arrows. Dust rose in choking clouds while the knights who had lost their horses grappled hand to hand with the emirs, and many foot soldiers threw down their bows and ran. But, for the most part the discipline was impeccable, the ranks held and the orderly march continued.

At last it grew unbearable, and Garnier de Nablus, the Master of the Hospital, rode forward to Richard and begged him to tell the trumpeters to give the order for the charge. But the king told him to bide his time, the moment was not propitious. For Richard was determined, if he could not avoid a general engagement, to wait until the main Saracen force had exhausted itself in unavailing attacks on the rear, and only then to break ranks and risk a decisive battle. But when he got back to the rear, Garnier de Nablus found his men in open revolt, and crying, "O Saint George, wilt thou suffer us to be thus confounded? Now ought Christendom to perish when against this pack none offereth battle!" and he rode up to Richard again. "Be patient, good Master," said the king, "I tell you it must be endured. I cannot be everywhere at once."

But by this time the Hospitallers had reached breaking point. "Sirs," they were saying, "let us charge! Never was seen such disgrace, nor never yet from misbelieving folk has our host suffered such reproach!" And shouting, "Saint George, Saint George!" the Marshal of the Hospital and one of Richard's companions from England, Baldwin de Caron (or Carew), wheeled about and plunged into the enemy. And as their brethren dashed after them, rank after rank of the army followed suit. As soon as he saw what was happening, Richard told the trumpeters to sound the charge and came thundering down the line himself. With his picked Anglo-Norman knights he drove the Turkish force attacking the rear down onto the shore and cut it to bits. His sword flashing before and behind in lightning strokes, he made a lane of dead wherever he rode.

It was now the turn of the Turkish right wing to be thrown into disorder. The rest of the heavy cavalry then charged the Turkish centre and left and put them to headlong flight. In the rout, Bohardin, Saladin's secretary, tried to reach the right wing, then the left, but found each in equal confusion and only seventeen men remaining to defend the standard on the hillside among the reserves. "But still the Christians pounded away with their swords until the Turks grew faint with terror." Many sprang from their horses and climbed up the trees, only to be shot down "with horrid yells". Others rode their horses into the sea. Those whom the knights unhorsed, the sergeants dispatched. Soon the plain was covered with severed limbs and corpses. The rout went on for two miles, and in the fury of the slaughter and dust the Christians began to slay each other.

As soon as the crusaders, after rallying to their standard, reformed their ranks and continued their march, Saladin launched another attack and more than 20,000 Turks fell upon the rearguard, "smashing, lopping and bruising the heads, arms and other limbs of our knights, till these went stupidly over their saddle bows". Then came another wave of Saladin's household troops, with their yellow pennants, led by his kinsman Taki-el-din, and attacked the Anglo-Normans round the standard. But William de Barres counterattacked "that noisome press of savage folk" with such fury that they dispersed and Richard pursued them right back into the wooded hills. "Helmets clinked as the enemy fell before him and sparks leapt out from the battery of his sword", while the army reorganized itself about the standard, fell into its accustomed ranks, and resumed its march into Arsûf.

But in this fight Jacques d'Avesnes was unhorsed and done to death. When they found him among the 7,000 Turkish corpses, his face was so swollen and coated with blood that it was almost unrecognisable. He was buried with great honour at Arsûf, a company of knights, King Richard and Guy de Lusignan attending his funeral on September 8th. After that, the army celebrated the nativity of the Virgin Mary, whose day it was.

The Battle of Arsûf, a great victory for the crusaders, thanks to the brilliant generalship of Richard and the admirable discipline of the army, was an unmitigated disaster for Saladin, chiefly for its effect on the morale of his troops. His army had proved ineffective outside Acre; now it had been defeated, with great slaughter, in open battle by a much smaller force of Christians. "No one but Allah," says Bohardin, "knew the great sorrow that filled his heart." It was in this battle that Malek Ric, as the Moslems called Richard, first won his reputation as an unconquerable paladin.

The Sultan Yûsuf Salâh ed-Dîn was fifty-four at the time of the Third Crusade. Unlike Richard, who was twenty years his junior, he never fought in person, though he delighted in the sight of a battle and was to be seen riding about the field quite fearlessly, bolts and arrows whistling round him, attended only by a groom leading a spare horse. His gentleness, courtesy and nobility of character, as well as his statesmanship, were conspicuous in his age, the classical age of Moslem culture. He seems to have had a genuine admiration for Richard. Though—in spite of Sir Walter Scott—the two men never met, he is reported to have said that if he had to lose Jerusalem, he would rather lose it to Malek Ric than to any other prince of Christendom. Indeed, had Richard followed up the victory of Arsûf with a rapid march against the Holy City the chances are that he would have taken it. And this was what Saladin evidently expected him to do, for on September 9th he moved his camp to Ramleh to intercept him.

But Richard had no intention of moving against Jerusalem without a secure supply base on the coast, and had he moved inland Saladin could have encircled him. The next objective, therefore, was Jaffa, which the army reached the following day.

From Ramleh, Saladin could observe the two possible routes of the Crusaders' advance, either through Ramleh itself to Jerusalem or along the coast to Ascalon, the Bride of Syria. But since the capitulation of Acre and the defeat at Arsûf, Saladin had lost much of his authority over his emirs, and they now refused to defend Ascalon, since none of them were anxious to share the fate of the garrison of Acre. He was therefore left with no alternative but to follow a scorched earth policy and create a desert in the path of his enemies. The only way of preventing Richard from laying siege to Ascalon and capturing it, was to defeat him in pitched battle, and this his army now shrunk from attempting. So he was faced with the prospect of destroying Ascalon, as he had been forced to destroy Haifa, Caesarea and Jaffa. But the destruction of Ascalon and the evacuation of its Moslem population, who had once more taken possession of it after the Battle of Hattin four years before, was a far greater humiliation. "I declare before Allah," Bohardin reports him as saying, "I would rather lose both my children than dislodge a single stone of Ascalon. But so Allah wills it." The governor was thereupon ordered to see to its immediate demolition, despite the cries and lamentations of the inhabitants, who were forced to depart on foot, homeless, either to Egypt or to Syria.

Some of the citizens of Ascalon, who had watched the methodical destruction of their homes, went, in their bitterness, to Jaffa, and found the Christian army camping pleasantly enough in the olive groves and beneath the orange and almond-trees outside the walls of that ruined city. When Richard heard what was going on at Ascalon, it seemed to him so incredible that he dispatched Geoffrey de Lusignan and William de l'Étang by sea to reconnoitre. Saladin began the destruction of Ascalon on September 12th and did not complete it until the 21st, by which time this fair city had become no more than a sickening heap of smoking ruins—a prospect with which we are only too familiar in the second half of the twentieth century.

Meanwhile life in the Christian camp at Jaffa was becoming as riotous as it had been at Acre. Much to Richard's disgust, the same type of undesirable visitors who had demoralized the soldiers of God in the latter city now began to arrive by the shipload. Soon there was feasting and music and Syrian dancing girls, and the object for which they had all come so far and endured so much seemed to be in danger of being forgotten under the influence of more seductive delights than any that Englishman or Norman, at any rate, had ever experienced at home. The king reminded them that there was work to be done. A deep trench had to be dug round the city, the walls and fortifications had to be rebuilt, and a subscription list was opened to raise funds for this purpose.

On October 1st Richard wrote to N—— his beloved and faithful servant:

Know ye that after the taking of Acre and the departure of the king of France who there, against the will of God and to the eternal dishonour of his kingdom, so shamelessly failed in his vow, we set out for Joppa. And as we were nearing Arsûf, Saladin came fiercely swooping down upon us. But, of God's mercy, we lost no man of importance that day, saving one only James of Avesnes—a man right dearly loved by the whole army: and rightly so too, for he had proved himself, by many years' service in the Christian host, to be vigorous, devout, and, as it were, a very column in holiness and sincerity of word. Thence by God's will we came to Joppa, which we have fortified with a ditch and wall in our desire to do everything that can promote the Christian cause. On that day, to wit on the Vigil of the Nativity of the Blessed Mary, Saladin lost an infinite number of his greatest men: and being put to flight, in the absence of all help and counsel, he has laid waste the whole land of Syria. On the third day before Saladin's defeat we were ourselves wounded with a spear on the left side; but, thanks to God, we have now regained strength. Know also that by twenty days after Chistmas we hope, through God's grace, to receive the holy city of Jerusalem and the Lord's Sepulchre, after which we shall return to our land. Witness our own hand at Joppa, October 1st.

On the same day he also wrote to the Abbot of Clairvaux, repeating most of what he had already said in the previous letter, but saying that they "had good hope of speedily recovering the heritage of the Lord". Part of it had already been recovered, but in its recovery he, Richard, had "borne the burden and the heat of the day". He continued: "Now that we have spent not only all our money, but our strength and our flesh, too, we signify to you our utter inability to stay in Syria beyond Easter." He adds that the Duke of Burgundy and the French will by that time also have gone home, unless by his preaching St Bernard can rouse the people to send out reinforcements of men and money.

"Wherefore, falling at your knees, we beg you with tears and earnest prayers to stir up the chiefs and noblemen and the folk throughout all Christendom to the service of the living God. Make it your business after Easter in defence of God's heritage; for with his favour, we shall hold till then what we shall win. . . . Do you therefore, in this extremity, rouse the people of God to the same vigorous action as you urged upon us and God's other people for the restitution of His heritage, before we started.

At the next council of war Richard spoke of the necessity of securing the coastline at their rear before marching inland over difficult terrain to Jerusalem. He was therefore in favour of continuing the advance down the coast to Ascalon, which they might still save from utter destruction. For the route through Ascalon, he pointed out, was recognized to be of the utmost importance to pilgrims the whole world over. The Duke of Burgundy and the French, however, argued that the shortest route to Jerusalem was from where they were at present and pleaded passionately for an immediate advance upon the Holy City. But the majority of the pilgrims were in no hurry to leave Jaffa, and Richard was already beginning to wonder whether, with the means at their disposal and with such unlimited forces against them, they would ever take Jerusalem. On October 3rd he sent an envoy to Saladin at Ramleh to propose peace. Meanwhile Conrad at Tyre was making overtures to Saladin for a separate peace.

One day, while reconnoitring in the neighbourhood of Jaffa, and exercising his hawks, Richard very nearly fell into the hands of the Saracens, whose spies kept a close watch on all his movements. Tired with his exertions, the king had laid himself down to rest with his companions when the Saracens suddenly swooped upon them as they slept. Richard, being of a nervous disposition was a light sleeper. Awakened by the thud of approaching hooves, he roused his companions, snatched his sword, sprang into his saddle, and engaged the enemy. But the Saracens, who had planned the attack very carefully, knowing the king's rashness in pursuit, led him into an ambush, and Richard would have been taken had it not been for the presence of mind of William des Préaux, who called out: "Saracens, I am Malek." William was at once surrounded and taken prisoner, while Richard galloped away on Fauvel, leaving behind him the bodies of Reynier de Marun, his nephew Walter, and Alun and Luke de L'Étable, and a golden belt studded with jewels. The belt, lost in the scrimmage, was, however, picked up and brought to him later by William de Tornebu, but the dead knights remained a prey for the vultures. It was in vain that Richard's companions implored him not to expose himself, saying: "Without you Christendom is lost. For when the head is parted from the members, the members are no more sufficient to themselves but straightway fail and languish."

Indeed, the religious enthusiasm of the pilgrims was even now visibly abating and many of them had returned to the wicked city of Acre. So, early in October, Richard sent Guy de Lusignan to recall them to some sense of their duty. But Guy's moralizing had little effect against the Arabic arts of love, and a few days later Richard went there himself. He exhorted the Genoese ship-owners to support the war effort, offering them part of his conquests in return and promising to bear half the expense of their ships as long as they remained "in the service of God". He also gave a charter to the Pisans, confirming all the rights and privileges which King Guy, Queen Sibylla and the Templars had granted them. Once again he tried to get Conrad to rejoin the crusade. But Conrad, who was already intriguing against him with Saladin, was far too comfortable at Tyre.

On October 13th Richard returned to Jaffa with Joanna and Berengaria, having meanwhile rounded up some of the strayed revellers. On the same day reinforcements and supplies arrived. Then, hearing that Malek el Adil was encamped at Ibelin, three miles to the south along the coast, Richard sent him the present of a fine horse. A few days later, at Yazour, "a goodly young man who was his secretary" arrived from el Adil. Richard sent the envoy back with two sets of peace proposals, one set to be transmitted to Saladin, the other for el Adil's consideration alone. To Saladin he wrote:

Greet him, O my letter, and tell him that both Musulmans and Franks are reduced to the last extremity, their towns destroyed and the resources of both sides in men and goods are reduced to nothing. Surely we have had enough of this state of things: it is only a question of Jerusalem, the Holy Cross and (our old) possessions. Jerusalem we are resolved not to renounce so long as we have a single man left; and, as regards the Holy Cross, to you it is nothing but a worthless bit of wood, whereas it has great value in our eyes and the Sultan will be doing us a great favour if he restores it. Everything will then come right of itself and we shall enjoy a pleasant rest after our long toils.

Saladin replied:

To us Jerusalem is as precious, aye more precious than it is to you, in that it was the place whence our Prophet made his journey by night to heaven and is destined to be the gathering-place of our nation on the last day. Do not dream that we shall give it up to you. As to the land, it belonged to us originally, and it is you who are the aggressors. When you seized it it was only because of the suddenness of your coming and the weakness of those Musulmans who then held it. So long as the war shall last God shall not suffer you to raise one stone upon another. Finally as regards the Cross, its possession is very profitable to us and we should not be justified in parting with it unless to the advantage of Islam.

To el Adil Richard proposed, somewhat surprisingly, that he should marry Joanna, the ex-Queen of Sicily; that they should live in Jerusalem together and reign over all the Frankish kingdom. In return, Richard is prepared to cede to Saladin Acre, Jaffa and Ascalon, which he already regarded as his. All Moslem and Christian prisoners are to be freed, the Cross to return to the Christians, and the property of the Templars and Hospitallers to return to them also, though the fortresses shall belong to el Adil and Joanna. When this is accomplished Richard shall return to his own country.

El Adil accepted these terms and at once sent Bohardin with them to his brother. When Saladin read them he roared with laughter, not believing for a moment that they were meant seriously. Nevertheless he professed himself pleased and ready to accept them and on October 23rd sent an envoy to Jaffa.

Unfortunately, the stumbling block was Joanna. When she heard of the proposals she flew into a Plantagenet passion and declared that nothing on earth would induce her to marry an infidel. So Richard informed Saladin's envoy that difficulties had arisen, but that everything would come right if only his brother would embrace the Christian faith! But el Adil declined the honour and negotiations were broken off.

So, on October 29th, hearing that the Christians were about to leave Jaffa on the first stage of their march to Jerusalem, Saladin, who was encamped at Ramleh, sent a body of troops to surprise the camp. But the attack failed. Next day, while "roving in the plains of Ramleh," Richard encountered a Moslem reconnoitring party. "Thundering on like a wild boar," he slew some of them and scattered the rest, leaving among the dead "a certain very noble emir lying headless on the plain."

On the last day of October 1192 the army moved forward to Yazour and pitched their tents between two crusader castles, Casal of the Plains and Casel Maen, both recently demolished by Saladin.

These they now rebuilt, to secure the road from Jaffa to the hills, an operation which occupied a fortnight. The Saracens, however, did not leave them in peace and their incessant raids provided Richard with plenty of exercise. On one occasion he pursued the raiders almost as far as the Sultan's camp at Ramleh, which he saw quite plainly before turning back. Another day a foraging party, who had gone out to seek grass for the horses and fodder for the mules, with a small escort of Templars, was suddenly surprised by a large body of Turkish horse and surrounded at Ibn-Ibrak. The Templars, "seeing it was a case of emergency", dismounted and, ranging themselves back to back, prepared to sell their lives dearly. Andrew de Chauveny, the Earl of Leicester, the Count of St Pol and others went to their rescue, but more and more Turks came up and by the time Richard arrived, the situation looked so bad that his friends begged him to retire and not risk his life. Richard, we are told, went pale with fury: "I sent those men there," he shouted, "if they die without me may I never be called king again." And setting his spurs to his horse, he hurtled into the midst of the Turks "like a thunderbolt", his sword flashing on all sides, before and behind, "laying many low by the mere vigour of his movements". The Turks turned and scattered, with the demon king in hot pursuit, "and he overtook them again, and hewed off hands and arms and heads. And they fled like cattle." Bohardin, on the other hand, describes the battle as a Saracen victory and makes no mention of King Richard's presence.

But Richard wrote to el Adil complaining of the attack and asking for an interview. Next day, on November 7th, el Adil arrived at the Christian camp at Yazour, but as Richard had just been bled he could not receive him. Instead, Stephen de Turnham deputized for the king and entertained the prince at breakfast. Next day Richard met him at Lydda. A large tent was set up for the purpose and each brought presents of special delicacies of food and drink. El Adil also presented the English king with seven camels and crowned the entertainment with Syrian dancing girls. Richard, as a musical connoisseur, expressed himself pleased with the Saracen mode of singing. The interview lasted all day, and when the two princes parted it was with mutual assurances of perfect friendship.

Meanwhile Saladin was entertaining Conrad's ambassador, Reginald of Sidon, who brought an offer from Conrad to break with the Franks and to restore Acre to the Saracens, if Saladin on his side would restore Sidon and Beyrout. But when Saladin asked whether the marquis was prepared to take up arms against Richard, Reginald became evasive. Nevertheless, after that Conrad grew even more friendly with el Adil than Richard and was frequently to be seen out riding with him, which made Richard still more anxious to press on with the peace negotiations. He had asked el Adil to get him an interview with the sultan, but Saladin had replied: "It would be a strange thing for kings to continue disputing after they have once met. Better let the questions at issue be settled first.... Moreover, I do not know your tongue any more than you understand mine; and so we should have to find an interpreter in whom we could each place confidence. Later, when definite terms have been agreed on, we will have a meeting to ratify our sincere friendship."

Richard was struck both with the wisdom and the courtesy of the reply and sent Humphrey of Toron, the best Arabic linguist in the camp, to the sultan with the message: "I love your uprightness and desire your friendship. You have already promised to give your brother all the coast. But it is absolutely necessary that we should have Jerusalem. It is my wish to make such a division that your brother may incur no blame from the Musulmans and none from the Franks." He hoped, he said, to be able to arrange the marriage with Joanna. Though he had aroused much opposition by proposing it, a papal dispensation might be got in about six months. Failing that, el Adil could have his niece, Eleanor of Brittany. "The sultan immediately replied with fair words," says Bohardin, "but his object was to shake the foundations of the treaty.... After the envoys had left he turned to me and said: 'If I were to make peace with this people nothing would secure us against their bad faith!'"

A strange paralysis of the will seems to have immobilized Richard at this time. It is as though he now realized that the task he had so confidently undertaken was too much for him. His military instinct told him that the correct move after the victory of Arsûf was an attack on Ascalon before it was demolished. Instead of ordering this, we find him "pleading" for it in the council of barons and in the end giving in to those who wanted to advance to Jerusalem. "You have heard that Saladin is demolishing Ascalon, and yet you do nothing!" Conrad exclaimed to Richard in astonishment, according to the Arab historian Ibn al-Athir. "By Christ's truth, had I been near thee, Ascalon had been in our hands this day and this without the loss of a single tower."

The best part of two months had been wasted at Jaffa in futile negotiations—negotiations which still continued even after the army had left the coastal plain and begun to move slowly up into the foot-hills towards the Holy City. In fact, the actions of the Lion Heart at this time, and for the rest of the crusade, show an unwonted perplexity of mind. It is clear that he really did not know what to do.

A week after his meeting with el Adil, Richard moved his camp to a place between Lydda and Ramleh, where he remained for over three weeks. Meanwhile discussions continued between Saladin and the son of Humfrey de Toron about the proposed marriage. This was something that the other soldiers of the Cross could never understand. To pacify them, and because he enjoyed the sport, Richard would return from his almost daily skirmishes with a large assortment of Saracen heads, which he stacked in a corner of the tent.

On November 17th, Saladin left his camp five miles south of Ramleh and took up his winter quarters in Jerusalem, for the rains were approaching. All through November the crusaders had suffered from what are now known as "scattered showers and bright inter-vals". In the middle of December the rains set in and continued for three months. Instead of blinding sun and dust, they had to contend with ever-deepening mud—particularly awkward for heavily mailed knights, siege engines and supply wagons dragging across slippery moorland tracks. In any case the rolling hill country was full of Turkish light horsemen, who would suddenly appear from nowhere, attack the column, and disappear again before the heavy Frankish cavalry could get under way.

Retiring upon Jerusalem, Saladin had destroyed everything in his wake, and Ramleh when the crusaders reached it on December 8th, was no more than a heap of ruins under the pelting rain. The army camped there in great difficulties and discomfort. Hitherto the Saracen forces had barred the way to Jerusalem at Latrun, but in the middle of December the sultan disbanded his army, leaving it to his guerrilla horsemen, the weather and difficult and unfamiliar country to discourage the crusaders from any further advance.

Jerusalem lies on the eastern slope of the central range of hills which form the backbone of Judea. From the plains along the coast, the road, or rather track, ascends first through the Shephelah, or low-lands, a sloping moorland breaking into ridges of rock rising to chalk or limestone hills, bare and featureless, and then, after crossing a deep valley, the track climbs by more precipitous ways through the

Judean hills to the Holy City. It was at the foot of these lowlands
that Richard's army was still encamped.

The first crusaders had marched upon Jerusalem in two days by
the road from Ramleh to Emmaus and thence via Bethhoron and
Gibeon. Richard, it seems, now decided to follow in their footsteps
if he could. But the country was a perilous one for an invading
army which had once left the plains. With its scattered boulders,
caves and thick scrub, its torrent beds and hidden tracks, it was
ideal for the harassing tactics of guerrillas.

The army remained at Ramleh for six weeks, waiting for provisions and reinforcements. They had to wait a long time, because
Saladin's horsemen attacked all the convoys from the coast, and at
night Bedouin arabs would creep up stealthily and take prisoners
in the camp itself.

Richard was very nearly captured one day late in December.
Riding with only a small escort towards the castle of Blanche-garde
on its chalky hill about thirteen or fourteen miles due south of
Ramleh, he learnt by chance that Saladin had already dispatched
three hundred chosen warriors to ambush him. Three days later he
moved his headquarters to Latrun, the "Post of Observation",
which lay on the edge of the Judean hills. Here he celebrated Christmas with Joanna and Berengaria and Guy de Lusignan. He does
not seem to have had any definite plan of campaign and remained
behind at Laturun when, after Christmas, the army moved on to Beit
Nuba.

From Beit Nuba they could see the road climbing up through the
barren hills of Judea to Jerusalem, now only twelve miles away as
the crow flies, but hidden from view, as it lay on the other side of
the central range. Now the enthusiasm of the army broke all bounds.
(Perhaps Richard had remained behind at Latrun so as not to see
it!) Throwing their helmets into the air, they cried: "Help us, O
God, Our Lady, Holy Virgin Mary, help us! O Lord, suffer us to
adore Thee and thank Thee and see Thy Sepulchre!" Even the sick,
brought up from Jaffa on litters, raised their feeble voices and lifted
wasted arms.

On the tableland of Beit Nuba the Christian camp was exposed to
the full fury of the wind and rain. The wind broke their tent-poles,
the rain rotted their stores of salt-pork, and reduced their biscuits to
a yellow mess, and rusted their arms and coats of mail—in spite of
their continual enthusiastic polishing of them. Many sickened from
the bad food and the cold and wet and horses died in large numbers.

Nevertheless, Ambroise tells us, the camp rang with joy as all waited for the command to "liberate" Jerusalem. But says Richard of the Temple, "the wisest set of men did not share the too-hasty zeal of the common folk". They knew that Richard had already missed his only chance of taking the Holy City. As a letter of September 1191 from the governor of Jerusalem to Saladin reveals, had the Franks attacked the city after the Battle of Arsûf, they would have found it poorly defended and without provisions for a siege. Next month Saladin had begun rebuilding the walls and fortifications, el Adil and his emirs themselves working on them till they were complete. By December Jerusalem was ready to meet any attack.

The week of Christmas 1191–92 was a disastrous one for the crusaders. A convoy from Jaffa had been attacked and annihilated; among those massacred were many of the sick, who were being carried up into the mountains in the hope of seeing the Holy Sepulchre and finding release from their miseries. For they believed that a glimpse of the Sepulchre would cure them.

The night of 2 January 1192 was spent by Richard and Geoffrey de Lusignan on the watch at Casal of the Baths. Richard's known headquarters was Latrun. The Saracens therefore would not expect to meet him as they came up from the direction of Lydda to attack the baggage train. But no sooner did they attack at daybreak than Richard was upon them. Taken by surprise, the Bedouins fled to the hills. But not fast enough. Richard had already unhorsed and maimed two before his followers overtook him, when twenty or more were either killed or taken prisoner.

A council of war was held at Latrun on January 10th. The Templars and Hospitallers pointed out that a siege of Jerusalem in the present circumstances was not practicable. Surrounded on all sides, the Christians would starve before the Saracens did in the city. And even if they managed to take the city, the majority of the pilgrims having reached the goal of their pilgrimage would then want to go home. They would certainly not want to stay in the Holy Land indefinitely to hold it against Saladin. That burden would devolve upon the military orders and the Pullani—those that is, with Frankish fathers and Syrian mothers, who lived in the country. The military orders strongly advised a retreat upon Ascalon, so as to intercept the Saracen caravans from Cairo—Saladin's main source of supply.

"Draw me a plan of Jerusalem," said Richard, according to Ibn al-Athir, "for I have never seen it." And when those who knew the country had drawn one for him, and he saw the great valley that surrounded the city except for a small space towards the north, and had asked a number of questions about its depth and how it could be crossed, he said: "It will be impossible to take this town so long as Saladin lives and the Musalmans are at peace with one another."

The decision to retire was seconded by the Duke of Burgundy and the French. But it came as a terrible shock to the army. Suddenly dashed down from their peak of wild enthusiasm, many simply lay down under the snow and hail and refused to move. The sick would have died at that time had not Richard given orders that they were to be sought out, provided with litters or set upon horses. But the poor horses could not carry their loads and many collapsed beneath them and were left behind as the prey of vultures. Nor could the men carry all the provisions, and as they retreated down the slippery hill-tracks in the sleet and mud, each nationality began to accuse the other of treachery and cowardice. By the time they reached Ramleh, feeling was running so high that the French deserted, many going back to Jaffa and Acre, and others to join Conrad at Tyre.

From Ramleh what was left of the army marched, on January 19th, ten miles through marshland and heavy mud to the ruins of the fortress of Ibelin, about four miles from the sea, where they spent an equally comfortless night, the king, we are told, "outworn with grief and toil such as no tongue nor pen can describe". But the wretchedness of that day's march was as nothing to what followed on January 20th, with twenty miles to cover to Ascalon. "For, as our men plodded on wearily, bitter snow drifted in their faces, thick hail stones rattled down, and pouring rain enveloped them. The marshy land, too, gave way beneath their feet; baggage-horses and men sank into the swamps, and the more they struggled the deeper they became involved. So battered, so weary and so worn, cursing the day on which they were born, and smiting themselves, they at last reached Ascalon, only to find it in ruins so that they could barely struggle through the gates over the heaps of stones."[2]

Camping outside the ruins of Ascalon, they had to wait eight days for provisions to arrive from Jaffa, for there was no harbour at Ascalon and the sea dashed all their ships to pieces. Undaunted,

[2] *Itinerarium Ricardi.*

Richard had the driftwood collected and built new galleys with it. He also sent messages to the discontented French to return and carry on with the crusade. They agreed to come back and serve under him until Easter, on condition that they would then be free to return home. "To these terms the king agreed, thinking it well to dissemble for a while."

Next month, in February, the rebuilding of the walls of Ascalon began. They all worked—"laymen, clerks, high and low, servants and masters, all shared the same labour: toil made all on an equality." Richard himself carried stones to set an example to the nobility, each of whom engaged to rebuild a section of the wall at his own expense—"and if any had to stop working from lack of money, this high-souled king, whose heart was greater than even his royal dignity, gave them of his own wealth so far as he knew them to be in want." Three parts of the city walls, it is said, were built at the king's expense.

While building operations were going on, Richard rode out one morning to reconnoitre Darum, a castle which had been the extreme south-west outpost of the kingdom of Jerusalem. It was now the first halting-place for caravans from Cairo. As luck would have it, just as Richard and his knights arrived, they met an Arab caravan comprising a thousand Christian prisoners on their way to be sold into slavery at Cairo. As soon as they saw Richard's banner approaching, the Saracen escort sought shelter in the Castle of Darum, but not before Malek Ric had caught up with them and lopped off the heads of a score or so.

Richard now made another attempt to get Conrad to join the crusade and render the military service due to the Crown of Jerusalem. Conrad refused, but agreed to meet Richard at Casel Imbert, between Tyre and Acre. Meanwhile the French began to ask the Duke of Burgundy about the pay owing to them, without which, they declared, they would not fight any more. The Duke being hard pressed and having no money himself, asked Richard for a further loan, but as the original loan had not been repaid—it was to have come out of the ransom of the Acre garrison—Richard refused. This became such a sore point that soon after that the Duke of Burgundy and the French left Ascalon and went back to Acre.

But trouble had now arisen at Acre, where King Guy reigned over a non-existent kingdom of Jerusalem and where he was supported by the Pisans. The Genoese, however, were scheming to oust him and put Conrad in his place. It was the old quarrel that had never been really settled. So when the Duke of Burgundy arrived with the French, the city was in an uproar. The Pisans refused to allow him to enter and shot his horse. Just then Conrad arrived by sea, but was kept off for three days by a bombardment from the mangonels of the Pisans, who sent word to Richard of what was afoot. Their messenger found the king at Caesarea, on his way to the meeting with Conrad; he immediately set spurs to his horse and arrived at Acre that same night. Then, calling the people together, the king "showed them by the clearest arguments that between colleagues nothing was better than friendship, peace and unity; nothing worse than quarrels."

The meeting between Richard and Conrad at Casel Imbert then took place, but without any practical result. So, after consultation with the other leaders, Richard gave out that Conrad had forfeited his rights and should be deprived of his revenues in the kingdom. In retaliation, Conrad immediately sent word to those French who were still at Ascalon to join him and the Duke of Burgundy at Tyre. "And on the Tuesday before Easter the king returned from Acre to the army at Ascalon, very sad and ill at ease."

On his arrival the chief men of the French greeted him with the demand that he should give them guides and leave to depart to Tyre. Not only did Richard give them all they asked, with an escort of Templars and Hospitallers, and Henry of Champagne, his nephew, but he rode out with them himself on April 1st, "praying them with many tears to stay with him a little while at his expense". As they still remained obdurate, he sent a swift messenger to Acre with orders that they should not be admitted to the city. By their defection Richard lost seven hundred of the best knights in his army. When news of this reached Saladin he at once sent out messengers to reassemble his forces.

The rainy season was now almost over and the country once more fit for campaigning. Nevertheless the French, on reaching Tyre, "abandoned themselves to wantonness, women's songs and banqueting with harlots". Those who saw them, writes the English author of the *Itinerarium* disgustedly, "brought us word how they applauded bands of dancing women, and how the very luxury of their costume bespoke their indolent effeminacy.... Round their necks were jewelled collars and on their heads garlands wrought with every kind of flower, goblets they brandished in their hands, not swords, their nights were spent in potations and profligacy.... Why should I say more?" The French had, as indeed was only human, after all their trials, succumbed to the pleasures of the East.

To put heart into the English, who were, probably even then, more accustomed to austerity, Richard held a great court outside the walls of Ascalon, offering food and drink in abundance to all who desired it. But on Easter Monday he set everyone to work again on the walls. He told them that they must all pull their weight and hang together and make Ascalon the strongest castle on the coast of Palestine. Next day the king rode out with a few comrades to inspect Gaza, twelve to thirteen miles to the south-west.

All this time negotiations had been going on with Saladin. But when Stephen de Turnham reached Jerusalem, he was perturbed to see Conrad's envoy, Reginald of Sidon, and Balien of Ibelin riding out of the gate together. Nevertheless on March 20th el Adil had met Richard's envoy, with an offer that the Christians should keep what they had conquered and should have the right of pilgrimage to Jerusalem, where Latin priests might officiate. They might annex Beirut, provided it was dismantled, and the Holy Cross was to be restored. Richard received the embassy favourably and even knighted one of el Adil's sons. By April 1192 it seemed that the war was almost over.

On the fifteenth of the month came disturbing news from England. Robert, prior of Hereford, arrived at Ascalon with letters from Longchamp begging the king to return at once "on the wings of the wind", for Earl John was making open war upon him and usurping the realm. Moreover, there was no money left in the king's treasury or anywhere else, "unless perchance what remained hidden in the churches". Queen Eleanor also wrote saying that Philip was preparing to invade Normandy and recover Alais from the tower of Rouen and that John was scheming to marry her himself and to repudiate the Countess of Gloucester, and she implored her son to abandon every other project and return to England "with all speed to save his own".

The news seemed to Richard hardly credible and after reading it he remained silent. The next day he summoned a council and announced that he would shortly be returning to England, but would leave 300 knights and 2,000 men-at-arms behind him to serve in the kingdom of Jerusalem at his expense. After consultation, the barons told him that unless he appointed as lord over the land someone with experience of war under whom they could serve that they would return to their own countries. This once more raised the question of the crown of Jerusalem, and Richard asked them whom they would rather have—Guy de Lusignan or Conrad of Montferrat. To his shocked surprise they one and all, on their bended knees, prayed that they might have Conrad for their chief and defender, "seeing that he was the more powerful man". Richard agreed to grant their request and sent Henry of Champagne to Tyre with the news of the election. When Conrad heard it, he said that he would now join the camp at Ascalon and fixed his coronation for a few days hence at Acre.

Then he fell on his knees and besought God that if he were unworthy of the crown it should not be given to him. On April 28th, as he was returning from a dinner party with the Bishop of Beauvais, his prayer was answered. Two young men ran up to him and, whipping out knives, stabbed him to the heart. The marquis fell from his horse and rolled over in the road a dying man. One of the assassins was cut down on the spot; the other, after taking sanctuary in a church, was captured and sentenced to be dragged about the city at a horse's tail till dead. While this sentence was being carried out he was questioned and confessed that he had long sought for an opportunity to murder the marquis, having been sent by the Old Man of the Mountain, Chief of the Assassins. "But you must know", says the author of the *Itinerarium*, "the Old Man of Musse has all men whom he judges unworthy of life cut off in the same way. The faith of this folk is very cruel and obscure." In this case, it seems, Conrad had offended the sheikh of Sinan by an act of piracy against a merchant ship carrying a cargo that belonged to the sect of the Assassins. Conrad had drowned all the crew and refused to return the goods. This was his payment.

The French, and in particular the Bishop of Beauvais, at once accused Richard of having contrived the murder, because, they said, he was not willing that Conrad should succeed Guy as king of Jerusalem. And, on his return to Tyre, Henry of Champagne was unanimously acclaimed king in place of Conrad. Two days later, his betrothal to the much-married Isabella, Conrad's widow but still only twenty-one, was announced. Richard was against the marriage on moral grounds, saying to Henry's messengers, "Sirs, I should greatly wish that my nephew might be king—if it please God, when the land shall be conquered, but not that he wed the marchioness, whom the marquis took from her rightful lord and lived with in such wise that if Count Henry trusts my counsel he will not take her in marriage. But let him acccept the kingship, and I will give him in demesne Acre and its port dues, Tyre, Jaffa and jurisdiction over all the conquered land. And then tell him to come back to the host and bring the Frenchmen with him, as quickly as he can, for I want to go and take Darum—if the Turks dare wait for me there!"

Richard was no politician, for it was evident that the kingship of Jerusalem could not be had without marriage to Isabella. Indeed, it is said that Isabella took matters into her own hands by coming to the handsome young Henry of Champagne and offering herself to him together with the keys of Tyre, and the marriage was celebrated a week after the assassination of her former husband, Conrad. Five years later, when Henry fell from a window of his palace at Acre and was killed, Isabella made haste to console herself with Amaury de Lusignan and became Queen of Cyprus.

Her marriage to Henry of Champagne should have brought about better relations between the French and the Anglo-Angevin armies, since Henry was nephew to both Philip of France and Richard.

As for Guy de Lusignan, he was no longer wanted after the death of his wife Sibylla, who had really worn the crown of Jerusalem, so Richard gave him Cyprus instead. For the Templars had grown tired of trying to hold down the Cypriots. At the moment the island was quiet, after a wholesale massacre at Nicosia, with which the Templars had celebrated Easter. According to the Greek chronicle of Makhairos, the Templars practised all kinds of abominations on the quiet. "The above Templars were very rich, and they cherished amongst themselves a great heresy and a most filthy order of life, but in secret." Curiously, the same charges were brought against them when Philip the Fair suppressed the Order early in the four-teenth century. Thousands of these incorruptible knights were sub-jected to the most horrible tortures to make them "confess", and the horror culminated with the burning of their Grand Master, Jaques de Molay, in front of Notre Dame. The case against them was, of course, prepared and carried through with the connivance of the Church, for whose salvation in the Orient they had fought and suffered. But their removal from the Levant made possible the final conquest of the Byzantine Empire by the Turks.

Guy de Lusignan was now crowned King of Cyprus, where he founded the Lusignan dynasty, which lasted until 1489, with most of the rulers assuming the title of King of Cyprus and Jerusalem. Among them were several women rulers. To the Lusignans we owe the exquisite abbey of Bellapaise, whose cloisters are full of dark-leaved orange trees and their yellow and golden fruit, "while bright green lizards crawl in the sunshine across the dead, stone face of some forgotten Crusader from the West".[3]

Messengers continued to arrive from England urging Richard to return. Others, equally insistent, urged him to remain where he was and finish the crusade to which his life had been dedicated.

What had been going on in England during the king's absence is described by Roger de Hoveden: "In the same year (1191), William Bishop of Ely, legate of the Apostolic See, Chancellor of our Lord the King and justiciary of all England, oppressed the people entrusted to his charge with heavy exactions. For in the first place he despised all his fellows whom the king had associated with him in the government of the kingdom, and disregarded their advice. Indeed, he considered no one of his associates in the kingdom his equal, not even John, earl of Mortaigne, the king's brother. Accordingly, he laid claim to the castles, estates, abbeys, churches, and all the rights of the king as his own. On the authority of his legateship, he came to take up his lodging at bishoprics and abbeys, and priories, and other houses of the religious orders, with such a vast array of men, horses, hounds and hawks, that a house where he took up his abode for only a single night was hardly able within the three following years to recover its former state. From the clerks and laiety he also took away their churches, and farms, lands, and other possessions, which he either divided among his nephews, clerks, and servants, or else, to the loss of the owners, retained possession of them himself, or squandered them away to supply his extraordinary expenses."

The result of this behaviour was a gradually mounting rage against the chancellor throughout the kingdom. All those who had a grievance against him looked to John, who had now returned to England to claim the castles and honours granted to him by his brother. He had made haste to do so, in fact, as soon as he heard that Richard had recognized Arthur of Brittany as his heir. John, however, was determined to succeed to the throne, and nothing was more useful to him than the general hatred of Longchamp. Matters came to a head when the chancellor arrested the king's other brother, Geoffrey archbishop of York, when he landed in England, contrary to his oath, in the autumn of 1191. Longchamp's sister, as warden of Dover Castle, had actually had him dragged away from the altar of a church where he was taking sanctuary and imprisoned. This was felt to be the final outrage and the chancellor was forced

[3]Clennell Wilkinson, *Coeur de Lion*, 1933. p. 94.

to seek refuge in the Tower. "As we entered the city at a late hour," writes Hugh de Nonant, Bishop of Coventry in a letter of October 1191, "many of his (Longchamp's) household in arms attacked us with drawn swords, and slew one of our knights, a nobleman, and wounded a great number". Next morning at a conference of nearly all the nobles of the kingdom, with John and the archbishops of Rouen and York and the other principal bishops, "and in the presence of the people of the city", and the justiciars of the king, it was agreed "that such a person should henceforth no longer rule the kingdom of England ... for, to suit other matters, he and his revellers had so exhausted the whole kingdom, that they did not leave a man his belt, a woman her necklace, a nobleman his ring, or anything of value even to a Jew". In all this, of course, the chancellor had been acting on the king's instructions to collect as much money as he possibly could, nor was Richard particular about how he did it. Nevertheless, the odium fell upon Longchamp, who was now hustled off to Canterbury, "that there, as became him, he might assume the cross of pilgrimage, and lay aside the cross of legateship."

After spending a few days at Dover Castle, which belonged to his brother-in-law, the chancellor disguised himself as a woman—"a sex he had always hated", says Nonant—"and changed the priest's robe for the harlot's dress". Then, hobbling with difficulty down from the heights of the castle, the little monkeyish dwarf came to the seashore in a green gown of enormous length, "having a cape of the same colour with unsightly long sleeves". As he sat on a rock waiting for a boat to take him to France, to his delight a half-naked fisherman came out of the sea and began embracing him in the freest possible manner. But it was not long before the fisherman discovered his mistake. "Come all of you and see a wonder!" he cried, "I have found a woman who is a man!" At this the chancellor's attendants came up and pushed the fisherman back "with a gentle kind of violence, and told him to hold his tongue". Next a woman came up to him and, noticing the length of cloth he held in his hand, asked him how much it was and if he would sell her a few yards. But as Longchamp was "utterly unacquainted with the English tongue", he made no answer. Then another woman came up and asked the same question and as he still remained silent, the two women pulled off his hood "and beheld the swarthy features of a man, lately shaved". Their cries of "Come, let us stone this monster!" soon attracted a large crowd who began dragging the

chancellor about the shore by the long sleeves of his gown and bang-
ing him against the rocks. After that they dragged him about the
streets of Dover and shut him up in a cellar. Nonant concludes the
long, malicious letter, in which he describes all this, by wishing
that the king would appoint people to govern the country by whom
the royal dignity might be preserved. Longchamp remained in his
cellar for eight days, till John gave orders for his liberation. On
reaching Normandy, he wrote to King Richard and the Pope complaining of his treatment. To Richard he said that the kingdom had
been seized by his brother John and that John would place the
crown upon his own head unless the king returned speedily.

In his perplexity, Richard continued reconnoitring in the region
of Ascalon, Gaza and the foothills. His purpose was, apparently, to
find another more direct route to Jerusalem than the Vale of Ajalon.
The most direct way was by the Wady es Surar (Valley of Sarek);
the third main route by the Wady es Sunt (Vale of Elah) was
blocked by the great castle of Blanchegarde seventeen miles away,
which the earlier crusaders had built to protect the route from
Ascalon.

When, on April 22nd, Richard attacked Blanchegarde, the
Turkish garrison fled at his approach. Leaving his whole force there
in occupation, he rode back to Ascalon alone. On the way he was
very nearly killed in a fight with a wild boar. Six days later, Roger
de Glanville, the commandant of Blanchegarde, made a daring
reconnaissance through the Vale of Elah, up the mountain pass on
the other side of the great valley, and on across the plateau at the top
of the pass to the very gates of Jerusalem, even returning with a few
Saracen prisoners. Next day (April 29th) Richard came upon eight
Saracens somewhere between Blanchegarde and Gaza; three of them
he killed straight away, making prisoners of the other five. But he
had a narrow escape during the night of May 1st. Camping at
Furbia (Herbiya), near the mouth of the Wady el-Hasi between
Ascalon and Gaza, he was surprised by a small party of Turks early
in the morning. Being a light sleeper, he was the first to wake, and
seized his sword and ran to meet his assailants. He killed four and
took seven prisoners. The rest, we are told, "fled before his face".
So the indecisive skirmishing and reconnoitring went on.

A more important operation was the capture of Darum, which
had taken the place of Ascalon as Saladin's main supply base from
Egypt. Moreover, there were rumours that the sultan's nephew

Taki-ed-Din, having died, his son, el Mansour, was in open revolt in Mesopotamia. Richard, whose treaty with Saladin was not yet ratified, saw this as an opportune moment to renew the war. And he was anxious to take Darum himself, before the Duke of Burgundy and the French arrived.

Sending his mangonels and siege engines down the coast by sea, while his army took a parallel route on land, he arrived before the walls of Darum on May 17th. The Turks laughed at the insignificant number of the besiegers, and, after the arrival of the fleet, were still more amused to see the king and his nobles sweating like packhorses as they staggered for nearly a mile across the sands with the various parts of their siege engines on their shoulders. The parts were swiftly assembled and the stone-casters and slings set to work, one manned by the Normans, another by the Poitevins, a third directed against the principal tower of the citadel by the king himself. The mangonels hurled their great millstones against the city day and night, while the famous sappers of Aleppo undermined the walls.

On the fourth day of the siege the castle gate was set on fire and shattered by a well-aimed millstone from Richard's mangonel. The garrison, laughing no longer, offered to surrender if their lives were spared. Richard told them to defend themselves as best they might and kept up the bombardment, till one of the towers, which had already been skilfully undermined, fell with a roar. The Franks rushed in, cutting down the Turks right and left, and made for the citadel. Seeing the Christian banners waving on the outer bailey, the garrison despaired of further resistance. Those who still held out on the battlements were flung into the ditch beneath, while three hundred in the citadel were kept under close guard, their hands tied so tightly behind their backs with leather thongs that they roared with pain. Next day they were sent to the slave market, with their wives and children. "Thus before the French came up, with the aid of his own men only did King Richard nobly get possession of Darum after a four days' siege." The first to set up his banner on the walls, says the writer of the *Itinerarium*, as though he were describing some sporting event, was Stephen de Longchamp, the second the Earl of Leicester, the third Andrew de Chauvigny, the fourth Raymond son of the Prince of Antioch. But the first to force his way into the citadel was Seguin Barrez, with his man-at-arms Ospiard.

When everything was over, Henry of Champagne and the Duke of Burgundy arrived. Richard greeted them joyfully and made the castle of Darum over to his nephew. "Then they all tarried at Darum for the great festival of Penticost." Afterwards the French went to Ascalon and Richard to Furbia, where he stopped to await the report of a scout sent to reconnoitre the southernmost approaches to Jerusalem through the Wady el Hesy (the Valley of the Wells). When he learned that the Emir Caysac was at the Castle of the Fig Trees, with more than a thousand men, Richard decided to give him a surprise.

Calling out the army from Ascalon, he set out from Furbia on May 27th and pitched his tents at the Canebrake of Starlings. At sunrise next day they were about to attack the Castle of the Fig Trees, when they found it deserted. For, hearing of Richard's approach, Caysac had decided not to wait for him. So the host returned to the Canebrake of Starlings. Next day, they were less successful, for when they attacked another fortress they were driven off.

While the army was still encamped at the Canebrake of Starlings, Richard's vice-chancellor John of Alençon arrived with the news that his brother John was intriguing with Philip of France. When he got this last and most disturbing piece of intelligence, the king said that he must go home "lest he be stripped of his ancestral soil and the kingdom of his fathers". Yet at the same time he felt that he could not desert the crusade just when another attempt on Jerusalem was about to be made. And while the king "tired out by the weight of his thoughts, sought his couch in angry mood", the leaders of the army, French, Normans, English, Poitevins, Angevins and the men of Maine, held a council and decided to advance upon the Holy City without him. At this there was such a general rejoicing in the camp that lamps were lit, the *jongleurs* sang their gestes, and they all danced till past midnight. But the choice that lay before Richard was between losing his inheritance to John and Philip, or failing in his life's mission. It was a terrible, a paralysing dilemma.

In the morning of June 1st the army struck camp and marched back down the Wady el Hesy to the plains, till they came to Ibelin of the Hospital (Beit Jibrin), a fortress with a village built round it. Here they halted for two or three days, draping themselves in veils against a plague of minute flies, which flew about like sparks and stung every exposed part of their bodies till they looked like lepers. The flies added to Richard's torment of mind. But as he sat brooding in his tent, he became aware of a man pacing up and down outside weeping bitterly. It was William the chaplain from his own land of Poitiers. Richard called out to him and asked him what was the matter.

"O King," said William, "remember how, when thou wert Count of Poitou, thou hadst no neighbour who did not yield to thy strength; remember the confusion of the Brabançons whom thou so often routedst with a little band. Remember how gloriously thou didst drive the Count of St Giles from the siege of Hautefort; how thou didst receive possession of thine own realm without use of shield or helm; remember how manfully thou didst conquer Messina, utterly crushing the Greek race that dared to war against thee. Remember how God enriched thee at the conquest of Cyprus—an enterprise which, before thee, no one ever dared to undertake; how thou didst subdue it in fifteen days and with God's assistance didst take the emperor prisoner; remember the destruction of that splendid ship near Acre harbour with the drowning of its eight hundred men and its serpents. Remember how thou didst reach Acre just in time to receive its surrender; and thy recovery from the *arnoldia* of which so many other chiefs died. Remember how God has entrusted this land to thy care; how its safety rests on thee alone now that the king of France has gone off so meanly.... Remember how, from the moment of leaving the western world, thou hast stood out as a conqueror and how before thy feet enemies have fallen prone and been consigned to chains.... Already does the Soldan dread thee, already are the recesses of Babylon struck with amazement; already does the valour of the Turks fear thy approach. What more? All men say commonly that thou art the father of all, the patron and champion of Christendom, which, if deserted by you, will lie exposed to the plunder of her enemies."

Richard listened in silence to this passionate harangue, and so did those who sat with him in his tent. And by this speech, we are told, the king's heart was changed. "And lo! on the morrow at the ninth hour he turned back with all his army and settled outside the city of Ascalon in the orchards". Breaking from his ominous silence, he told Henry of Champagne and the Duke of Burgundy that "for no other concern or need, no messenger and no tidings, nor for any earthly quarrel, would he depart from them or quit the land before next Easter"—that is, March 1193.

Then, calling for his herald Philip, he bade him proclaim the same throughout the host—"that all men should make them ready, with whatsoever means God had given them, for they were all going to Jerusalem."

VI

RICHARD WILL NOT LOOK UPON JERUSALEM

EARLY on the morning of June 1st 1192 the Christian host set forth
once more on the road to Jerusalem. It seemed that the spirit of the
first crusade had revived again. For many were the deeds of charity
and courtesy, when knights and noblemen dismounted and set poor
pilgrims on their horses, themselves going on foot behind. The heat
was intense. That night they camped at Blanchegarde, and rested
two days, and on the third resumed their march, into the foothills.
"All the host marched in close order," says Ambroise, "the roads all
filled with warriors iron-clad, meeting no man nor encountering any
hindrance, straight on to Toron of the Knights." They reached
Toron on June 9th, and that night intercepted a party of Turks
returning from a raid on Jaffa.

The siege engines not yet having come up, Richard next day went
on ahead to Castle Ernault, built by his great-grandfather Fulk of
Anjou on one of the highest hills of the Shephelah about three and
a half miles north-west of Beit Nuba and commanding views of two
roads to Jerusalem. On June 10th the French arrived and the whole
army advanced to Beit Nuba. Here they pitched their tents to wait
for Henry of Champagne, who had gone to Acre to round up the
people who were living there at their ease.

That same night a scout returned from his post of observation on
the hill of Gibeon, which the Franks called Montjoie—for from
there they had had their first glimpse of Jerusalem—to report a
Turkish ambush near the Fountain of Emmaus.

Richard was in his saddle before dawn. At daybreak he and his
knights surprised the Turks at Emmaus, killing twenty of them
and capturing three camels, several fine horses and two mules laden
with silks and spices. Saladin's herald was spared, but the rest
Richard chased over the hills. They gave him a fine run and he had
just transfixed one caitiff with his lance, when, looking up, he saw
the towers and domes and slender minarets of Jerusalem lying like
a bride in the early morning light on the eastern ramparts of
Judea. It was but a momentary glimpse. Knowing that he would
never take her now, he covered his face with his shield and, addressing God, his ultimate feudal overlord, he cried, "Fair Lord God, I

pray thee not to let me see thy Holy City if so it be that I may not deliver it out of the hands of thine enemies."

What Richard saw from Montjoie was a prospect of rugged hills covered with scanty herbage, an empty desolate area, and Jerusalem beyond on a still higher ridge. Below, the hills rolled away to the horizon in undulating green waves, broken by patches of grey rock. And beyond that, thirty miles westward, shone the sea.

To advance farther towards Jerusalem would, as Richard knew now, have been to court disaster. Reinforcements had just arrived for Saladin from Jezireh and Mosul, and next day two hundred horsemen came down from the heights and threw the whole Christian camp into confusion. Otherwise, skirmishing continued and provided opportunities for exhibitions of prowess. In the battle of June 12th Robert de Bruges, a Hospitaller, distinguished himself by riding out alone and driving his lance right through the body of a Turkish horseman—"a goodly feat of arms," says Ambroise, "had he not broken the rule of his Order". That is, Robert had no business to break ranks and attack the enemy single-handed as though he were at a tournament. For this, the Grand Master made him dismount and sent him back to the lines on foot in disgrace, till all the other knights and barons knelt to Garnier de Nablus and prayed that "he forgive Robert for the prowess he hath wrought".

On June 17th a large convoy from Jaffa was attacked near Ramleh by Turkish cavalry, who cut their way through the rearguard and unhorsed Baldwin de Carron, Richard D'Orgues and Theodoric. "Indeed with such a multitude of Turks closing round our men," says the *Itinerarium*, "it is no wonder that the bravest warriors got unhorsed." But Baldwin was unhorsed a second time and Clarembald de Montchablon fled. Then Baldwin was unhorsed a third time and battered senseless. Menasses de Insula, who came to his rescue, was also flung down and struck with maces. Complete disaster seemed inevitable, when "lo! God sent the valiant Earl of Leicester as their champion and liberator", together with Stephen de Longchamp, and the Turks were put to flight. But not before they had taken many prisoners and left the field littered with Christian dead and maimed.

The garrison at Jerusalem were cheered by the sight of the prisoners, just as the camp at Beit Nuba was thrown into ecstacies of religious fervour at the sight of a blackened bit of wood which the Syrian Bishop of Lydda said was a fragment of the True Cross. Shortly after that, the Abbot of St Elias, a monastery on the road from Jerusalem to Bethlehem, reported that he had hidden another bit of the Cross in his garden and would give it to Richard if he would come and get it. Richard thereupon rode with a suitable escort to the appointed place and returned in triumph with the miracle-working piece of wood. The sight of this wrought the camp up to such a pitch of enthusiasm that they were for going on to Jerusalem then and there, till Richard brought them back to facts. The army was too small, he said, to fight a rearguard action as well as to besiege the Holy City. To advance now into the waterless mountains at the height of summer would merely be to court a repetition of the Battle of Hattin, and he, for his part, refused to lead the army to certain destruction. He knew well, he added, that there were many people, especially some in France whom he could name, who would be only too glad to see this so that he might be for ever discredited. But he had no mind to satisfy them. Neither he nor the French knew the land. It was for the military orders and the Pullani to advise. "Let them decide," he concluded, "whether we are to attempt the siege, or to go and take Babylon (Cairo), or Beyrout or Damascus. So shall there be no more discord among us."

The decision was left to a jury composed of five Templars, five Hospitallers, five Syrian knights and five barons of France. The first fifteen voted for the expedition to Cairo; the French remained adamant in their desire to go on to Jerusalem. Richard did his best to persuade them of the advantages of the Cairo plan. "See, my fleet lies at Acre," he said, "ready to carry all the baggage, equipments, and accoutrements, biscuits and flour; the host could go all along by the shore and I would lead from here at my own charges seven hundred knights and two thousand men-at-arms; no man of mine should be lacking. But if they (the French) will not do this, I am quite ready to go to the siege of Jerusalem; only be it known that I will not be the leader of the host; I will go in the company as leader of my own men, but of no others."

He then bade the nobles assemble at the headquarters of the Hospitallers to discover exactly how much each of them could contribute to the siege of Jerusalem in men and money. The inquiry was interrupted, however, by the arrival of Richard's scout Bernard and some other spies, so well disguised and so fluent in Arabic as to be practically indistinguishable from Saracens, bringing news of the approach of a great caravan from Egypt. Everybody was delighted when Richard at once decided to attack it and sent to the Duke of Burgundy inviting him to join the expedition. The French accepted in consideration of a third share of the booty. So Richard set out with five hundred knights and a thousand men-at-arms.

The king rode in advance of the rest, as was his custom, "beneath the splendour of the moon to Galatea", where they rested and sent to Ascalon for supplies. Saladin, however, was kept informed by his scouts of Richard's movements and sent five hundred picked troops under the Emir Aslam to escort the caravan to Jerusalem by a less-known route over the mountains. Aslam met the caravan that evening at the waters of Kuweilfeh, which the Franks called the Round Cistern. His force, together with those already escorting the caravan made a total of over two thousand horsemen, without counting the foot-soldiers.

When Richard heard that the first part of the convoy had reached the Round Cistern, Bohardin says that disguising himself as a scout, he made a circuit of the Egyptians' camp and, finding them all asleep, rode back and gave the order to attack. Crossbowmen and archers were sent to delay the Turkish advance. The Turks, thereupon, withdrew to the hills and opened fire with darts and arrows, which fell "thick as dew". But when Richard charged with his knights the entire Moslem force "took to headlong flight as hares before dogs". Bohardin corroborates it. "Those of our men", he says, "who were reputed bravest were glad to save their lives by the fleetness of their horses." The slaughter of the flying army was appalling. Richard's lance became so sodden with blood that it crumbled in his hand like rotten wood.

While the knights were enjoying themselves in this way, the foot-soldiers were busy looting the caravan. Seeing this, the Emir Aslam sent down a party of horsemen to attack them. But the Earl of Leicester, "laying about him right and left", came to the rescue, with Stephen de Longchamp. "Then was the slaughter renewed, the heavens thundered, the air was bright with sparks struck from the swords. The ground reeked with blood, dismembered corpses were everywhere; lopt off arms, hands, feet, heads, and even eyes. Our men were hindered in walking over the plain by the corpses of the dead Turks, and the bodies which they had just dismembered caused our men to stumble.... With such prowess did our men capture the caravan." Thirteen hundred Turkish horsemen were killed, not counting the foot-soldiers. The booty was enormous, more than four thousand camels laden with jewels, gold, silver, silks, fabrics from Baghdad and Grecian textiles; arms of every kind, chess tables, tents, hides, leather water-bottles; barley, wheat, flour.

For Saladin, the Battle of the Round Cistern was a major disaster. Now, he was sure, the Christians would advance on Jerusalem. The walls of the city were manned and everything was put in a state of defence; all the wells in the neighbourhood were poisoned, cisterns destroyed, springs dammed up. But still the Christians did not come. Richard did not return to the camp at Beit Nuba till June 29th. On the way, at Ramleh, he met Count Henry of Champagne with the stragglers from Acre and the Duke of Burgundy. The French began to clamour once more for an immediate advance on Jerusalem. But the Syrian Franks repeated their former arguments and said that if they went up into the mountains of Judea, they would all die of thirst. The French objected that they could get water at the Tekora River. "How," said King Richard, "shall we manage to water our beasts there?" They replied that the army could be divided into two parts, while one party was besieging Jerusalem the other could fetch water from the river. "Yes," said Richard, "and as soon as one division has gone off with its beasts for water, the garrison will sally out upon those who are left, and then it is all over with the Christian host."[1] But the French were unconvinced and there were murmurs of treachery and cowardice.

So while Saladin was fervently praying in the Mosque of Al Aksa, prostrating himself and calling upon the Lord in an agony of inde-cision whether to evacuate Jerusalem or to defend it and risk a pitched battle with the Christians outside the city, it was reported to him on July 2nd that the whole army of his enemies had ridden out to the top of a hill, where they could be plainly seen from the city, and then ridden down again. Next morning at daybreak his scouts brought a still more astonishing report. The Christian army was in full retreat. Saladin could hardly believe his good fortune. Mounting his horse, he rode out to witness the spectacle. "And yet," says Bohardin, "as he knew the enemy to have plenty of camels and other beasts of burden, he had fears for Egypt, a land that the king of England had many times shown an inclination to invade." But, as his spies informed him, three hundred knights had been appointed as arbitrators in the Christian camp between Richard and the Duke of Burgundy; these three hundred elected twelve others, and these twelve chose three umpires to settle the matter, and the final decision had been to retire.

[1] Another Christian host under Allenby, seven centuries later, suc-ceeded where Richard failed, though they followed exactly the same road.

On one of the last nights at Beit Nuba, Richard received an urgent message from a hermit who dwelt on Montjoie, bidding him come in God's name without delay. When he reached the joyful mountain for the second time, the holy man, who was covered all over with matted hair like a monkey, led him into an oratory, removed a stone from the wall and took out a wooden cross, which he said was made from the Tree of Calvary. He prophesied that the king would not at this time win the land of Jerusalem, however hard he strove for it. He also foretold his own death that day week. Richard took him back with him to the camp to see whether his last prophecy, at any rate, would come true. Seven days later the hermit died.

The army fell back from Jerusalem for a second time on July 4th. It was an occasion of great bitterness and mutual recrimination, and as they retired the Saracen horsemen galloped down from the hills and harried their rearguard. Each night, as they marched back on the road to Ramleh, the French, to show their disgust, pitched their tents apart from the English. The Duke of Burgundy even made up a scandalous song about Richard, the words of which, according to the *Itinerarium* were "shameful and such as ought not to have been given to the public, if those who wrote it had any sense of shame left in them; for it was sung not only by the men, but by women who surpassed men in their license." To set half the army singing about such a subject, added Richard of Holy Trinity, Aldgate, only went to show what the French were really like.

Richard was quite equal to the occasion and wrote a *sirvante* against the Duke of Burgundy in reply, which was taken up and sung throughout the Anglo-Angevin camp. But, comments Richard of Holy Trinity sadly, such an incident could never have occurred when "our people took Antioch by force of arms—a period we hear sung of in the Gestes". Those were the days when Bohemund Prince of Antioch, and Geoffrey de Bouillon won glorious victories, "their deeds now flow as food from the mouth of the *jongleurs*. God gave them the reward for which they toiled, because they served Him out of no faint heart." Now they lived in decadent times, and the cause of the Lord had fallen upon evil days when the Soldiers of the Cross made up obscene songs about each other almost within sight of the Holy City itself. . . .

Instead of going to the rescue of the Sepulchre, Richard, it was said, was again negotiating with the infidel. Everything seemed to point to the fact that he had lost interest in the crusade and that his only object now was to make as favourable terms as possible with Saladin and to return home before he lost his throne, leaving Henry of Champagne to rule over the kingdom of Jerusalem. But on July 6th Henry sent an arrogant message to Saladin. "The King of England," he said, "has given me all the towns along the coast, and I have them in my hands. Deliver up to me, then, my other towns that I may make peace with you and be as one of your children." Saladin was so annoyed at this that he made the messenger stand upright before him in order to cut off his head. He then changed his mind and a more conciliatory letter arrived from Richard a few days later. According to Bohardin, Richard wrote:

I desire to merit your affection and friendship. I have no wish to play the Pharoah in this land any more than I suppose you have. You must not make all your Musalmans perish nor I all our Franks. Here is Count Henry, my sister's son, whom I have put in possession of all these countries, and now I put him and his army at your disposal. If you invite him to accompany you on an expedition to your Eastern provinces he will obey.... Many monks and men of religion have begged churches of you, and you have granted their petitions generously. And now I ask you to give me a church. As to what displeased you in my former communications with Al-Malek Al-Adil I renounce them and entertain them no more. If you will give me a farm or a village, I will accept it and give you an equivalent.

A modest letter! It had been reported to Saladin that the Franks were now so weakened that they could not undertake any expeditions, but his council advised him to be equally conciliatory in tone and he replied:

Since you address me in so conciliatory a manner and since one good turn deserves another, the Sultan will regard your nephew as one of his sons; and you will soon learn how he has treated this prince. To you he grants the greatest of all churches, the Church of the Resurrection and he will divide the rest of the country with you. The seacoast towns which you already hold you shall keep; the fortresses that we have in the mountain regions shall remain ours; while what lies between the mountains and the sea coast shall be divided between us. Ascalon and its neighbourhood shall be ruined and belong to neither. If you wish to have some villages from us you shall have them. What I objected to most up till now was the matter of Ascalon.

"See the cunning of this cursed man," comments Bohardin of the English king, "who to gain his ends at one time would employ soft language, at another violence. Although he saw that he was obliged to depart he persisted in the same line of conduct. God alone was able to protect the Musulmans against his malice. Never have we had to meet the hostility of a subtler or bolder man than he." Richard, hitherto regarded as a plain, blunt soldier, was now acquiring some skill in diplomacy and showed that he could play at the same game as the sultan himself.

So Saladin replied that as to the villages the king asked for, he did not care about them himself, but the Musulmans would never consent to yield them and he offered Lydda in exchange for Ascalon. Richard replied: "It is impossible to let one stone of the fortifications of Ascalon be pulled down. The limits of the two countries are well fixed and admit of no discussion."

After this the negotiations, which had lasted from July 6th to 19th, came to an end and Saladin prepared to renew hostilities. Richard sent three hundred Hospitallers and Templars to demolish Darum and transfer its garrison to Ascalon, while he himself, with the rest of the army, went first to Jaffa, where he left the sick, and then on to Acre with the fleet, arriving there on July 26th. Saladin, watching his movements, inferred that he intended to sail forthwith for Europe.

"Thus," writes Richard of Holy Trinity, "the army returned to Acre, unspeakably saddened and amazed at its immeasurable misfortune in that God did not yet deem it worthy of a fuller favour."

VII

THE EPIC OF JAFFA

Before leaving the Holy Land, Richard had set himself one final task. Beyrout was still in Moslem hands and had to be liberated. But the day on which he arrived with the army at Acre, Saladin, advancing rapidly from Jerusalem, appeared with a greatly reinforced army before the walls of Jaffa. Next day he began the assault.

The garrison at Jaffa was only a small one and the majority of those who had remained behind in the town were invalids. Saladin

ranged his huge forces outside the walls in three divisions—under
his brother el Malik el Adil, under his son Ed-Daher, himself commanding the central division. He set up his mangonels before the
weakest point of the ramparts near the Eastern Gate. Then he sent
his sappers forward to undermine the wall. When part of the curtain wall fell, the defenders filled up the breach with blazing wood.
"The Sultan conducted the attack on the besieged with the greatest
conceivable energy; but what fine soldiers they were," writes Bohardin in admiration of the Christian garrison, "how brave and
courageous! In spite of all they suffered they did not barricade the
gate, but came out to fight incessantly. Our men maintained a desperate struggle with them, till night intervened and put an end to
the fighting."

The Saracens then collected a great quantity of stones from the
ravines and set up five mangonels and bombarded that part of the
wall that had been already undermined. The sultan himself and his
son Ed-Daher took an active part in the attack while el Adil, says
Bohardin, attacked the city on the opposite side. "Then a mighty
shout was raised, the drums sounded, the trumpets blared, the
mangonels hurled their stones, and the enemy saw nothing but
disaster threatening them on every side. . . ."

On the second day of the siege the wall fell with such a crash that
everyone thought the end of the world had come. There was only
one cry heard: "The curtain has fallen!" and a cloud of dust and
smoke rose that overcast the sky. "The sun lost its light, and none
of the besiegers dared enter the breach and breast the fire. But when
the cloud as it cleared away let us see the ramparts of halberds and
lances that now took the place of what had fallen, closing up the
breach so well that not even the eye could pierce it—then indeed it
was a terrible sight to see the courage, the fearless aspect, and the
cool precise movements of the enemy. . . . I myself saw two men
standing on the ruins and repelling all who attempted to clear the
breach. One of them a stone from a mangonel hurled back within
the enclosure, whereupon his comrade took his place, thus exposing
himself to the same fate which overtook him in the twinkling of an
eye." The Turks then poured into the town. They amused themselves by putting the sick to death, whom they found lying helpless
in the houses, by various forms of torture.

On July 30th the garrison retired into the citadel and agreed to
surrender if help did not arrive by 3 p.m. next day. Aubry de Reims,
their commander, had already taken refuge on a ship in the harbour,

and was forcibly carried back into the citadel again. He was then handed over as a hostage to Saladin, together with Theobald de Troies, Augustine of London, Osbert Waldinus and Henry de St John, who were all taken as prisoners to Damascus.

At the first sight of the approaching Saracen host on July 26th, urgent messages had been sent to Acre. These arrived on the evening of the 28th as the king sat in his tent making his final preparations for the attack on Beyrout. He had already sent forward seven galleys with troops and siege engines. When he received the news of the desperate plight of the Jaffa garrison, he exclaimed: "God yet lives and with his guidance I will do what I can." The French, however, declared that "they would not stir with him one foot". So Richard set off for Jaffa on July 29th with all the men he could collect and various knights, including the Earl of Leicester, Andrew de Chauvigny, Roger de Sacey and others, and some Pisans and Genoese. He and his knights went by sea, while the army kept a parallel course by land. On reaching Caesarea, the army, headed by the Templars and Hospitallers, heard that Saladin had set ambushes for them along the coast. They struggled on, nevertheless, to Arsûf, where they remained, not wishing to engage an army of whose numbers they knew nothing.

Richard had also been held up by contrary winds off Mount Carmel and his fifty ships dispersed. It was not till the evening of July 31st that the well-known galley, with its scarlet sails emblazoned with the three lions of England, was sighted from the citadel of Jaffa. The garrison had already surrendered and were on the point of laying down their arms and passing into captivity.

But even then the king did not land. "God have mercy!" he cried, as he waited impatiently for the rest of his fleet to arrive. "Why dost Thou keep me here, when I am going in Thy service?" God kept him waiting outside the harbour all night. Fortunately for the garrison, Saladin's troops were too exhausted by the day's fighting to make an assault on the citadel, though the sultan had learned that afternoon that Richard had given up his expedition against Beyrout and was hastening to the relief of Jaffa.

Richard had no idea how matters stood there until a priest swam out to his ship next day and told him that the garrison were still alive but already surrendering with their wives and children. For as soon as he sighted Richard's fleet on the morning of August 1st, Saladin had sent Bohardin with a body of troops to get the garrison out of the town. Bohardin says that he had first to clear the town of Musulman troops in order to prevent a general masacre of the Christians as they came out of the citadel. The Frank chroniclers, however, say that as each man and woman surrendered the Turks at once struck off their heads.

But as soon as the men of the garrison saw the king's ship, they mounted their horses and drove Bohardin's troops out of the town. Saladin at once sounded the call to arms and drove the garrison back into the citadel again, where, filled with despair that the king still did not come to their aid, they once more laid down their arms and sued for peace through that mountain of a man, the Patriarch of Jerusalem. Until the swimmer reached him, Richard could not possibly know whether the citadel was still holding out or not, for the whole town, including the shore, had the appearance of being entirely in Saracen hands.

"How? Are any of them still living? Where are they?" cried the king, as soon as the dripping priest was lifted on board his galley. "Before the tower, awaiting their death," the priest spluttered. "God sent us here to suffer death, if need be," the king reproved him sternly. "Shame on him who lags behind now!" he roared, as he gave the command to land. And even as the keel of his ship grated on the shingle, he leapt waist-deep into the sea like one of his remoter Viking ancestors and waded ashore. The Turks reeled back beneath the blows of his battle-axe. Other ships followed and disgorged their knights and men-at-arms and the shore was soon cleared. After setting his men to barricade the harbour on the land side with planks, barrels, pieces of old ships and anything they could find, Richard entered the town by a stairway that led to the house of the Templars. Once in the town, he set up his banners on the walls. The Turks were so busy looting that they did not see the golden lions floating above them till they were caught between Richard's men and the garrison. A tremendous slaughter now took place in the streets. When the first fugitives fled past his tent, Saladin was in the act of putting his name to the terms of surrender he had just granted to the patriarch of Jerusalem. Bohardin whispered in his ear, the sultan laid down his pen, called for his horse and rode off in haste, while Richard pursued the routed Moslem army right out of the town and finally pitched his tents on the same spot just vacated by Saladin.

Many of Saladin's Mamelukes had been captured and Richard invited el Adil's chamberlain Abu Bekr to visit him in his tent. "Your

Sultan is truly admirable," he was saying pleasantly to the assembled Mamelukes when the chamberlain arrived. "Islam has never had a sovereign greater or more powerful than he. But why did he run away at my first appearance? By God, I was not even armed or ready to fight. See, I am still wearing the shoes I wore on board ship. Why, then, did you retreat? Great and good God, I should have thought he could not have taken Jaffa in two months, and yet he made himself master of it in two days!"

Then, turning to Abu Bekr, he said: "Greet the Sultan from me, and tell him that I beseech him, in God's name, to grant me the peace I ask at his hands; this state of things must not be allowed to go on; my own country beyond the sea is being ruined. There is no advantage either to you or to me in suffering the present condition of things to continue."

Saladin replied the same night. It was still August 1st. "You began by asking for peace on certain terms, and at that time the question of Jaffa and Ascalon formed the main points at issue. Jaffa is now in ruins; you can have the country from Tyre to Caesarea." Abu Bekhr took this answer back to Richard and returned to Saladin again the same night accompanied by an envoy of the Franks, with the king's reply: "The King sends you this answer. Among the Franks it is customary for a man to whom a city has been granted to become an ally and servant of the giver. If, therefore, you give me these two cities, Jaffa and Ascalon, the troops I leave there will be always at your service, and, if you have any need of me, I will hasten to come to you and be at your service, and you know that I can serve you."

Saladin's reply was subtle. "Since you trust with such trust in me, I propose that we share the two cities. Jaffa and what is beyond it shall be yours, whilst Ascalon and what is beyond it shall be mine."

When the envoys returned, Saladin went to Yazour, three and a half miles south-west of Jaffa and demolished it. He also demolished Beit Dujan and left his miners there to make a thorough job of it under the protection of his rearguard, while he fell back to Ramleh. Here on August 2nd, Richard's envoy came to him again, thanking him for the cession of Jaffa and with a renewed request for Ascalon, adding that if peace was concluded within six days there would be nothing to keep him in Syria. Saladin replied that it was absolutely impossible for them to give up Ascalon and that in any case Richard would have to remain in Syria for the winter.

He knows full well that if he departs, all the country he has conquered will fall into our hands without fail. But that will most certainly happen, please God, even if he remains. If he can manage to spend the winter here, far from his people, and two months' journey from his native land, whilst he is still in the vigour of his youth and at an age that is usually devoted to pleasure, how much easier is it for me to remain here not only during the winter, but during the summer also? I am in the heart of my own country, surrounded by my household and by my children, and able to get all I want. Moreover, I am an old man now, I have no longer any desire for the pleasures of the world; I have had my fill of them, and I have renounced them for ever. The soldiers who serve me in the winter are succeeded by others in the summer. And, above all, I believe that I am furthering God's cause in acting as I do. I will not cease therefrom until God grants victory to whom He will.

The next few days were spent repairing the walls of Jaffa. They filled up the breaches with whatever materials were available. Count Henry of Champagne had arrived by sea, though the bulk of the army that had set out from Acre was still immobilized near Caesarea. At Jaffa, with about fifty-five knights, foot-soldiers and balistarii, the Genoese and Pisans, the garrison amounted to no more than two thousand all told. Of horses, good and bad, there remained but fifteen. Meanwhile the Mamelukes, smarting at having been routed by so small a force, had planned to seize Richard at night in his tent. "But God, taking care lest the unbelieving should surprise His own champion while asleep, inclined the mind of a certain Genoese to go forth into the neighbouring plains at dawn. As he was returning he heard with astonishment the neighing of horses and the tramp of men, and saw the gleam of helmets against the distant sky." He hastened back to the camp and roused the king. Richard leapt up, slipped on his hauberk over his nightshirt, sprang bare-legged onto his horse, and, with the Earl of Leicester, Henry of Champagne, Bartholomew de Mortimer and a few others, including Henry the Teuton his standard-bearer, and about two hundred foot soldiers, prepared to give the Mamelukes a warm reception.

On their arrival at the little camp with its dozen odd tents, the Saracens found Richard prepared for them. But there were only five horses, several of them not even war horses, between seventeen odd knights. "The Franks displayed such hardihood in the face of death," says Bohardin, "that our troops lost heart at their sturdy resistance, and were obliged to draw off, and content themselves with completely surrounding the camp, though at a little distance."

One party of Saracens tried to force an entry into Jaffa. The terrified townsfolk sent a message to Richard to say that they were all lost, for "a countless host of heathen were taking possession of the city". Richard silenced the messenger by threatening to cut off his head if he repeated his message to anyone. He then went on methodically constructing a low palisade of sharpened stakes behind which he arrayed his tiny army, setting his knights in pairs and kneeling on one knee, their shields held before them in their left hands like a fence, their lances grasped in their right hands, with the butts firmly fixed into the ground. Between each of these pairs he placed two crossbowmen to one bow, it being the duty of one man to stretch the bow and of the other to keep discharging it. Thus the Christians presented a solid wall and left no opening for attack, on much the same principle as the famous British squares at Waterloo.

Having arrayed his men with the utmost skill, Richard told them to have no fear of the foe and rode off with a detachment of knights and a few crossbowmen to see what was happening in Jaffa. He soon cleared the town of Saracens and ordered part of the garrison to come down from the tower and guard the gates. Then, riding down to the beach, he collected most of the sailors and rounded up stragglers, and with these reinforcements rejoined his little army in the field.

Saladin had disposed his army in seven divisions of a thousand horsemen each, and as the first of these advanced to attack, Richard said to his men: "Remember, there is no chance of flight. The enemy hold every position and to attempt it would be certain death. Only keep your ranks unbroken and if we stand firm against the first onset we may laugh at the next, and by God's help we shall defeat them. But even if it means martyrdom we ought to receive it thankfully. After all, it is the death we came here to find."

As he finished speaking the first wave of Saracen horse charged and drew up short before the palisade of stakes and the bristling wall of steel behind it. And even as the horses reared, the crossbowmen discharged their bolts at close range, creating havoc. The Saracens wheeled and cantered back to their lines.

Richard burst out laughing. "There! What did I tell you. Now they have done their utmost. We have only to stand firm against every fresh attempt, till by God's help the victory is ours."

Five or six times, from prime almost to nones, the Turks charged down upon the little band of crusaders, but each time their horses reared back. At one point, according to Ibn al-Athir, Richard rode out between the lines and challenged any Turk to single combat. As none stirred, he asked them for food, and when it was brought him, calmly dismounted to eat it in the no man's land between the two armies. By his example alone, he had the whole Moslem army cowed. Even the sceptical Gibbon exclaims: "Am I writing the history of Orlando or Amadis?" Indeed it was more like the *Chanson de Roland* than sober fact.

In vain Saladin rode up and down his lines urging his men on to another charge, but they would not, for they were thoroughly discontented with the conduct of the whole campaign. They had been tricked by the Jaffa garrison, and not only had they needlessly lost the town after capturing it, but many of them had been trapped there by Richard's sudden arrival. And now the flower of the Moslem world was being put to shame by a contemptible little army of unbelievers. Then Ed-Daher, Saladin's son, rode out to answer Richard's challenge, but was instantly recalled by his father. Apart from that, the Moslem ranks stood immobile watching Malek Ric eating his lunch.

At last, however, the emirs sullenly yielded to the sultan's exhortations and urged on their unwilling horsemen once more towards the Christian lines. They were met with a flight of arrows and steel crossbow bolts under cover of which Richard and his knights charged. The Christians charged so furiously that they broke right through the Turkish ranks and came out facing the rearguard. As he wheeled, Richard saw the Earl of Leicester unhorsed and fighting for his life on foot, and at once went to his rescue. The Turks now directed their attack against the lion standard of Ralph de Manleon, whom they took to be the king. They had already captured him when Richard came up, "laying about him as if he had done nothing that day". Indeed so energetically did he wield his sword that he broke the skin of his right hand. One emir, "vaunting much and reproaching his comrades with cowardice," galloped up to Richard, who received him with a blow from his sword which sliced off not only his head but his shoulder and right arm as well. The others fled from him "as from the face of a furious lion".

In admiration of his prowess, Malek el Adil sent the king a splendid Arab horse. But Richard would not mount, suspecting a trap. And when he told one of his sergeants to mount instead, the spirited animal refused to obey the bit and carried its rider off to the Saracen camp. El Adil, we are told, was very angry at this and sent the king another horse with the message that if by Divine grace he should issue from his present awful peril, he might bear this service in mind and recompense it afterwards as he thought fit.

The guard who had been left at Jaffa, seeing how matters stood, joined the battle and the Moslem defeat became a rout. As he rode from the field "the king's body was everywhere set thick with arrows, as a hedgehog with bristles". His horse presented the same appearance.

When Saladin's troops returned discomfited, he taunted their former arrogance, saying: "Where are those who are bringing me Malek Ric as my prisoner? Who was the first man to sieze him?" Whereupon a certain Turk who came from the extremities of the Moslem world, cried: "Know, O king, for a surety that this Malek Ric of whom you inquire is not like other men. In all times no such soldier has been seen or heard of: no warrior so stout, so valiant, and so skilled. In every engagement he is the first to attack and last in retreat. Truly we tried hard to capture him but all in vain; for no one can bear the brunt of his sword unharmed: his onset is terrible: it is death to encounter him; his deeds are more than human."

The defence of Jaffa was Richard Coeur de Lion's crowning effort in the Holy Land. But the city itself was little more than a festering cemetery with dismembered corpses rotting, black with flies, in the August heat. Before leaving the town, the Turks had slaughtered all the pigs and, as a final insult, mingled their bodies with those of the Christians. Garbage and ordure, which had not been cleared for days, added to the mortifying stench from the streets and helped to spread infection and disease. And now, after the last five days of intense strain, Richard succumbed to the prevailing epidemic.

Nevertheless, on August 7th he sent his defiance to Saladin, who had retired to Natrun. For el Adil, who was also lying sick at Gibeon, had sent his chamberlain to Richard proposing a renewal of talks. "How far am I to put myself in the sultan's hand before he will deign to receive me?" Richard replied impatiently. "Truly I was very desirous of returning home, but now I have decided to stay through the winter, and want no further conferences with you."

Ill as he was with typhus, it was hardy a time for such a reply. Those of his troops who were not in the same state as himself were already dead. As for the French, they refused to budge beyond Caesarea. Richard was soon sending to Saladin to beg for fruit and snow and writing to el Adil to intercede for him with his brother for Ascalon. But on this issue Saladin remained adamant.

Then, calling his nephew Count Henry and the Templars and Hospitallers about his bed, Richard told them that he was so ill that his only hope of recovery was to go to Acre to be properly nursed, and begged them to keep watch on Ascalon and Jaffa. At this, both his nephew and the knights declared brusquely that they would do neither without him and left the tent. "The king lay very sick on his couch," says Richard of Devizes, "the typhus continued and the leeches were whispering about the greater semi-tertian fever. They began to despair, and wild despair spread through the camp." Had it not been for Hubert Walter, Bishop of Salisbury, who told them that they must put a bold face on it before the enemy, whatever their real feelings, what was left of the army would have melted away altogether. Hubert Walter told them that they must stay at least until the truce was signed, then they could do as they liked.

On the most critical day of his illness, Richard heard that the Duke of Burgundy had fallen very sick at Acre. He was so pleased that he at once began to get better, and raising his hands cried out: "May God destroy him because he was unwilling to help me destroy the enemies of our faith, although he had long been fighting at my expense." Three days later the duke died.

At once the Bishop of Beauvais hurried back to France to tell Philip that Richard had sent two assassins into his country to kill him. When he heard this, Philip, "contrary to the custom of the land, set choice guards to keep his body safe; moreover he sent envoys with gifts to the emperor of Almain and anxiously inclined the imperial mind against the king of England." As a result, Henry VI of Germany issued an edict that should Richard land in any part of his dominions on the way back from the Holy Land, he was to be taken alive or dead.

Richard now issued a proclamation throughout the coastal towns of the kingdom of Jerusalem calling upon all fit men to come and serve under him at his expense. The response was poor. A crowd of out-of-pocket foot-soldiers came indeed, but very few knights, for the majority were enjoying themselves in Acre. "If our men were to live too sparingly just once in a week they would feel the effects of this for the next seven weeks," says Richard of Devizes sarcastically. "A mixed crowd of French and English used to banquet, and, no matter what the price of things, so long as the money lasted they banqueted daily with splendour, and, saving the respect due to the Frenchmen, I may add, with nausea. But for all that, they kept up the memorable English custom and with due devotion drained their goblets dry, even though the trumpets were sounding to horse and the drums beating. The country merchants who brought food into camp wondered, even after they had got used to it."

But as it became evident that the king must leave the pestilential purlieus of Jaffa or die, the conclusion forced itself upon him that the only thing left to do was to make what terms he could with Saladin and return home. By the end of August, too, many fresh troops had reached Saladin from Mosul and Egypt, and, seeing that the crusaders were in such a bad state, he was in favour of making a surprise attack upon either Jaffa or Ascalon. "Meanwhile," says Bohardin, "the king constantly sent messengers to the sultan for fruit and snow, for all the while he was ill he had a great longing for pears and peaches. The sultan always sent him some, hoping by means of these frequent messages to obtain the information of which he stood in need. In this way he managed to ascertain that there were three hundred knights in the city, according to the highest computation . . . he also learned that Count Henry was using every endeavour to persuade the French to remain with the king, but that they were one and all determined to cross the seas. He heard more-over that they were neglecting the walls of the city, centring all their attention on getting the fortifications of the citadel into good order. And the king of England had expressed a wish to see Abu Bekr, the chamberlain, with whom he had become very intimate."

Saladin therefore advanced from Latrun to Ramleh and dis-patched a body of troops to attack Jaffa. They sent him this mes-sage: "We made an expedition against Jaffa and they sent only about 300 knights against us, the greater part of whom were riding upon mules." Shortly afterwards a messenger from Richard, accom-panied by Abu Bekr, arrived at Saladin's camp. The chamberlain told Saladin that on one occasion when he was alone with Richard, the king had said to him: "Beg my brother el-Malik el-Adil to consider what means can be used to induce the Sultan to make peace and ask him to request that the city of Ascalon may be given to me. I will take my departure, leaving him here, and with a very small force he will get the remainder of his territory out of the hands of the Franks. My only object is to retain the position I hold among the Franks [in England and France]. If the Sultan will not forgo his pretensions to Ascalon, then let el-Malik el-Adil procure me an indemnity for the sum I have laid out in repairing its fortifications."

Hearing this, Saladin sent the chamberlain to his brother, with a confidential servant whom he had instructed to say: "If they will give up Ascalon, conclude the treaty of peace, for our troops are worn out by the length of the campaign, and have spent all their resources."

On August 28th negotiations were opened between Bedr el-Din Dolderim, commander of the Saracen advance guard, and "one Houat", as Bohardin calls him—evidently Hubert Walter, Richard's closest adviser. A message reached Saladin that the king of England in his "most hearty desire for peace", had agreed not only to surrender Ascalon but to give up all claim to compensation. For in these talks, says Richard of Devizes, Hubert and Count Henry quickly came to terms with Bedr el-Din, and the sick, bewildered king was only told what had been decided when it was too late for him to do anything about it.

Saladin then called a council and drew up the terms for a truce as follows: Ascalon was to be dismantled, nor was it to be refortified until three years had elapsed, after which it was to go to the most powerful party. The king was to have Jaffa and its dependent territory, except Ramleh, Lydda, Ibelin, Yebna and Mirabel; also Acre, Haifa, Arsûf and Caesarea, with their dependencies, except Nazareth and Safforia. The Christians were to have free access to Jerusalem and liberty to trade anywhere in the land; and there was to be an inviolate peace between Christians and Moslems for three years, as from the previous Easter.

The truce was signed on September 2nd. When its terms were read over to Richard, he denied that he had ever waived his claim for compensation for the fortification of Ascalon, but as they all declared that he had, he replied, "If I did say it, I will not go back on my word. Tell the Sultan I agree to these conditions; only appeal to his generosity, and acknowledge that if he grants me anything further it will be of his own bounty." He then sent the envoys on to Malek el-Adil requesting him to sue his brother for the cession of Ramleh. When the final draft of the treaty was sent back by Saladin, Ramleh and Lydda had been made over to the Franks, or, if they agreed, were to be shared equally between Franks and Moslems. But Richard said he was too ill to read it and had already confirmed the agreement by giving his hand on it. When the Moslems asked him for his oath, he said that kings in the West did not swear on such occasions. So Count Henry and Balian, the son of the Lord of Tiberias, swore for him and the Templars and Hospitallers and all the other leaders gave their assent to the terms. Then several of the Franks returned to Saladin's camp and were received with great honour.

Next day the king's ambassador was introduced to the sultan and, taking his hand, said that he accepted peace on the terms proposed. Saladin at once sent 300 masons and miners to demolish Ascalon. They were to be assisted in their operations by a detachment of Franks, but when the demolition party arrived the Frankish garrison would not let them in protesting that the king owed them arrears of pay. "Let him pay us," they shouted from the ramparts, "and we will leave the city. Or, if you like, pay us yourselves." Hearing this, Richard sent an order to the garrison that they were to help in the work of demolishing Ascalon "and when you have demolished it you have leave to depart."

Peace was proclaimed in the camp and in the market places of the cities, and there was great rejoicing on both sides. Much to Richard's annoyance, most of his remaining troops now went off on the pilgrimage to Jerusalem, and he wrote to Saladin asking him to put what obstacles he could in their way and only to allow those with passports through to the holy places. In any case, Richard had determined not to issue passports to the French, to pay them out for not coming to help him at Jaffa. But Saladin was delighted to see them and invited many of the pilgrims to dinner. We are told that he "entered into familiar conversation with them, taking care to let them know that he should thereby incur the reproaches of the king". He seems to have thoroughly enjoyed the situation, writing to Richard: "There are men here who have come a long way to visit the holy places, and our law forbids us to hinder them." To Hubert Walter, who had just been eulogizing Richard, he said: "I know the great valour and bravery of your king well enough, but, not to speak too severely, he often incurs unnecessary danger and is too prodigal of his life. Now I, for my part, however great a king I might be, would much rather be gifted with wealth (so long as it is compatible with wisdom and modesty) than with boldness and immodesty."

Richard himself was still too ill to risk the journey to Jerusalem. But doubtless the thought of being carried there in a litter, instead of entering the city as a conqueror, did not commend itself to him.

"His lofty spirit," says Richard of Devizes, "would not suffer him to accept from the grace of a heathen ruler a privilege which he had been unable to obtain as a gift of God."

Saladin now had forebodings about the truce, saying confidentially to Bohardin, "I am afraid of making peace, and I do not know what may happen to me. The enemy will increase their forces, and then they will come out of the lands we are leaving in their possession and recapture those we have taken from them. You will see that each one of them will make a fortress on some hilltop. I cannot draw back, but the Moslems will be destroyed by this agreement." And this foreboding was soon confirmed by a message from Richard himself. He was only asking for a three years' truce, he said, to enable him to return to his own lands to collect men and money, with which to liberate the entire kingdom of Jerusalem from Saladin's sway. To this the ever-chivalrous sultan replied that if he had to lose Jerusalem, he would rather lose it to Malek Ric than to any other prince he had ever known.

Shortly after making peace, early next year, Saladin died. Though he had united the Moslem world in resistance to Western aggression, he was himself a quiet and modest man. Slight of build, his usually melancholy face would on occasions light up with a charming smile. In manner he was gentle, hating all forms of vulgarity and ostentation.

Richard left Jaffa for Haifa on the night of September 9th accompanied by Count Henry of Champagne, to whom he had given the command of the army. He remained at Haifa for several weeks, recovering his strength, and then went on to Acre, where he rejoined his wife and sister and gave orders for his fleet to be loaded with arms and stores for the passage to England. His last act in the Holy Land was to ransom William des Préaux, who had so gallantly given himself up to the Saracens in his defence when a small party of them had been surprised the year before while out hawking. In exchange for William, Richard gave up ten of his noblest Turkish prisoners.

He then proclaimed by his herald that he was about to depart from the Holy Land and called upon all his creditors to come and be paid, "and even over-paid, lest there should be any complaints or disputes after he was gone about anything that they had lost through him."

After dispatching the two queens, Berengaria and Joanna, on

September 29th, the king put to sea ten days later. He left such fear behind him that when children of even the next generation cried, their mothers would silence them with: "Be quiet! England is coming!"

PART THREE

THE RETURN

Ricart li Peitevins
Murra en Limousins

I

GUEST OF THE HOHENSTAUFEN

THE same storms that scattered Richard's ships as he approached the Holy Land eighteen months before, scattered them again as he left it early in October 1192. "Whence it was sufficiently clear," says Ralph of Coggeshall, "that God was wroth at their return before completing their pilgrimage."

The king put in at Cyprus, to visit Guy de Lusignan; then went on, tempest-tossed, towards the coast of Barbary, until after a month's sailing he came within three days of Marseille. Unfortunately, on their way home, some of the Anglo-Norman knights had invaded the territory of Raymond V Count of Toulouse, whose father Queen Eleanor is said to have poisoned. Moreover a revolt of the Aquitainian nobles had only recently been suppressed by Richard's brother-in-law Sancho of Navarre, thus all the princes and nobles whose lands he planned to pass through were not too well disposed towards him. They were, in fact, in league with Philip of France and had determined to seize him as soon as he set foot on land.

Getting wind of this while still at sea, Richard changed his course, went back the way he had just come, and landed at Corfu on November 11th. Here he is said to have chartered a pirate vessel. "The king, knowing their bravery and boldness, went on board with these pirates," says Ralph of Coggeshall, "taking with him also Baldwin de Bethune, Master Philip his clerk and Anselm his chaplain. Certain brothers of the Temple also went with him." Some writers mention a fight with the pirates, who had attacked the king's galley off Corfu and that, falling under the spell of the king's bravery, they had invited him on board their ship and agreed to take him up the Adriatic to Venice. If this was the case, how does one account for the fact that the king's ship—the one, that is, in which he embarked from Palestine—was seen approaching Brindisi, where Berengaria and Joanna had already arrived? For, as Agnes Strickland quaintly remarks, "better fortune attended the vessel that bore the fair freight of the three royal ladies." Richard may merely have taken the pilot of the pirate ship on board to negotiate the dangerous Dalmatian coast.

Whatever the explanation, his movements after leaving the Holy Land are most peculiar. Possibly, by doubling back on his tracks from Marseille to Corfu, he intended to join his wife and sister at Brindisi. Why, then, did he not do so? Perhaps he was driven willy-nilly up the Adriatic, for the little boats of the period seem to have been completely at the mercy of the winds and waves, though one would have thought that if he had managed to get near enough to Brindisi for his boat to be recognized, he could have landed. Then why choose the domains of his arch-enemy Leopold of Austria as a way home? It would surely have been better to have travelled through his own domains of Aquitaine and risked the rebellious nobles of Toulouse. The fact is, that Richard was surrounded by enemies whichever way he turned—Greeks, Austrians, Germans, French being alike hostile. He seems to have had some muddle-headed idea about getting through in disguise to Saxony where, presumably, he had friends, since his sister was duchess. Richard's strange behaviour is usually attributed to "a schoolboyish love of adventure", though anyone might have foreseen the outcome of such a ridiculous escapade. It looks rather as if the king were at his wits end and did not know which way to turn.

Fortunately, in England, his mother was still there to look after his interests, and though John had gained much power and was now more or less regent, the barons were in the main loyal. But it was obviously in the interest of both John and Philip, who was already in league with the emperor against him, that Richard should never return. It was a miracle he ever did.

The "pirate" boat with the king and Baldwin de Bethune and the Templars on board was finally driven ashore on the little island of Lacroma half a mile south of Ragusa (Dubrovnik), then an independent republic. As soon as the rulers of Ragusa heard of the king's somewhat unimpressive arrival on their shores, they invited him to lodge in the city. In his terror of the storm, Richard had vowed that he would spend 100,000 ducats on building a church on the spot where he was brought safely to land. He must have been very frightened to have wanted to spend so much money. He now, therefore, offered to rebuild the monastery on the island of Lacroma, till it was pointed out to him that the money would be much better employed in building a church at Ragusa. But as he had promised God to build a church on the spot where he was delivered from the peril of the sea, he said that he would have to get the Pope's sanction for deviating from his vow. He agreed to dedicate a splendid church at Ragusa, however, if the Benedictine monks would rebuild their monastery on Lacroma. The king then borrowed a large sum of money and work was at once begun on the basilica, which stood for the next five hundred years without a peer in Illyria, until destroyed by the earthquake of 1667.

From Ragusa, Richard took ship about December 10th and continued his journey up the Adriatic. After passing Pola and Zara, storms drove him ashore with his companions somewhere between Aquileia and Venice. The emperor was already on the look-out for him. But Richard had assumed a disguise and sent a messenger with a magnificent ruby ring to the lord of the district, Count Maynard of Gortze, requesting permission to pass through the country. The Count not unnaturally asked the names of those for whom a safe conduct was requested and was told that they were pilgrims returning from Jerusalem. "One of them is called Baldwin de Bethune," said the messenger, "the other, who has sent the ring, is called Hugh the Merchant." The count looked at the ring for some time in silence. Then he said: "Nay he is not called Hugh the Merchant but King Richard. Though I have sworn to take prisoner all the pilgrims coming from those parts, and to receive no gift at their hands, yet by reason of the noble gift and the lord who sends it as a gift of honour to me whom he does not know, I will return him his gift and give him free leave to depart."

Meanwhile Richard and his companions were "trembling greatly" for the outcome of the interview, and when the messenger returned they "got their horses ready in the mid of the night, stealthily quitted the town, and in this fashion set out through the land." Richard had now disguised himself as a Templar. But their fears were well-founded, for as soon as he heard they were gone, Maynard (who was a nephew of Conrad of Montferrat) sent after them and arrested eight of their party. Richard and the rest escaped through Friuli to Freisach, 120 miles from Aquileia, in the Carinthian Alps. But they had been followed by spies, and these now warned Maynard's brother, Frederic of Pettau, to seize the king as soon as he reached Freisach.

Now Frederic had in his household a Norman knight, Roger de Argenton, whom he sent to search all the houses where pilgrims were known to lodge, to see if by any chance he could discover the king "through his speech or any other sign", promising him half the town if he succeeded. "So this Roger, routing and enquiring at every inn, at last found the king, who, after long attempts at hiding his personality, in the end yielded to the earnest prayers and tears of his dutiful questioner and confessed what rank he held. Upon this, Roger, anxious for his safety, gave him a goodly steed, begging him to take flight secretly and without delay." Roger then returned to his own lord and said that the report about the king was no more than idle rumour, the strangers being Baldwin de Bethune and his comrades. Upon this, Frederic, "mad with rage", gave orders that all six of the pilgrims should be arrested, but finding that Richard was not among them he set them free.

Riding for three days and three nights, without food or sleep, accompanied only by William de l'Etang and a boy who could speak German, on the third day, December 17th, Richard reached the suburbs of Vienna, having covered a distance of about 145 miles. Hunger now drove him to put up at an inconspicuous inn, where he remained in hiding for another three days. On the first day he sent the boy to Vienna to change some money and the silly boy began to show off, boasting about the wealth and importance of his master. This at once aroused the suspicion of the authorities who were already on the look-out for Richard. The boy then hurried back to the inn and begged the king to leave the neighbourhood at once. But Richard was too exhausted to move. Foolishly, he sent the boy to Vienna several times again, until finally, on December 20th, when swaggering about the market-place with the king's gloves in his belt, the boy was seized and beaten by the magistrates, who threatened to tear out his tongue unless he told them who his master, was. The little creature blurted out everything. A dispatch went at once to Duke Leopold, who happened to be in the city at the time. Taking the boy with him as a guide, Leopold immediately rode to the inn. But when they entered it, they found only a Templar there and the kitchen folk. For Richard, knowing nothing of their approach till the last moment, "took a mean jacket and threw it over his back to disguise himself and so entered the kitchen and sat down to turn capons at the fire. And the boy went up to him and said: 'Master, get up; too long hast thou tarried here already.' "[1] Another account says that as he sat by the kitchen fire he was recognized by the fatal ruby ring he had forgotten to remove from his finger.

Seeing himself surrounded by a crowd of "barbarians" and

[1] *Chronicle d'Ernoul.*

realizing that the game was up, the king threw off his disguise and made them understand that he would only surrender to the duke in person. Then, going outside, he surrendered honourably, giving up his sword to Leopold, who with no more ado sent him to Dürrenstein, a remote fortress on a rock above the Danube, with a strong guard to keep watch over him day and night. The guards, it is said, stood round the king in a circle with drawn swords, allowing no one to approach him.

The three people who received the news of Richard's imprisonment most joyfully were John, Philip Augustus and Henry VI of Germany, the Holy Roman Emperor. In fact Henry could hardly wait to get so valuable a prize into his hands, writing to his "beloved and especial friend" Philip on December 28th to tell him that:

> ...while the enemy of our empire and the disturber of your kingdom, Richard King of England, was crossing the sea for the purpose of returning to his dominions, it so happened that the winds brought him, the ship being wrecked on board of which he was, to the region of Istria.... A faithful subject of ours, the Count Maynard of Gortze, and the people of that district, hearing that he was in their territory, and calling to mind the treason and treachery and accumulated mischief he had been guilty of in the Land of Promise, pursued him with the intention of making him prisoner.... Shortly after, the king proceeded to a borough in the archbishopric of Saltzburg which is called Frisi, where Frederic de Botesowe took six of his knights, the king hastening on by night, with three attendants, in the direction of Austria. The roads, however, being watched, and guards being set, on every side, our dearly beloved cousin Leopold, Duke of Austria, captured the king so often mentioned in an humble house, in a village in the vicinity of Vienna. Inasmuch as he is now in our power, and has always done his utmost for your annoyance and disturbance, what we have above stated we have thought proper to notify to your nobleness, knowing that the same is well pleasing to your kindly affection for us and will afford most abundant joy to your own feelings. Given at Creutz, on the fifth day before the calends of January."

Indeed the emperor could not have sent Philip a more welcome Christmas present than this letter.

When those of Richard's knights who had left the Holy Land after him reached England, they expected to find the king already there, and, on being asked where he was, replied: "We know not, but his ship, on board of which he embarked, we saw nearing the shore of Brindisi in Apulia." Rumours of his capture by the emperor soon began to reach England and Walter of Coutances, the chief justiciar, wrote to "his venerable brother in Christ" Hugh Puiset enclosing a copy of the emperor's letter to Philip, passed on to him by his secret agents in Paris, with the comment: "Now there is need not of your tears but of your promptness, as we must not meet the attacks of fortune with lamentations, but, concealing our sorrow, must endeavour to make trial of our prowess." Walter therefore proposed a meeting at Oxford with his fellow justiciars to decide what was to be done in face of this trouble, "momentous beyond all conception".

On 6 January 1193 the emperor held his court at Ratisbon and Richard was brought before him by Leopold. Henry charged him with conspiring with the usurper Tancred to the detriment of his own claims to Sicily and Apulia, with the betrayal of the Holy Land and the murder of Conrad of Montferrat Prince of Tyre. After that, he was taken back to prison, either to Dürrenstein or Wurzburg. Philip then wrote to Leopold urging him to keep Richard in close confinement until they have both had a chance to consult the emperor. At the same time he sent his defiance to Richard and declared war against him. Next he wrote to the emperor offering him a vast sum to keep Richard in prison. Then he invaded Normandy, John having previously done him homage in Paris for all Richard's continental possessions, swearing at the same time to marry Alais. In return Philip promised to help him to the English throne. John went back to England with an army of mercenaries, occupied Windsor and Wallingford Castles, and demanded the kingdom from Walter of Coutances and the other justiciars, saying that the king was dead. The justiciars, however, replied by exacting general oaths of allegiance to Richard. Walter of Coutances laid siege to Windsor, Archbishop Geoffrey of York besieged Doncaster and Hugh Puiset attacked Tickhill. A truce was then signed with John to last until November 1193.

Meanwhile in Normandy, Philip demanded in John's name that Rouen should be surrendered to him, and his sister Alais delivered. But the Earl of Leicester, Justiciar of Normandy, suspecting treachery, replied that he had received no notification of the change in the succession. Nevertheless, he offered Philip and his company hospitality at the castle. Philip realized that he had fallen into a trap, and, setting fire to his siege engines in a rage, promised to return and visit the city with a rod of iron.

Leopold and the emperor met again at Wurzburg on 14 February 1193 and drew up a treaty for the terms of Richard's ransom. By this treaty Leopold agreed to give up Richard to the emperor on the payment by Richard of 100,000 marcs, of which 50,000 should be settled as dower on Constance the daughter of Richard's brother Geoffrey of Brittany so that she might be married at the feast of Michaelmas to one of Leopold's sons. The remaining 50,000 to be paid over at the beginning of next Lent (23 February 1194) and to be divided equally between Leopold and the emperor. The emperor further agreed to give Leopold 200 hostages as surety that should he die while Richard was in his hands, Richard would be given back to Leopold. If, on the other hand, Leopold should die, then the agreement should be performed by that one of his sons who married Richard's niece. Further, Richard should provide the emperor with fifty galleys and a hundred knights and go in person with another hundred knights to aid the emperor against Tancred in the conquest of Sicily. As surety for this Richard should give the emperor two hundred hostages of the highest condition. After Richard had complied with these terms, the emperor to keep the hostages until Richard shall have obtained the Pope's absolution of Leopold—the Pope having excommunicated Leopold for laying hands upon a brother crusader. Richard shall be detained until the emperor of Cyprus and his daughter are freed. Finally, if Richard shall not have fulfilled any of these conditions by 23 February 1194, then he shall be given back to Leopold with fifty hostages. If Richard should die, the hostages to be kept until Leopold has received his share of the ransom. And then, to improve his health, the emperor loaded him with so much iron that as Richard said afterwards: "Scarce could a horse or an ass have stood under the weight of it."

When the Queen Mother, Walter of Coutances and the justiciars met at Oxford, they decided that the first thing to do was to find the king. The abbots of Boxley and Pontrobert (Robertsbridge) were thereupon dispatched to Germany to look for him. "After having passed through the whole of Germany, and not finding the king," writes Roger de Hoveden, "they entered Bavaria, and met the king at a town the name of which is Oxefer [Ochsenfurt on the Maine, ten miles from Wurzburg] where he was brought before the emperor, to hold a conference with him on Palm Sunday [March 21st]. On hearing that the before-named abbots had come from England, the king showed himself courteous and affable to them; making inquiries about the state of his kingdom and the prosperity of the king of Scotland, in whose fidelity he placed a very strong reliance; on which they testified to what they had heard and seen."

What the abbots of Boxley and Robertsbridge had heard and seen could not have been very welcome news to the king. But, as usual, he did not take John's doings very seriously. "My brother John," he said, "is not the man to subjugate a country, if there is anyone capable of making the least resistance to him."

Meanwhile Berengaria had seen Richard's jewelled belt for sale in Rome and there were stories that he was kept in the darkest of dungeons and loaded with chains. Queen Eleanor began writing anguished letters to the Pope. "O Mother of Mercies," she cried, breaking off in her appeal to Celestine to address the Virgin, "look upon a wretched mother! If thy son, the Fount of Mercies, avenges the sins of the mother on the son, let Him launch his vengeance on her who has sinned: let Him punish me, the guilty, and not let His wrath diverge on my unoffending son. If I leave my son's dominions, invaded as they are on every side with enemies, they will on my departure lose all counsel and solace; if I remain I shall not behold my son whose face I long to see. There will be none to labour for his redemption, and what I fear the most he will be goaded by an exorbitant ransom: and unused as his generous youth is to such terrible calamities, he will not survive all he has to endure."

It is clear that Eleanor, like all mothers, looked upon Richard as a boy, and a boy who could do no wrong, to be protected and shielded by maternal love from the buffets of the wicked world. She is a tragic figure, guilt-ridden in her old age, for Richard, she confessed, was "the light of her eyes".

On March 23rd Leopold officially delivered his royal prisoner to the emperor and at the Easter court at Speyer Richard was charged with a long list of crimes—aiding and abetting the traitor Tancred, the rape of Cyprus, the imprisonment of Isaac Comnenus and the unlawful retention of his daughter, the murder of Conrad Prince of Tyre, the betrayal of the Holy Land to Saladin and, finally, the wanton insult offered to Leopold Duke of Austria. It all sounded very bad. Leopold and Henry Hohenstaufen had done their best to give Richard as black a record as possible to justify their own unlawful retention of him.

Richard's defence was noble and eloquent.

"I am born," he told the Court, "in a rank which recognizes no superior but God, to whom alone I am responsible for my actions: but they are so pure and honourable that I voluntarily and cheerfully render a full account of them to the whole world. The treaties I have concluded with the King of Sicily contain no infringement of the law of nations. I do not understand how I can be reproached for the conquest of Cyprus. I avenged my own injuries and those of the human race in punishing a tyrant and dethroning a usurper; and by bestowing my conquest on a prince worthy of the throne, I have shown that I was not prompted by avarice or ambition. So much so that the emperor of Constantinople, who alone has the right to complain, has been wholly silent on the subject. In reference to the Duke of Austria, he ought to have avenged the insult on the spot, or long since to have forgotten it. Moreover, my detention and captivity by his orders should have satisfied his revenge. I need not justify myself against the crime of having assassinated the Marquis of Montferrat; he himself exonerated me from that foul charge and, had I my freedom, who would dare accuse me of deliberate murder? My pretended correspondence with Saladin is equally unfounded; my battles and victories alone disprove the false assertion, and if I did not drive the Saracen prince from Jerusalem, blame not me, but blame the king of France, the Duke of Burgundy, the Duke of Austria himself, all of whom deserted the cause and left me almost single-handed to war against the infidel.

"It is said I was corrupted by presents from the Sultan, and that I joined the Crusade from love of money; but did I not give away all the wealth I seized on capturing the Baghdad caravan, and what have I reserved out of all my conquests? Nothing but the ring I wear on my finger. Do you then render justice to me. Have compassion on a monarch who has experienced such unworthy treatment and put more faith in my actions than in the calumnies of my deadly foes."

He looked so splendid, he spoke so well and with such obvious sincerity, that the assembled bishops and barons burst into spontaneous applause and even the emperor was shamed into giving his prisoner the kiss of peace and, outwardly at least, receiving him back into his favour. The tears streaming down his face, he made a treaty of friendship with Richard, promised to reconcile him to the king of France, and loaded him with honours and presents, while the whole Court dissolved into tears of joy at the spectacle. Henry even promised that if he failed in his attempts to make peace between Richard and the king of France, he would send him back to his own kingdom without claiming any ransom at all!

As long as the Easter festivities continued Richard was treated as an honoured guest. At the end of the period of rejoicing, however, he was sent to an even worse prison than before, to the gloomy fortress of Trifels in the mountains between Swabia and Lorraine, which had been built for the reception of traitors. From the dungeons of this castle very few ever emerged again. Here, once more Richard was placed under a guard of picked soldiers who kept watch on him day and night with drawn swords. We are told, however, that in spite of everything, he remained perfectly serene and self-possessed, joking and wrestling with his lubberly guards, and at night drinking them all under the table—feats which must have won their admiration.

Believing that he was soon to be freed, Richard wrote to England for robes of scarlet and green, a fur doublet and furs for his retinue.

II

THE RANSOM

WHILE at Speyer, Richard had written to the prior of Canterbury telling him that he had to pay the emperor 100,000 marks (£66,000 odd) for his freedom and asking the prior to lend him the money out of the church's treasure. He also wrote to his mother, addressing her as the queen of England, as though Berengaria did not exist, and thanking her for her devotion in the defence of his kingdom. At the same time he sent over Hubert Walter, who had lately arrived from Rome and whom he wished to reward with the vacant see of Canterbury and the justiciarship, telling his mother that she can accept what the chaplain William de Ste Mere Église and Master John Bridport tells her about that admirable man. For Hubert Walter had not only fought at his side in the Holy Land and acted as his envoy to Saladin, but had also put his case before the Pope. This letter was reinforced by another to Walter of Coutances and the other justiciars.

The indefatigable and faithful Longchamp now arrived in Germany and got the emperor's permission to visit Richard at Trifels, and as a result of his intercession he succeeded in getting him moved to much better quarters at Hagenau. From Hagenau Richard wrote to his mother and the justiciars on April 19th to tell them that he had been "honourably received" by the emperor.

> Here, too, our lord the emperor and our lady empress honoured us with many and various presents, and, what is of special importance, a mutual and indissoluble bond of friendship was formed between our lord the emperor and ourselves; whereby each of us is bound to aid the other against all living men in gaining his rights and in retaining possession of the same. For becoming reasons it is that we are prolonging our stay with the emperor until his business and our own shall be brought to an end.

This business was the matter of the ransom and the hostages. The letter continues:

> Wherefore we beg of you, and by the fealty by which you are bound to us, do adjure you, that you use all earnestness in raising the said sum of money, and that you, our justiciars, who are placed above the others in our kingdom, will set an example to others, that you may honourably and nobly afford of your own means for our assistance.... He whom, in the moment of our necessity we shall find to be prompt, in his necessity will find us a friend, and ready to reward. Under the golden bull of our lord the emperor, our chancellor brings to you the attestation above mentioned.

The gold and silver of the churches throughout the realm was to be collected and melted down and inventories and receipts made out. Both the money and the hostages were to be delivered to Eleanor, "our much-beloved mother".

Richard evidently thought that this letter would produce swift results, for he sent his military accoutrements back to England by Robert de Turnham and requested that ships be got ready under the command of his pilot Alan Trenchmer. But when Longchamp arrived in England with his commission and another letter from the emperor urging the English to show loyalty to their king, "his dearly beloved friend", no one would have anything to do with him.

Before he was allowed to land he was made to swear that he would not meddle with anything except the king's redemption, and then the people of London were so hostile that he had to be received at St Albans. But though Longchamp appeared before the justiciars with all humility as nothing but a bishop and the king's envoy, Walter of Coutances could not bring himself to give him even the customary kiss of peace.

It was decided, *pro redemptione regis*, that the clergy as well as the laiety should give up a quarter of one year's income. The Cistercians lost the whole of their crop of wool for that year. The churches were plundered by the king's commissioners, who took the very crosses from the altars and unscrewed the silver hinges from the coffins of the saints. What this meant to the people of that age is clear from the letter of Peter of Blois to the Bishop of Mainz. "Those children of perdition, the Germans," he wrote, "were levying a treasure that would not be drawn from the royal exchequer, but from the patrimony of Christ, the pitiful substance of the poor, the tears of widows, the pittance of monks and nuns, the dowries of maidens, the substance of scholars, the spoils of the Church". And to make it worse, the hated Longchamp had been sent over with a list of the hostages required, many of whom were still children, the prospective heirs to estates. The chancellor aroused so much opposition that Richard had to recall him and employ him on diplomatic business abroad.

Inscribing herself, "Eleanor, by the wrath of God, Queen of England", the Queen Mother now wrote to the Pope furiously upbraiding him for his slackness in coming to the aid of her son.

> The kings and princes of the earth, she wrote, have conspired against my son, the annointed of the Lord. One keeps him in chains while another ravages his lands; one holds him by the heels while another flays him. And while this goes on the sword of St Peter reposes in its scabbard. Three times you have promised to send legates and they have not been sent. In fact they have rather been leashed than sent (*potius ligati quam legati*). If my son were in prosperity, we should have seen them running at his call, for they all know the munificence of his recompense. Is this the meaning of your promises to me at Chateauroux?

It is such a display of impotence as this, she tells the holy father, that gives people such a poor opinion of him.

But actually the Pope was in a most embarrassing position. He had already excommunicated Leopold of Austria for laying violent hands on a brother crusader; he had threatened Philip with an interdict, and an interdict hung over England should it fail to collect the ransom. But it was more difficult to excommunicate the Holy Roman Emperor, although Henry's agents had pulled out the beards of the papal nuncios and cut their throats. In fact Celestine had already done all he could in the circumstances.

Meanwhile John reacted to the situation in his own way. As soon as he heard that money was being collected for the king's ransom, he had a duplicate of the chancellor's seal made and began collecting contributions to fill his own coffers. It was some time before the fraud was discovered. But when it was, Richard sent his messengers into England warning his officers not to trust his brother.

Ostensibly true to his word, the emperor now proposed a conference between Philip and himself to settle all differences between Philip and Richard through the mediation of the Archbishop of Reims, and fixed June 25th for the meeting to take place between Vaucouleurs and Toul. Richard at once scented danger, fearing that should the meeting ever take place, he would in all probability find himself in a French prison instead of a German one. He knew that Henry was most anxious to get Philip's support against his own discontented prelates and nobles, whom he had antagonized by complicity in the murder of the Bishop of Liège. A strong confederation had been in fact formed against him by the Archbishops of Cologne and Maintz and the Dukes of Louvain, Limberg and Saxony. Knowing his duplicity, Richard had a shrewd idea that Henry was about to buy Philip's support by surrendering him to his most implacable enemy. Richard's ignominious position at this time comes out clearly in the letters of May 28th and June 8th from Worms. From these it appears that Savaric, Bishop of Bath, had been blackmailing him for the archbishopric of Canterbury—Savaric having been one of the first to intercede for him with the emperor, to whom he was related. In the first letter to the prior and convent of Canterbury, Richard confirms that his former letters in favour of Savaric are genuine, although he had shortly before urged them to elect Hubert Walter. On June 8th he writes to his mother to say that she is to give no credence to any letters of his in favour of either Savaric or Longchamp, and once more urging her, the justiciars and the bishops of London, Winchester, Lincoln and Rochester to proceed in person to Canterbury and secure the election of Hubert Walter to the archbishopric, if, indeed he had not been elected already. Master Bridport, in whom she can have perfect faith, will give her further information. He is forced, he says, during his captivity to write in favour of persons he does not wish to be promoted.[1] But by the time he wrote on June 8th, Hubert Walter had already been elected.

In June, too, Richard received a visit from Samson, Abbot of St Edmundsbury, Carlyle's Abbot Samson of *Past and Present*. For when the news of the king's imprisonment first reached London and a great council of the barons was held, Samson "sprang forth before them all, saying that he was ready, secretly or otherwise, to seek his lord the king until he found him or had sure knowledge of him". Samson was also at the siege of Windsor in May, "at which, with certain other abbots of England, he carried arms having his own standard and leading a number of knights at great expense, though shining rather in counsel than in prowess. But we cloister monks judged that that conduct was hazardous.... When a truce was concluded on that occasion (i.e. with John), he went to Germany and visited the king, bringing him many gifts."[2] Doubtless the king was cheered by the visit of this good, loyal and enthusiastic man.

Meanwhile, at Worms, Richard was exerting himself to bring about a reconciliation between the emperor and his nobles, as the best means of preventing a Franco-German pact. His success in this was a major diplomatic defeat for Philip. For on June 25th, at Richard's urgent request, Henry opened a great court at Worms attended by a crowd of his vassals and four representatives of King Richard—Savaric and Longchamp (as Bishop of Ely) and two justiciars from England. Then Henry swore on his soul that he had had nothing to do with the murder of the Bishop of Liège and restored to all those who had rebelled against him in this cause their castles and lands.

At the same time the conditions for Richard's liberation were finally settled. The amount of the ransom was raised to 150,000 silver marks, that is, twice the annual revenue of England—the extra 50,000 being paid in lieu of military service against Tancred in the reconquest of Apulia and Sicily. Hostages were then demanded against the payment of the extra 50,000. But not till the

[1] C. M. Church, Some Account of Savaric, bishop of Bath and Glastonbury 1192–1205. *Archaeologia*, Vol LI, 1888.
[2] *The Chronicle of Jocelin of Brakelond*, translated and edited by H. E. Butler.

100,000 marks had been paid and the hostages handed over would the king be liberated. If, however, the king kept his promise to reconcile the emperor and his rebellious vassal Henry the Lion of Saxony, then the extra 50,000 would be remitted. Under the new agreement Leopold's "rake-off" was reduced to 20,000 marks, the lion's share of the whole gigantic political blackmail going to the emperor, who raised his price the longer Richard remained in his hands. Then the terms of the earlier treaty of Wurzburg, drawn up between the emperor and Leopold, were ratified.

As soon as he got news of the signing of this treaty, Philip wrote to John saying, "The devil is unchained"—meaning that Richard was now free. For by this time, Philip had worked himself up into a state of neurotic dread—an effect Richard seems to have had on many people. John, of course, had good reason to fear his brother, just as Conrad is reported to have said that he feared Richard more than any man on earth. Utterly ruthless, cold-blooded and implacable as he could be, Richard hardly differed in this respect from the other rulers of his age—whose behaviour often reminds us of particularly evil-minded children. Philip, however, was by this time quite convinced of the devilry of Richard. After all, did not the Angevins come from the Devil? They said so themselves. Who but the Devil could come to a brother crusader as he lay desperately ill and tell him that his son was dead? Who but the Devil would keep his sister shut up in the tower of Rouen all this time, purely as a bargaining piece, after having sworn to marry her? So Philip must have argued—and he went everywhere closely guarded, like a modern dictator, even carrying a bludgeon against imaginary assassins.

But Richard had still to come to terms with him. So he sent Longchamp to France, granting to the French king as much of the land he had taken from him as he wished to keep and promising to do him service for all the lands he himself had in France. And he promised to pay him 20,000 marks. As security for this payment, Richard delivered up the castles of Loches and Châtillon-sur-Indre, and to the Archbishop of Reims the castles of Driencourt and Arques. When these four castles are delivered up, reads the treaty, "the French king will receive the king of England into his grace and will ask the emperor to release him." And William du Hommet constable of Normandy, Robert de Harcourt and Stephen de Longchamp swore that they would surrender themselves at Paris if Richard failed to fulfil these conditions. At the same time Richard made his peace with various French and Aquitainian nobles, including Aimar Count of Angoulême and Geoffrey Count of Perche, who also owned lands in England.[3]

As for Count John, if it could be proved in the French king's court that he had issued letters to procure money for the king's release, he should be made to repay it. Nevertheless, he should continue to hold all his lands in England and Normandy which he held at the time of the king's setting forth on crusade. He should also be released from his oath not to enter England.... In all things Richard wished to appear conciliatory, though, of course, now he had not much choice in the matter. Had he not been still subject to blackmail, he might have ruled England through Hubert Walter as effectively from Worms and Speyer as he did later from Château Gaillard and Chinon. But on 10 July 1193 we find him once more writing urgently to the prior and convent of Canterbury to proceed no further in the election of Hubert to the archbishopric and to recall any messenger who may have been sent to Rome. But as the election had already taken place on May 29th, this may be one of the forged letters, except that we know Savaric to have been at this time bringing pressure upon the king to give him the abbey of Glastonbury, the most ancient and wealthy abbey in England. Berengaria and Joanna left Rome in March or April 1193 escorted by Cardinal Melior and reached Marseille, where they were met by Alfonso II of Aragon. Raymond the young Count of Toulouse, then brought them to the borders of Poitou. Three years later he married Joanna and the southern frontier of Aquitaine was at last secure.

As the king's ransom was brought to London, it was received by a committee consisting of Hubert Walter, the Treasurer Bishop fitz Nigel, two earls and the Lord Mayor. Walter of Coutances was in charge of the collection from the Norman and Angevin lands. Richard had many sources to draw upon, though the Aquitainian barons, some of whom he had only just released from prison, could not have paid up too willingly. But a rich haul was netted from the abbeys along the pilgrim route from St Martin of Tours to the shrines of the paladins near Bordeaux. In England a second and third levy was made, and as the money, the gold and silver plate,

[3] "The treaty," remarks Sir James Ramsay, "does not give a high idea of the diplomacy or the honesty, of either the king or of his ministers (*Angevin Empire*, p. 333).

the jewel-encrusted goblets and crosses were brought in, all was methodically accounted for, weighed, valued and sealed up in bags with German thoroughness by the emperor's messengers, who then handed them over to the king's messengers for delivery at the king's risk at the borders of the Reich. But after all, the tax of 5s in the £ from clergy and laity was as nothing compared with modern income-tax. To this was added, it is true, a fourth part of their moveables. But, in those days, the heavier the tax the greater the difficulty in collecting it.

By December 1193 a sufficient sum had apparently been dispatched to Germany, for the emperor wrote on the 20th of the month to say that he had fixed 17 January 1194 as the day of the king's liberation and the week following for his coronation as king of Provence—an area which Henry had always claimed as part of the Holy Roman Empire, but which he had never been able to subdue. The title was, therefore, an empty one. On December 22nd Richard wrote as follows to Hubert Walter:

Richard, by the grace of God, King of England, duke of Normandy and Aquitaine, and earl of Anjou, to the venerable father in Christ and his most dearly beloved friend, Hubert, by the same grace, archbishop of Canterbury, health and the fullness of his sincere affection. Inasmuch as we feel certain that you greatly long for our liberation, and that our liberation will very greatly delight you, we do therefore desire that you should be partakers of our joy. For this reason it is that we have thought proper to make known to your affection that his lordship the emperor has appointed a certain day for our liberation, namely, the Monday next ensuing after the twentieth day from the day of the Nativity of our Lord: and on the Lord's day then next ensuing we shall be crowned king of the kingdom of Provence, which he has given to us. Wherefore, we do send into England to you the letters patent of our lord the emperor relative thereto, and also to the rest of our friends and well-wishers; and do you in the meantime, to the best of your power, endeavour to console those whom you know to love us, and whom you know to long for our release. Witness myself at Spires...

The emperor's letter confirming this spoke of "our dearly beloved friend, your lord Richard, the illustrious king of the English" and went on to refer to his coronation as the king of Provence—"for it is our purpose and our will to exalt and most highly to honour your aforesaid lord, as being our especial friend". One can only say that Henry Hohenstaufen had a strange idea of friendship.

Richard then sent for his mother. Eleanor was now an old woman of seventy-two, "worn to a skeleton, a mere thing of skin and bones", as she described herself in a letter to the Pope. Walter of Coutances brought her over to Germany together with the hostages, the bags of ransom money and Richard's royal regalia for his crowning as king of Provence. The old queen reached Cologne on January 9th.

But when the joyful day appointed for Richard's liberation arrived, it transpired that the emperor had had second thoughts about liberating his especial friend, and adjourned the day of the diet until February 2nd. Richard was still presumably under guard at Speyer, where he remained for the next three weeks.

Then on February 2nd at Mainz, before a great assembly of ecclesiastics and nobles, Henry proposed another adjournment, on the grounds that while at Speyer he had received in private audience mesengers from King Philip and Count John who offered him 80,000 marks if he would keep Richard in custody till Michaelmas— or alternatively a thousand pounds of silver for every month that he kept Richard in Germany. But if he kept him in prison for another year, or delivered him over to them, then Philip and John would give him 150,000 between them—that is, the whole amount of the ransom money. And Henry was not ashamed to say that he had not yet made up his mind whether to accept their offer or not. He even gave Richard their letters to read, and we are told that "the king was much disturbed and confused, and despaired of his liberation". But, "with the eloquence of Nestor, the prudence of Ulysses", he appealed to the assembled nobles, as sureties for the emperor's fulfilment of the Worms treaty. Again he spoke so well, his presence was so splendid that, as before, the whole court broke into spontaneous applause and "reproved the emperor most severely for attempting in so shameless a manner to recede from his agreement, and prevailed upon him to release and dismiss the king of England from his custody". Richard produced a letter from the Old Man of the Mountains vindicating him from the murder of Conrad of Montferrat and charging the emperor to recognize the inviolability of a Christian warrior vowed to crusade.

Before releasing him, and as a final humiliation, Henry Hohenstaufen demanded that Richard should divest himself of his king-

dom of England and grant it to him as "the lord of all men". Queen
Eleanor advised her son to humour the emperor's megalomania. So,
kneeling down, Richard took off his cap and gave it to Henry. But
Henry had only wanted the formal gesture of homage and immediately regranted his kingdom to Richard to hold of him by the
yearly payment of £5,000. He then invested Richard with a double
cross of gold and released him from his fetters.

"It ought to be known," says Roger of Hoveden, "that the king
of England was in captivity with the emperor during a period of
one year, six weeks and three days"—that is not counting the three
months' close imprisonment at Dürrenstein on the Danube. It is
perhaps to the Dürrenstein period that the romantic legend of
Blondel belongs, of how the *trouvère* wandered over all Bohemia
singing outside every castle a song which he had composed in col-
laboration with the king, until at last he heard Richard's voice from
the dungeon of Dürrenstein, taking up the song and completing it.
It is a story which first makes its appearance in the completely
unreliable *Recits d'un menéstral de Reims* of the mid-thirteenth
century.[4] In the same way, as Ida Farnell remarks in *The Lives of
the Troubadours*, "whether Richard composed the only two songs
left us by him in French and Provençal can hardly be decided". All
we can say is that the writing of poetry was traditional in his family
and that he was probably as familiar with Provençal as with French,
and there is every reason why he should have beguiled the tedium
of prison with poetry and music—if, that is, there was time for it
with all his diplomatic activities. The prison song is a graceful and
accomplished piece which, addressed to his sister Marie de Champagne, complains of his friends, "Englois, Normant, Poitevin et
Gascon", for allowing him to remain so long in jail unransomed
while his feudal overlord Philip ravages his lands. One looks in vain
for any more personal note, so that the poem might have been
written by almost any poet of the time.

> No prisoner can tell his honest thought
>   Unless he speaks as one who suffers wrong;
>   But for his comfort he may make a song.
> My friends are many, but their gifts are naught.
> Shame will be theirs, if, for my ransom, here
>   I lie another year.

[4] The subject is discussed by Leo Wiese in his edition of Blondel de
Nesle, Dresden, 1904. The original Blondel came from Picardy.

They know this well, my barons and my men,
    Normandy, England, Gascony, Poitou,
      That I had never follower so low
Whom I would leave in prison to my gain.
I say it not for a reproach to them,
      But prisoner I am!

The ancient proverb now I know for sure:
    Death and a prison know nor kind nor tie,
      Since for mere lack of gold they let me lie.
Much for myself I grieve; for them still more.
After my death they will have grievous wrong
      If I am prisoner long.

What marvel that my heart is sad and sore
    When my own lord torments my helpless lands!
      Well do I know that, if he held his hands,
Remembering the common oath we swore,
I should not here imprisoned with my song,
      Remain a prisoner long.

They know this well who now are rich and strong
    Young gentlemen of Anjou and Touraine,
      That far from them, on hostile bonds I strain.
They loved me much, but have not loved me long.
Their plains will see no more fair lists arrayed
      While I lie here betrayed.

Companions whom I love, and still do love,
    Geoffroi du Perche and Ansel de Caieux,
      Tell them, my song, that they are friends untrue.
Never to them did I false-hearted prove;
But they do villainy if they war on me,
      While I lie here, unfree.

Countess sister! your sovereign fame
May he preserve whose help I claim,
    Victim for whom am I!
I say not this of Chartres' dame,
    Mother of Louis!

      Translated by Henry Adams, *Mont-Saint Michel and Chartres.*

"Chartres' dame", thus rebuked, was his other sister, Alix, mother of Count Louis of Chartres, who, together with Geoffrey of Perche and Philip, was ravaging Normandy. Later, after his release, both young Louis and Geoffrey of Perche, whom Richard had already reinstated in his English possessions, joined him to war against Philip.

As soon as he was free and had embraced his mother, Richard sent Saut de Bruil to Palestine to his nephew Count Henry of Champagne to say that, if God would grant him vengeance on his enemies and peace, he would come at the appointed time to succour them against the paynim. On the same day the emperor and the bishops, dukes and counts of the empire wrote to Philip and John commanding them to restore to Richard all the towns and castles they had taken from him during his captivity and saying that, unless they did so, "they were to know for certain that they would aid the king of England to the uttermost of their power, in recovering everything that he had lost". After this Richard confirmed by charter to a number of magnates of the empire yearly revenues for their homage and fealty and for their aid against the king of France. This homage appears to have been merely formal, for there is no evidence that the German nobility ever gave him any help in the French wars which occupied the rest of his life.

Meanwhile Philip, in league with John had denounced the truce and once more invaded Normandy, while John sent Adam de St Edmund over to England with letters to the constables of his castles ordering them to make preparations for a siege by the king's forces. The justiciars, however, with the vigorous Hubert Walter at their head, were prepared for him. They arrested Adam on his arrival in London and at a meeting of the council at Westminster John's letters were read and orders sent out to seize all his lands and to lay siege to his castles. On the same day (10 February 1194) the assembled bishops passed sentence of excommunication on John and all those of his followers who would not renounce their hostility to the king. Another truce was then declared in Normandy until June 5th, Lent being near at hand, and a closed season for fighting.

While all this was going on in England and Normandy, Richard and his mother were making a leisurely progress down the Rhine. They spent three days at Cologne, where they were feasted by the archbishop. When they attended Mass at the cathedral the archbishop sat in the choir and diplomatically chanted the introit "Now know that the Lord hath sent his angel and snatched me from the hand of Herod". Certainly Eleanor was no angel, but she may have seemed like one to Richard at that time. His journey down the Rhine became a triumphal progress and he won all hearts by his graciousness and liberality. None of this could have been very pleasing to either Henry Hohenstaufen or Philip Augustus, who now wrote to the emperor charging him with having let Richard off altogether too lightly. As a result, according to William of Newburgh, Henry sent pursuivants after Richard to arrest him, while Philip's fleet was sent to intercept him in the channel. But nothing came of this, for Richard had an imperial safe conduct and was accompanied by Adolph, Archbishop of Cologne as far as Antwerp. He reached Louvain on February 16th; on March 4th he sailed from Antwerp, where his own ships were waiting for him. The wind, however, was against them, and Alan Trenchmer was some days negotiating the islands at the mouth of the Scheldt. Richard spent each night aboard "a large and very fine ship which had come from Rye", till they reached Sweyne in Flanders. After spending a further five days at Sweyne waiting for a wind, the king finally put out to sea at five o'clock in the morning on March 11th or 12th, arriving at Sandwich the day after about the ninth hour.

As his fleet put into port, the sun stood at about a man's height above the horizon and shone with such a ruddy and welcoming glow that all men took it as a good omen.

III

THE DEVIL IS UNCHAINED

IMMEDIATELY after landing the king made a pilgrimage to the shrine of St Thomas of Canterbury to offer up thanks for his deliverance. The unobtrusive landing was very different from the triumphal embarkation from Dover three years before. But we are told that Richard was hailed with joy upon the strand and the news of his arrival flew faster than the north wind. The Warden of St Michael's Mount, one of John's castles, hearing of it, died of fright on the instant.

Three days later Richard entered London in triumph and was given a great popular welcome. The majority of the nobles were too busy besieging his brother's castles to attend the thanksgiving service in St Paul's. As for the German knights who accompanied him, they remarked sourly that if only the emperor had known that London was so wealthy he would never have let the English king go so easily.

Richard spent the day of March 16th in London, then set off on another pilgrimage, this time to the shrine of St Edmund at Bury. From there he hastened to the siege of Nottingham. Marlborough and Lancaster had already surrendered and Hugh de Puiset was besieging Tickhill.

Richard arrived at the siege of Nottingham in a black mood and his first act was to set up an enormous gallows beneath the walls. So near to the walls had he pitched his camp that the archers within the castle killed his men "at his very feet". Angered by this still more, Richard put on his armour and ordered his army to make an assault forthwith. A sharp engagement took place, and many fell on both sides. Richard himself, wielding a cross-bow, killed one knight with an arrow, then drove the defenders back into the castle, capturing the earthworks and burning the gates.

Operations were then interrupted by an altercation between the Archbishop of Canterbury and Richard's bastard brother Geoffrey Archbishop of York, who resented the fact that Hubert Walter had entered the camp, which was within the diocese of York, with his cross carried before him. Hubert answered tartly: "I carry my cross throughout the whole of England, and I ought to carry it, as being primate of the whole of England; whereas you do not carry your cross and, perhaps, you ought not to carry it; and therefore matters standing as they do I make appeal to my lord the Pope."

After hanging some of John's men-at-arms, who doubtless would have been hanged in any case if they had not fought against him, Richard had the stone-casters assembled and set up on March 27th. Then, as he sat at dinner, the constables of Nottingham, still not believing that the king was really there, for John had given out that he was dead, sent two envoys to see him.

"Am I the king? What think you?" said Richard.

"Yes," they replied.

"Then you may go back; go free as is right, and do the best you can."

When the constables heard this, they came with twelve others, and threw themselves at the king's feet. Next day the castle, which was so enormous and so well-stocked with men and provisions that it could have withstood a long siege, surrendered. All those who could not ransom themselves, the king imprisoned.

March 29th was spent in a visit to Clipstone and Sherwood Forest. Richard had never seen his father's great hunting-preserve before and, we are told, it pleased him greatly. He returned to Nottingham the same day and on the 30th held a great council at which the Queen Mother was present with Hubert Walter, the chief justiciar, sitting on his right hand, Geoffrey Archbishop of York on his left hand. Also present were Hugh de Puiset, Bishop of Durham, Hugh Bishop of Lincoln, William Longchamp Bishop of Ely—it is notable that Richard still stood by his unpopular chancellor—Hugh Bigod, the Bishops of Exeter, Worcester, and Hereford, Earl David brother of the King of Scots, and other magnates.

The council lasted four days, during which the principal offices of the country were again confiscated and put up to auction. This time the king could cheerfully repudiate old concessions on the charge of treason or political unreliability. Longchamp hastened to bid for Yorkshire, Lincolnshire and Northamptonshire, but he was beaten at the post by Geoffrey Plantagenet, Archbishop of York, who bid 3,000 marks (£2,000) for Yorkshire and got it. Only the Queen Mother's intercession saved John's English possession from going in the same way, for doubtless Eleanor pointed out that it would be better to have John on their side than, by depriving him of everything, to make his retreat from the French camp impossible. Nevertheless on the second day of the Council Richard asked for formal judgement against John and his accomplice Hugh de Nonant Bishop of Coventry for allying themselves with the King of France, and they were summoned to appear before the Court by May 10th. If John did not appear, it was decreed that he should be considered banished the kingdom, and the Bishop of Coventry should be sentenced by the bishops as to clerical matters and by the king's Court as to other matters.

On the third day of the Council the king adopted more orthodox methods of raising money. A carucage of 2s on the hide—that is, a land tax—was called for to meet the balance of the ransom and a scutage of £1 the knight's fee to finance an expedition to Normandy. Those who wished to be exempted from the fighting had to pay for the privilege, though a third of all those liable for military service were called up. Scutage yielded quite a large sum— £1,666 11s 3d., much more than the carucage, which only brought in £635 5s 10d.[1]

The fourth day of the council was devoted to hearing complaints brought by his own chapter against Geoffrey Plantagenet. These "were many in number, as to his extortions and unjust exactions".

[1] Sir James Ramsay, *A History of the Revenues of the Kings of England*, 6 Richard I, 1193–1194.

Geoffrey, however, "gave them no answers".[2] Then Longchamp, only too delighted to get his own back for his previous banishment and humiliation, brought serious charges against de Camville. But both accusations were allowed to stand over and de Camville made his peace with the king for 2,000 marks. Lastly, in response to popular demand, the king fixed April 17th for his re-crowning at Winchester, "to wipe out the stain of his homage to the emperor and his imprisonment".

The week-end of April 2nd was spent at Clipstone Palace on the edge of Sherwood Forest, when, according to the well-known ballad, the king dressed up as an abbot and had a jolly meeting with Robin Hood and his merry men under the greenwood tree. Unfortunately the king whom late Plantagenet ballads connect with "the good yeoman" Robin Hood is not Richard at all, but "Edwarde our comly kynge", and it is not till the late sixteenth century that Robin Hood (originally a woodland elf of great antiquity) became the Earl of Huntingdon in disguise. Nevertheless, as Richard is credited in these stories with relaxing the barbarous forest laws, which prescribed blinding and castration for anyone under the rank of knight or clerk caught poaching in the royal hunting-preserves, it may be as well to point out that what relaxation there was, was due to Queen Eleanor, who sought to win popularity for her son at the time of his coronation. On his return from the Holy Land Richard enforced the game laws in all their savagery.

From Clipstone Richard went to Southwell to meet William the Lion, King of Scots, who had come to attend his second crowning, and as they rode together to Melton Mowbray, the King of Scots asked that Northumberland, Cumberland, Westmorland and Lancaster should be restored to him, "the dignity and honours of which his predecessors had in England." Richard replied diplomatically that he would act according to the council of his barons. The rest of Holy Week was spent in progress by Geddington to Northampton, which was reached on April 9th, and where they spent Easter. After consulting his barons, Richard "told the king of Scotland that he ought on no account to have made his demand about Northumberland, especially in those days, when nearly all the nobles of the French kingdom had become his (Richard's) enemies; for if he were to grant this, it would look as if he did it more from fear than favour".

[2] As these "exactions" were an attempt to make his canons give up a fourth part of their income towards the king's ransom, Richard had good reason to waive the matter.

The royal party left Northampton on April 12th and travelled via Silverstone, Woodstock and Fremantle to Winchester Castle which they reached on April 15th. Next day the king moved to the Priory of St Swithun and slept there. On Sunday the 17th, after being ceremonially washed and purged, he was robed and crowned in his chamber at St Swithun's Priory by the Archbishop of Canterbury. Present at the ceremony were the Queen Mother and a great concourse of bishops and earls. Berengaria the queen was conspicuously absent. Geoffrey of York was also absent. Having been warned that he must not carry his cross in the province of Canterbury, rather than appear without it, he stayed away altogether.

Then the king, "arrayed in royal robes and having a crown of gold on his head, and carrying in his right hand the royal sceptre, on top of which was a representation of the cross, and in his left hand a wand of gold, on the top of which was the figure of a dove", went in solemn procession under a canopy of silk to the minster, the massive and terrifying building of the Conqueror's cousin Walkelin. Preceded by bishops, earls, abbots, monks and clerks and followed by the common people, the king, falling on his knees before the altar, "devoutly received the benediction from Hugh Archbishop of Canterbury". Eleanor, the Queen Mother, seated with her maids of honour, watched from the north transept. After Mass, Richard returned to the priory. He took off his more weighty vestments and his crown and, putting on lighter garments and a less ponderous crown, went to dine in the monks' refectory, the citizens of London, we are told, serving in the wine cellar, the citizens of Winchester serving in the kitchen. "On the same day, at a late hour after dinner, the king returned to his mansion in Winchester Castle."

Richard's second coronation was followed by another great auction of public offices and favours in the great hall of Winchester Castle. Longchamp, though restored to the chancellorship, had to buy it a second time. All prisoners taken in John's castles had to ransom themselves or stay in prison. Bishop Godfrey Lucy was deprived of the sheriffdom of Hampshire and the castles and estates which he had bought only five years before and Hugh de Puiset was induced to make a "voluntary" resignation of the earldom of Northumberland, returning to the status of a simple bishop. Puiset, however, made another offer for Northumberland, but being unable to agree with Hugh Bardolf, the sheriff, on the business details of the transaction, the king lost his temper and told Bardolf to take

both the bishop's money and the county away from him. Whatever appointments could be recalled, were put up to auction. At
the same time, the king could still assume a lofty moral tone
when pointing out to some unfortunate scapegoat the impropriety
of attempting to urge any private rights against the interests of the
Crown.

Then the Scottish king raised the question of Northumberland
again, offering 15,000 marks for it. This was too good an offer to
miss and Richard agreed to let him have the county after all, though
without the castles that controlled it. But as this was as good as not
having the county, William withdrew his offer. Next day he made
another attempt and Richard told him bluntly that he could not
trust him with the castles, but that he would reconsider the matter
on his return from Normandy. On April 22nd the King of Scots
returned to Scotland "sorrowful and in confusion". On the same
day Richard left Winchester for Portsmouth. On the way there, at
Bishop's Waltham, he was met by his half-brother Geoffrey of York,
who had upset Hubert Walter again by having his archiepiscopal
cross carried before him. Richard told Walter somewhat impatiently
that that was a matter for the Pope to decide and restored to
Geoffrey his estates in Anjou. While at Bishop's Waltham he also
issued two charters to the citizens of London confirming the privileges granted to them by John. He then hastened to make his
departure.

At Portsmouth a fleet of over a hundred ships had been assembled.
But storms delayed the departure of the royal party for more than
three weeks. After waiting at Portsmouth for a few days the king
went to Stanstead to hunt. In his absence the Welsh and the
Brabantines came to blows and many were killed on both sides. The
king had therefore to interrupt his hunting and come back unwill-
ingly to Portsmouth and pacify them. At the same time he also
made peace between Geoffrey and Longchamp—a more difficult
feat, for Longchamp had arrested Geoffrey on the latter's return
to England contrary to his oath during the king's absence on
crusade.

After three more inactive days at Portsmouth, a place which, we
are told, he found very tedious, Richard put out to sea, contrary to
all advice. Although the wind was still against him, he refused to
return and, after tossing about helplessly all day and night, was
forced to put in at the Isle of Wight. And so back to Portsmouth,
where he remained, chafing with impatience, for the next eight days.

On the ninth day the wind and the seas abated in their fury, and the whole fleet set sail for Normandy.

Landing at Barfleur, Richard and his mother made straight for Caen to look at the exchequer. The king, we are told, was welcomed everywhere by the common people, who had suffered from the ravages of Philip and John, as a deliverer and was led from place to place with dance and song.

> Dieu est venu avec sa puissance;
> Bientôt s'en ira le roi de France.

The crowds were so dense that no one, it is said, could have tossed an apple into the air without hitting someone else's head. There was still, however, no sign of Berengaria, but the unfortunate Alais, shut up in the Tower of Rouen, may have hoped that her hour of delivery was at hand.

From Caen the Court went to Lisieux stopping at the house of John of Alençon. And presently another John came humbly and on foot seeking forgiveness of his brother. But he dared not enter the archdeacon's gate without first sending to his mother and begging her to intercede for him. The loss of his castles and his revenues had reduced him to a sad state, and Philip had no use for him in that condition. So that it was as plain John Lackland that he came and threw himself weeping at his brother's feet in abject penitence. But from the point of view of the Plantagenets, treacherous as he was, John was after all the only hope for the succession. As king, after his brother's death, he could, presumably, be at least depended upon to fight for his inheritance against Philip Augustus.

"John mistakes me if he is afraid," said Richard hearing that the prodigal was waiting at the door, "bring him in. After all, he is my brother." And as the little elvish man lay weeping at his feet, Richard stretched out his long arm and raised him up saying, half contemptuously: "Don't be afraid of me, John. You are a child and have been led astray. Your counsellors shall pay for this. Come, get up, and have something to eat."

A fresh salmon had just been brought in and Richard gave it to his brother. He did not, however, give him back his castles or lands, but sent him with a troop of knights to relieve Evreux. Another account says that Philip had given Evreux to John, and that he now surrendered it to Richard.

On May 22nd Richard dispatched a force to relieve Verneuil,

which was being held against Philip by William de Mortemer. Eight days later he entered Verneuil in triumph, and the garrison, who had been desperately holding out against every sort of bribe and lie, as well as against assaults, embraced one another for joy. Once Verneuil had been retaken, the rest of Normandy was to all intents and purposes safe, for Verneuil opened the way to Rouen and the Lower Seine. Meanwhile Philip, who had good reasons for not meeting Richard, fell back upon Evreux and destroyed it, slaughtering the population, levelling the churches and carrying off the relics of its saints.

Next, hearing that the people of Anjou and Maine were besieging Montmirail, Richard hastened to its assistance, but arrived just in time to find the place a heap of smoking ruins. Then, "more swift than a stone from a Balearic sling", he turned south to recapture the castles of the Loire surrendered by John. At Tours he ejected the canons of St Martin from their houses and confiscated their rents. As soon as he heard about this, Philip confiscated the revenues of the churches and abbeys of the archbishopric of Rouen in his territory. But the citizens of Tours made haste to propitiate the Lion Heart with a gift of 2,000 marks.

From Tours Richard moved down to recapture the enormous fortress of Loches, which he had surrendered to Philip during his captivity. Sancho of Navarre, his brother-in-law, had already collected a band of Navarrese and Brabantine mercenaries to besiege the castle, and when he got there Richard found them encamped around its base in very low spirits, despairing of ever taking it. Those who know the castle and its site will readily understand their feelings, though the present castle is mostly of a later date. But Richard at once began a furious assault, battering at the impregnable-looking walls that soared above them day and night, and the garrison surrendered on June 13th. Within the castle were only five knights and twenty-four men-at-arms.

Meanwhile negotiations had been opened and a meeting between French and Anglo-Norman magnates had been arranged to take place at Pont-de-l'Arche to discus terms for a truce. But the French contingent failed to arrive. Instead Philip attacked Fontaine near Rouen and after a four day's siege took the castle and sacked it. The Earl of Leicester and John were at Rouen at the time, but their forces were too small to intervene. Nevertheless, as Philip left Fontaine on his way back to his own territory on June 15th, the Earl of Leicester sallied out with a few knights to harry his withdrawal and was taken prisoner. On the 17th a truce of one year was proposed at a meeting at La Vaudreuil between French and Anglo-Norman ambassadors, but the talks broke down because Richard would not agree to forgo his vengeance against the Poitevin barons who had done homage to Philip in his absence. "He would not," he said, "violate the laws and customs of Poitou and of his other lands where it was customary from of old that the magnates should fight out their own disputes among themselves." After that the war became more bitter on both sides and the country was reduced once again to misery and chaos as the mercenaries ran loose burning, killing and raping to their hearts' content, and the common people who had welcomed the king's return so gladly ceased to sing.

After carrying fire and sword through Poitou, Richard turned north to intercept the French king at Vendôme on July 6th. Philip sent him his defiance and a message to say that he might expect an attack that very day. Richard replied that he was quite ready for it and that if the French king did not come to him he might expect a visitor on the morrow. But instead of attacking, the French retired, and when Richard and William the Marshal fell upon them in the woods near Fréteval the retreat became a rout. Among the booty taken was Philip's treasure, his seal, his chapel and the charters of those who had transferred their allegiance from Richard to Philip and John. In this engagement many French were killed or taken prisoner. Richard dashed ahead with Mercadier, the captain of his mercenaries, to take the French king dead or alive. He rode, we are told, "breathing forth threats and slaughter". But Philip, instead of riding on through the marshes of the Isle de France, was calmly hearing Mass in a church some distance from the high road. Richard rode on until his horse dropped dead beneath him, and then returned to Vendôme.

After the rout of Fréteval, Richard went on a punitive expedition into Aquitaine. He now had all the traitors' names and could deal with them singly at his leisure. Foremost among them were his old enemies Geoffrey de Rancogne and the Viscount of Angoulême, whose castles lined the valley of the Charente and whose vast domains stretched between Poitiers and Bordeaux. These lords, fighting against each other and against his seneschals during his absence on crusade, stirred up by the *sirventes* of Bertran de Born and by Philip of France, had managed to turn the smiling land of Aquitaine into a wilderness of blood and misery. What life was left,

or just about to revive, had been beaten down again by the brutal
mercenaries of Sancho of Navarre, on his way to join Richard at
Loches. This, of course, made Richard's reconquest comparatively
easy and after three weeks of it, on July 22nd he wrote to Archbishop Walter from Angoulême:

> Know that by the grace of God, who in all things has con-
> sideration for the right, we have taken Taillebourg and Marsillac,
> and all the castles and the whole of the territory of Geoffrey de
> Rancon, as also the city of Angoulême, and Neufchatel, Mon-
> tignac, Le Chése, and all the other castles and the whole of the
> territories of the Viscount of Angoulême, with all things thereto
> appendent and appurtenant. The city of Angoulême and the
> borough we took in a single evening; while on the lands which
> we have captured in these parts, we have taken full three hundred
> knights and forty thousand armed men.

In a matter of ten weeks Richard had once more asserted his
authority over all his Norman, Angevin and Aquitainian domains,
lands stretching from the Channel to the Pyrenees. But, of course,
no engagement was decisive. As soon as he moved on, the revolt
flared up again. Then the king of France attacked; Richard counterattacked, took reprisals, and lands and castles changed hands again.
Richard's life had, in fact, once more assumed the same pattern of
futile, bickering warfare it had before he went on crusade. The
southern nobles enjoyed it, for they had nothing better to do. But
it is hardly surprising if the majority of people of Languedoc embraced the Catharist faith which told them that the world as it is
was the Devil's creation and that the Good God had no part in it.
For many must have said at this time with Marlowe's Mephisto-
philis: "Why this is hell, nor am I out of it!" And when they saw
the princes of the Church viciously engaged on one side or the other
in their struggle for worldly power and aggrandizement, it is natural
that they should have come to regard them as of the Devil's party
also.

So to add to the general confusion, the Albigensian heresy grew
and spread and took such a grip of men's minds in the southern
provinces of France that to the indiscriminate ravages of the mercenaries were added the Pope's inquisitors. What, indeed, should
the Church have aroused in the hearts of the people but loathing and
contempt, when its methods resembled nothing so much as those of

the Nazi and Soviet political police of our own time? For it could only re-establish its rule with the aid of the torturer's tools and the stake, though its full ferocity was not loosed upon the south of France until early in the next century.[3] Meanwhile the name of God was used as a rubber stamp by Richard and his kind to endorse any kind of atrocity.

By the end of July 1194 matters had come to such a pass that even Richard and Philip saw the necessity of calling a halt, and a year's truce was declared to last until 1 November 1195. Under the terms of this truce Philip was left in possession of almost all the territories that John had ceded to him and in August we find Richard living near Beauvais, at Bresle, in the heart of French territory!

Leopold of Austria now wrote to say that he would put to death all the hostages in his hands unless Richard immediately handed over his niece Eleanor of Brittany, who, under the terms of the treaty made between them, was to have married Leopold's son. So Richard sent both Eleanor and the princess of Cyprus to Austria in the charge of Baldwin de Bethune. But Leopold was still under sentence of excommunication for his imprisonment of a brother crusader and during the Christmas festivities at Gratz his horse fell on him and crushed his foot. When gangrene set in no one dared amputate the foot, so the duke himself, with his own hand, held an axe close to the bone of his leg while his chamberlain wielded a mallet. The foot was not finally severed until after three blows of the mallet. Next day the duke was obviously dying. Terrified lest he should die excommunicated and lie unburied and consequently go to hell for all eternity—for such was the penalty of the Church— the wretched man hastily released all Richard's hostages and excused him from the balance of his ransom. According to Hovedon, all Austria suffered from the duke's excommunication, the cities were consumed by mysterious fires, the Danube flooded the country, and when the crops came up they were seen to change into worms. "All these things were done by God," writes Hoveden, "that He might abase the haughty and manifest His power before mortals." But when Baldwin de Bethune heard of Leopold's death as he

[3] "The early thirteenth century gradually built up a machinery of repression which was unprecedented in world history for systematic completeness.... The Church anticipated in discipline the Soviet-Nazi theory of Totalitarianism." Coulton, *Medieval Panorama*, p. 470.

approached Austria, he at once returned to Richard with little Eleanor and the Cyprian princess.

Meanwhile Henry Hohenstaufen was making good his claim to Apulia and Sicily. At Salerno he put to death all the more powerful citizens and auctioned their wives and children among his troops. After that he entered Messina "with such honour and glory, that it had never been heard of any person entering that territory with greater honour and glory." On Christmas Day 1194 he had himself and his wife Constance crowned emperor and empress of Sicily in Palermo Cathedral. Afterwards he dug up the bodies of Tancred and his son Roger and despoiled them of their crowns and other royal ornaments. He then blinded and castrated William III of Sicily, Tancred's son, and left Constance de Hautville as regent. Three years later the rule of the detested Germans caused an insurrection. The Hohenstaufen returned and roasted the rebels alive in the tradition of Phalarius, tyrant of Agrigentum.

Richard spent Christmas 1194 at Rouen. His main concern was not peace on earth and goodwill towards men, but how to collect enough money to go on with the war against Philip. On his way northward from Aquitaine in the summer he had called together at Le Mans all his feudatories and told them of the "willing, unbroken and well-proved fidelity shown to him by the English in his time of adversity", for the English had, as usual, paid up and shouldered all the burdens laid upon them, whereas the French had contributed as little as possible. Accordingly, Richard now compelled all his bailiffs of Anjou and Maine to pay him a "fine" for their offices— which only meant that they extorted more money from those beneath them in the feudal hierarchy. Another source of revenue was the licensing of tournaments, which hitherto had been forbidden in England and severely condemned by the Church, though, once again, the French had always gaily disregarded this prohibition. Richard, of course, had been brought up in Poitou, where the tourney was regarded as a necessary part of the education of a gentleman, say the Church what it might. His disregard of other prohibitions was equally flagrant, for about this time "there came a hermit to King Richard and, preaching the words of salvation to him said: 'Be thou mindful of the fate of Sodom, and abstain from what is unlawful: for if thou does not a vengeance worthy of God shall overtake thee.'" But, we are told, the king "despised the person of his adviser" and "was not able so readily to withdraw his mind from what was unlawful".

Five years before, it will be recalled, he had made a public confession of his vices at Messina, in an agony of self-abasement. Now he was in no mood to repent—until, during Easter week 1195 he was suddenly struck down with a violent illness. At this "manifest sign of God's wrath", he once more gathered his clerics about him and "was not ashamed to confess the guiltiness of his life, and, after receiving absolution, took back his wife, whom for a long time he had not known, and putting aside all illicit intercourse, he remained constant to his wife, and they became one flesh, and the Lord gave him health both of body and of soul."[4] After that, for a time at least, Richard changed his life and his conversation for the better. He got up early and went to church and did many works of charity, feeding the poor daily, both at court and in the cities. And certainly there was need for this charity, for the constant wars and devastations had produced a famine in the land. Richard also had a great many chalices of gold and silver made to replace those that had been taken from the churches for his ransom, and this he could well afford to do since all his ransom money had been returned to him by the terrified Austrian nobles.

A change was also observed in his manners. At table he was mild and affable with his familiars, though to covert insinuation he replied with caustic wit. A joke of long standing seems to have been his non-existent children. One day a preacher, Fulk de Neuilly, said to him with great boldness:

"I warn thee, O King, on behalf of Almighty God, to marry as soon as possible thy three most shameless daughters lest worse befall thee. Oh, place thy fingers on thy lips for he will prove an accuser who has told thee the truth. No man is born without faults, blessed is he who is burdened with the fewest."

"Hypocrite!" cried the king, "to thy face thou liest, inasmuch as thou knowest I have no daughters whatever."

"Beyond doubt I do not lie," replied Fulk, "because, as I said, thou hast three most shameless daughters, of whom one is Pride, the second Avarice, and the third Lust."

The king called round him his barons and earls and said: "Listen, all of you, to the warnings of this hypocrite, who says that I have three shameless daughters, namely Pride, Avarice, and Lust, and recommends me to get them married. I therefore give my pride to the Knights Templars, my avarice to the monks of the Cistercian Order, and my lust to the prelates of the Church."

[4] Hoveden.

Of this, Hoveden, who relates it, cries: "O great disgrace to raise a laugh at the expense of the wretched!" For this same Fulk went about healing the sick and doing miracles ("even harlots he converted to the Lord") and when imprisoned, he is reputed to have broken his fetters and walked forth unharmed, and gone on his way "rejoicing that he had been deemed worthy to suffer reproach for the name of Christ."

And so, we are told, Richard became reconciled to Berengaria. Whether her failure to present him with an heir was due to some physical deficiency in her or psychological inhibition in him we have no means of knowing, though the inhibition is more likely to have been Richard's since he continued to allow his mother to usurp the place of his wife. Apart from Queen Eleanor and Berengaria, tradition does not associate his name with a single woman. While historians have for the most part contented themselves with doubtful shakings of the head and dark hints in the matter of his sexual habits, they credit his brother John with every form of twelfth-century vice. Indeed, John, with his completely sceptical and cynical temper, appears to have looked upon everything as a racket, though his family always seems to have been fond of him and prepared to forgive him anything. In May, for instance, Richard granted him an income of 8,000 livres Angevin and restored to him his counties of Mortain and Gloucester and the honour of Eye. At the same time he also restored all his lands to John's chief supporter Hugh Nonant Bishop of Coventry, whom he had earlier impeached for treason. Now, we are simply told that he had "put away his anger against him". There is, however, no doubt, that with his accessibility and flow of wit and engaging conversation, John appealed to the English and was popular with them—at least as a prince—as any prince or king who is ready with a joke is popular here. When he came to the throne, however, his political irresponsibility exasperated the barons. For Richard had undone much of the good work of his father's reign, when everyone was subject to the law, and had left the king at the mercy of his barons and his bishops. Richard, however, knew how to make himself feared; John Lackland was never a very impressive figure.

In spite of the truce between Richard and Philip, sporadic raids on each other's territory continued, until Philip, in a rash moment, perhaps forgetting the Lion Heart's love of single combat, proposed that the quarrel between them should be settled in a judicial combat between picked champions, five to a side. "So," as he expressed it, "the issue should make manifest to the people of both realms what was in the mind of the Eternal King as to the rights of two earthly sovereigns." Richard leapt at the idea—provided one champion on each side should be the sovereign himself. When he received this reply, Philip quickly dropped the scheme.

Then, at the end of June or early in July 1195, the emperor, after his successful campaign in Sicily and Apulia, sent a golden crown to Richard, exhorting him by the fealty he owed to his imperial suzerain and as he cared for his hostages' lives, to invade the French king's land, promising that he would send "help sufficient to avenge the injuries done by Philip to both of them". But in this Richard saw merely a plan to use him as a cat's paw in the conquest of France for Germany. He therefore sent Longchamp to the emperor to find out "in what manner, how much, and where and when" Henry would help him against Philip, and it soon became apparent that no help was forthcoming at all.

As soon as Philip got wind of these negotiations he tried to capture Longchamp on his return through France, failed, and declared the truce at an end. By the middle of July, the two kings, with their forces, were encamped on opposite sides of the river not far from Le Vaudreuil. But when peace talks were interrupted by the walls of the castle of Le Vaudreuil crashing to the ground—for Philip, doubting his ability to defend the castle, had ordered his sappers to undermine the walls—Richard at once called his men to arms and hunted the French from the conference. He crossed the Seine with such haste that the bridge broke down and he and his nobles and knights had a ducking. Indeed it must have been difficult to swim in chain mail. All the same, the French were routed and many prisoners were taken from Philip's household. Then, gathering together a large army from his dominions on both sides of the channel, Richard "entered the territories of the king of France in many places and made a great slaughter of those who resisted, reaped the standing corn though not yet ripe, rooted up the vines and fruit-bearing trees, and burned the towns".[5]

These vicious operations were temporarily halted by bad news from Spain, where in July 1195 the Moorish emperor of Morocco, marching into Castille, had utterly defeated King Alfonso at Alarcos and was besieging Toledo. This was bad news from every point of view, because Richard had been hoping for help from his

[5] Hoveden.

brother-in-law Alfonso against Philip. Now, far from that, it was suggested that, instead of fighting in France, Richard would be better employed helping Alfonso to defend Christendom against the infidel—that, in fact, another crusade in Spain was due—and the Pope urged the kings to unite. Early in August, therefore, another parley took place between Richard and Philip, when, at the urgent instigation of clergy and nobles, the unfortunate Alais, who, during Philip's invasion of Normandy had been hurriedly moved about from castle to castle, was at last let out of prison and restored to her brother. To cement the new friendship, a marriage was proposed between Philip's heir, Louis and Richard's niece Eleanor of Brittany, who should bring as her dowers Gisors, the Vexin, and various castles as well as 20,000 marks Angevin. If seriously meant, nothing could have been more foolish. On his side, Philip agreed to recognize Richard's claims in the county of Angoulême, his claim to the counties of Aumale and Eu, and to restore to him Arques (near Dieppe) and other castles he had seized while Richard was a prisoner in Germany. The ratification of these terms, however, was deferred until November, to give Richard time to consult the emperor. Nevertheless, when on August 20th Philip married Alais to William Count of Pontieu, the county of Eu and the town of Arques formed part of her dowry! The marriage was of course quite cold-bloodedly political, for William of Pontieu's lands formed a wedge between the domains of Richard and Baldwin of Flanders on the lower Somme.

Early in November Longchamp returned from Germany to say that the emperor disapproved of the proposed peace terms, but that he pardoned Richard the 17,000 marks still due on his ransom to enable him to recover the territory he had lost while in jail. The day was then fixed for the conclusion of a lasting peace with Philip. But when, on November 8th, Richard went to Verneuil, he was told that the king of France was otherwise engaged and could not meet him. Richard waited until the following afternoon; then, hearing nothing further from Philip, went to the king's quarters and demanded an interview. Here the Bishop of Beauvais met him and accused him in the king's name of bad faith, "inasmuch as thou didst plight thy word and swear to come to a conference with him this morning at the third hour, and didst not come, and therefore he defies thee."

Fighting thereupon broke out again. Richard besieged Arques, and Philip, only a few miles off, burned Dieppe and all the shipping in the harbour. Hearing this, Richard left the siege of Arques in an attempt to intercept the French on their way back to Paris, but only managed to catch up with the rearguard, who suffered in the usual way. After that Philip turned his attentions to Berry, recapturing Issoudun and setting fire to the castle. Richard, who was at Vaudreuil on the Norman frontier, on hearing this at once set off post haste and reached Issoudun in three days. His sudden appearance took everyone so much by surprise that he had no difficulty in retaking the castle. But as soon as Phillip saw Richard and his men arrayed for battle a few days later he asked for a parley and the two kings rode out to meet each other on December 5th at a place between Issoudun and Charost. The watching armies saw them dismount, bare their heads and exchange the kiss of peace. According to French sources, Richard renewed his homage to Philip as his feudal overlord. The armies were then disbanded and a truce was proclaimed until 7 January 1196, when the kings would meet again near Louviers to make a "final peace". After that Richard went to Poitiers for Christmas.

> And the two kings became niggardly and covetous, and would neither call together their hosts nor spend aught, save on falcons and hawks, and dogs, and greyhounds, and buying lands and possessions, and on doing evil to their barons. And full woe were the barons of the king of France and King Richard that they had brought about the peace, for that it made the two kings churlish and niggardly. And Sir Bertran of Born was more angry than any other of the barons, for that he could no more delight himself in wars of his own nor of others, nor in the warfare of the two kings . . .[6]

So in disgust Bertran renounced everything and went into a monastery, where he died soon after.

Some time during 1195 the "emperor" Isaac Comnenus also died, forgotten in the dungeons of the Syrian fortress of Margat, his silver chains by this time doubtless extremely rusty.

[6] Farnell, *Lives of the Troubadours.*

IV

CHÂTEAU GAILLARD-LES-ANDELYS

Now there was trouble in London, where the citizens had become exasperated by rising prices and the king's ever-increasing demands for money. "The rich men, sparing their own purses, wanted the poor to pay everything," says Roger of Hoveden. But a certain lawyer, William Fitz Osbert, popularly known as Longbeard, took up the people's grievances and demanded that the taxation should be born by rich and poor according to their property and means. He even bearded the nobles in every public assembly and accused them of robbery and extortion. Unable to get satisfaction in London, Longbeard crossed over to Normandy, with a pathetic faith in the even-handed justice of the king. Richard listened to him, as he was always ready to listen to any scheme for raising money. But he was not interested in the people's grievances, though he promised to see what could be done.

Returning to London in triumph, Longbeard, the first poor man's lawyer, continued to address great popular demonstrations in St Paul's churchyard till a general rising of the poor against the rich seemed imminent. When Hubert Walter summoned this "king of the poor" to appear before him, he came surrounded with such a threatening mob that the terrified justiciar "could only act with gentleness", says William of Newburgh, and "cautiously defer judgement for the purpose of averting danger." Then, discovering where and when Longbeard might be found alone, the justiciar sent some men-at-arms to arrest him. However, as one of the sergeants was "pressing him hard", Longbeard slew him with his own axe. After that he fled with a few adherents and his concubine to take sanctuary in St Mary-le-Bow. Troops then surrounded the church and set fire to it. Smoked out at last, Longbeard found the son of the man he had killed with an axe waiting for him. This youth suddenly whipped out a knife and "cut open his belly". The poor man's lawyer was then tied to a horse's tail and dragged to the Tower, where he was condemned to be drawn asunder by horses. The bits were hung up on a gibbet along with those of eight accomplices. So ended one of the first recorded working-class movements in English history.

Walter's action of countenancing the infringement of the right of sanctuary, however, brought about his downfall two years later, when Innocent III demanded that he should be relieved of his secular duties. And since he had shown himself rather too scrupulous in his methods of collecting money, the king was quite ready to comply with the Pope's demand.

Richard now demanded that the Bretons, who had become practically independent of the English crown under Constance, should give him the guardianship of little Count Arthur. He therefore invited Constance to a conference in Normandy, but on the way she was captured and imprisoned by her husband, Earl Ranulf of Chester, whom Henry II had obliged her to marry on the death of Geoffrey of Brittany. The Bretons at once took up arms to liberate her, calling upon the mythical King Arthur to come to their aid. But instead of Arthur and his Knights of the Round Table, Richard and his knights invaded Brittany and celebrated Easter 1196 by a grand massacre, "sparing neither grown man nor child, not even on the day of Our Lord's Passion". Compelled to make peace, the Bretons managed to convey Arthur to Paris, where he became a useful tool in the hands of Philip.

From Minihy-Trequier in Brittany, on 15 April 1196, Richard wrote to Hubert Walter thanking him for dealing with the disturber of the peace William Fitz Osbert and telling him at the same time to notify all those, the heads of whose baronies were in Normandy, to report to him at once for military service, and to summon all those who owed him military service in England to be in Normandy by June 2nd, prepared for a long spell of fighting; to summon all bishops and abbots who owed military service to send knights; and to send to Normandy as soon as possible all the money he had in hand, for, he added, "we think we are nearer to war than to peace with the King of France".

In England the year 1196 saw an outbreak of the plague as a result of the famine on the Continent and the spread of diseases imported by returned pilgrims from the East. This sickness, says Holinshed, "was a pestilential fever or sharp burning ague" of which so many died that "they could not have time to make for every one a several grave. This mortalitie continued for the space of five or six months."

Early in July fighting in France broke out again. Philip laid siege to Aumale and Richard took the castle of Nonancourt. Then, after confiscating all the property of the four abbots who were Philip's sureties for the Treaty of Louviers, Richard went to the relief of Aumale, only to be driven off. In the siege of Gaillon a bolt from the crossbow of Philip's famous captain of mercenaries Cadoc struck his knee, a wound which laid him out for a month. During this forced inactivity, Richard had to ransom the garrison of Aumale for 3,000 silver marks—a bitter pill.

When at last he was able to get up and mount his horse, he was in a very ill humour indeed. It was an ill-humour which was to last more or less for the rest of his life, for he saw himself condemned to an apparently endless and indecisive war with Philip. As Bertran de Born said, he was in the position of a falcon attacking an eagle, for he could never summon sufficient forces to his aid for a decisive victory and with each year that passed his resources dwindled and his vassals became more discontented. Forced more and more to rely on mercenaries, he no longer had the means to pay them. This meant that, unlike his father, he could not keep them under control. This hardly commended his cause, especially as each fresh rebellion of vassals was put down with ever-increasing severity. It would, he must have foreseen, only be a matter of time before Philip overran all the Angevin domains and united them beneath the crown of France.

Rouen itself, indeed all Normandy, had been threatened by the rash cession of the Vexin, and it was to block this route of advance from Paris that Richard began to build his famous castle on the island of Andely—against the consent and prohibition of the Archbishop of Rouen. Walter of Coutances had already protested to both Richard and Philip about the damage to his churches and the slaughter of his priests in the endless wretched border warfare, and he now set out in November to lay his case before the Pope, putting the whole of Normandy under an interdict before his departure. But military considerations took precedence over religious sentiment and Richard continued to build his castle on a great loop of the Seine to command the traffic up and down the river. That he had previously agreed not to fortify the rock of Andely was a mere detail. The castle was to be the wonder of the age. Château Gaillard, he called it, Saucy Castle, and it was indeed a marvel of engineering skill. Nothing like it had ever been seen before in Europe.

As the work progressed, under the personal direction of the king, the masons were continually harried by the French. To protect them Richard had impressed a host of wild Welsh who harried the French

border with a ferocity scarcely equalled by the Brabantine mercenaries themselves. At length two or three thousand of them were
slaughtered at the entrance to the Vale of Andely. Richard was so
enraged by this that he determined to take it out of his French
prisoners. Three of these he flung down from the top of the rock
of Andely and, blinding fifteen others, sent them as a present to
Philip under the guidance of a one-eyed man. A good joke, this last
touch! But Philip was equal to it and retaliated by having three
English prisoners thrown down from the cliffs on the other side of
the river. He then blinded fifteen others and sent them back to
Richard under the guidance of one of their wives—"lest," says his
poet-historiographer Armor, "he should be thought inferior to the
English king in power or spirit". Roger of Hoveden, however, says
that it was Philip who initiated these "acts of impiety" and provoked Richard, "unwilling as he was". However this may be,
Richard had never shown himself unwilling in the matter of reprisals. He was not the Lion Heart for nothing. After that red rain
was observed to fall at Les Andelys.

In December Richard sent Longchamp, with the Bishop of
Lisieux, the Bishop of Evreux and Philip Bishop of Durham, to
defend his operations at Les Andelys before the Pope. But on the
way, Longchamp died at Poitiers and was buried at the Abbey of
La Pin. "As long as he appeared to be in mortal agony, a wooden
crucifix in the cathedral church of the same city, which is called the
cross of S. Martial, was seen to weep so vehemently that streams of
water, as it were, poured down from its eyes." In Rome, Richard's
envoys pointed out that the king had repeatedly promised to make
full reparation to the Archbishop of Rouen for Andely, "according
to the estimate of honest men", but that he was forced, by reason of
the French king's continuing attacks on Normandy, to fortify the
island. The Pope, therefore, washed his hands of the whole matter,
advised Walter of Coutances to settle with the king of England as
best he could, and revoked the interdict on Normandy.

Meanwhile, earlier in the year, Richard had raided the coast of
Ponthieu, burnt Saint-Valerie to the ground and, having killed all
the monks, carried off the shrine and relics of the Saint. He then
burnt all the ships in the harbour and hanged the sailors. In May
John and Mercadier followed this up by ravaging the country round
Beauvais. They also captured the Bishop of Beauvais, who had come
out of the city to engage them with a company of knights and armed
citizens. In this engagement several French knights were taken

prisoner and all the common folk (not worth ransoming) butchered. After that John and Mercadier knocked down the bishop's castle, Milly. "And then, gloriously triumphing, they returned to Normandy."

After sending the prisoners taken at Beauvais to Rouen, Richard bought over to his side Baldwin of Flanders for 5,000 marks and scattered largesse among "nearly all the most powerful men of the kingdom of France, as his bounteous hand in its gifts surpassed all others". He also made magnificent presents to the people of Brittany and Champagne. To his prisoners Richard was not so generous. Philip Bishop of Beauvais, a relative of King Philip and one of Richard's most malignant enemies, was loaded with chains and thrown into a dungeon at Rouen, and when two priests of his household came to intercede for him, according to William of Newburgh, Richard replied: ·

"Judge ye between me and your lord. Let all the evils which he has actually inflicted upon me or plotted against me, be consigned to oblivion but one. Truly, on my return from the East, and detention by the Roman Emperor, out of respect for my royal person I was treated with gentleness and served with befitting honour. But one evening your lord came, and for what purpose he was come, and what manner of business he had with the emperor at night, I in the morning became aware of, for the emperor's hand was laid heavily upon me, and soon after I was loaded with so much iron that scarce could a horse or an ass have stood under the weight of it. Pronounce justly, therefore, what sort of imprisonment your lord should look for at my hand, who procured such for me at the hands of my gaoler?"

So the bishop complained at once to the Pope. But he got no sympathy from the Celestine, who replied: "That it has turned out unfortunately for you is not to be wondered at ... you sought and you found; you struck and were struck again; you have been levelled with the ground; into the pit which you have made you have deservedly fallen.... Still, we have addressed letters of entreaty to the king of England in your behalf." In the meantime the bishop was advised patiently to endure his chains.

In July Richard was campaigning in Berry with William the Marshal, his half-brother William Longsword and Aubrey de Vere, and took several castles, while Philip seized the opportunity to pounce upon the castle of Dangu in Anjou, which had surrendered to Richard a month before. And so it went on until in August

Philip was trapped in Flanders by Baldwin, who had flooded the country so that the French king could neither retreat nor advance, nor receive supplies. By this time, too, Richard had almost completely encircled the royal domain of France both by his own territories in the north and the west and by a system of alliances in the north-east (Flanders) and east (Champagne). There were still pockets of resistance, however, in the counties of Blois and Chartres and the little county of Ponthieu, to whose count Alais had been married. But to the east, beyond Champagne, lay Hainault and Richard's German allies. To the south, the Count of Toulouse Raymond VI was now his brother-in-law, having recently married Joanna of Sicily.

Philip was now forced to sue for mercy and entreated Baldwin of Flanders "not to sully the honour of the French Crown". Baldwin replied by offering to act as an intermediary between the two kings, and a conference took place between Gaillon and Les Andelys early in September 1197, when a truce of sixteen months was agreed to. Baldwin then went on a pilgrimage to St Thomas of Canterbury and Henry of Champagne, the king of Jerusalem, fell from the window of his palace at Acre and was killed. On his way to the Holy Land the Emperor Henry VI was suddenly taken ill in Sicily, after his atrocious suppression of the rebellion there. Terrified at the prospect of death, he sent Savaric of Bath to Richard offering to repay him all the ransom money for extracting which he had been excommunicated by the Pope. By the end of September, Henry Hohenstaufen was dead, and the Pope gave out that his body was not to be buried, unless with Richard's consent, until the ransom had been repaid in full.

It was probably in September 1197, at the conference between Gaillon and Andelys, on the Isle of Kings, that Philip first saw the swiftly rising walls of Château Gaillard. Gerald of Wales says that his courtiers could not refrain from expressing their admiration. This irritated Philip, who exclaimed that he cared not if the walls were built of iron, he still intended to bring all Normandy and Aquitaine under his rule. When this was reported to Richard, he roared: "By God's throat! If yon castle were built of butter, I would hold it against him and all his men!"

Château Gaillard, begun a year before, was completed by May 1198. It formed the key point of a system of fortifications spanning the river between Vernon and Gisors that completely blocked access to Rouen from Paris, designed rather belatedly to repair the mistake of surrendering this vital frontier area to the French under the Treaty of Issoudun. The fortress became the key to Normandy and was promptly lost by John after Richard's death. It was not retaken again by the English until 1419, in the wars of Henry V. Now nothing remains but gigantic crumbling ruins, which seem to have grown out of the very rock itself.

First of all, on a little island in the middle of the Seine, where the river forms a great loop near Gaillon, Richard built a strong octagonal work with towers, ditches and palisades. This was connected with the two banks of the river by a narrow bridge passing through the fortifications. At one end of the bridge, on the right bank of the river, he established a *tête de pont* which was soon filled with houses and came to be known as Petit Andelys, isolated by the water that surrounded it on all sides. Grand Andelys, standing at the end of an inlet of the river, opposite the rock of Andelys, was also fortified and surrounded with ditches. The principal fortress was built upon a promontory of chalk cliff which rises to a height of more than a hundred yards above the Seine.

At the base of the escarpment, and enfiladed by the castle, a stockade composed of three rows of piles was driven into the river bed, to block the approach by water. This stockade was further protected by palisaded works erected along the side of the right bank and by a work descending from a tower built half-way up the hill. The peninsula being made thus secure, it was impossible for an army to find encampment upon ground cut up by ravines and covered with enormous rocks. The only way the fortress could be attacked was from the tongue of land which connected it with the hills on the south. At this vulnerable point a ditch was dug out of the solid rock forty feet deep, with a perpendicular counterscarp.

At the apex of the triangle formed by the walls of the outer ward, which followed the natural slope of the rock, Richard placed a round tower with walls ten feet thick. This commanded the summit of the hills opposite. Towers of the same design were built at the other two angles of the curtain wall. Another great ditch, also dug out of the rock—there were no rock-drills or dynamite in those days!—separated the outer ward from the inner ward, whose eight-foot thick walls were flanked by two towers similar to those of the lower ward. The longer stretches of wall running north were sufficiently protected by the steep slope of the rock itself, except that on the river side. Here Richard placed a great tower and flank-works stepped along the cliff in which they were cut. At its northern end the wall terminated in two rectangular bastions behind one of which stood another round tower, which formed the base of the third ward or citadel. Thus, built up out of the rock itself, standing at the end of a narrow isthmus, the castle was practically impregnable and a work of tremendous engineering skill.

Beneath the first or outer courtyard of the castle vast cellars were excavated, supported on piers of solid rock and lit by lancets giving onto the castle moat, which divided the outer ward from the citadel and communicated with the outside by two tunnels, also bored through the rock. The entrance gate to the citadel was defended by the overhanging rock excavated to hold the portcullis. Near by another flanking tower planted against the cliff communicated with the body of the castle by stairways and galleries (again cut out of the rock face) which connected with a wall which acted as a barrier across the foot of the escarpment and the river banks. This again covered the approaches to the palisade of piles across the river. Beneath this another great ditch some fifteen to twenty feet wide was dug in the rock to form an elliptical rampart facing the river. This was overlooked by a series of seventeen semicircular bastions with two feet of curtain wall between every two. On the eastern side a bridge led from the rampart of the outer ward into the inner enclosure and directly opposite this bridge the bastions abutted onto a mighty keep-tower, or donjon, with walls twenty feet thick at the angles and nowhere less than twelve, commanding a tremendous view over the river valley and wooded Vexin, as in Turner's water-colour. Towards the bottom the walls of the donjon splayed outwards, both to give greater thickness to its base and to throw outward missiles dropped from the parapet. It was also furnished with machicolations commanding the foot of the wall—that is, a narrow gallery with holes in its floor through which the defenders could shoot or drop stones and burning pitch. "This," says Sir Charles Oman in his *Art of War in the Middle Ages*, "is a very early example of stone machicolation; the majority of builders at the time were only employing wooden galleries projecting so as to overlook the ground below the walls. It seems that stone machicolation was invented in the Holy Land, where large timber was so scarce that the architects of the crusaders were forced to replace it by solid masonry." In the same way, when Richard built Château Gaillard the rounded keeps were only just beginning to supersede the old square Norman keeps, though Henry II (or rather, his mason Arnold) had experimented at Orford with an eighteen-sided polygonal keep and gave Gisors an octagonal keep.

Château Gaillard, every detail of which Richard had planned with extreme care, was the last word in fortification. Its design was not concentric in the strict sense, for each of the three wards was not encircled by the others. But the concentric castle, of which the Tower of London as developed by Henry III is a perfect example, did not come into general use until the next century. T. E. Lawrence, gathering material for his thesis on crusader castles, wrote to his mother from Evreux in 1907 of Château Gaillard: "Its plan is marvellous, the execution wonderful, and the situation perfect. The whole construction bears the unmistakable stamp of genius. Richard I must have been a far greater man then we usually consider him." Richard had, in fact, learnt much about fortification in the Near East.

At Château Gaillard no sculpture or mouldings of any kind were to be seen. Everything was severely functional. "The masonry", says Viollet-le-Duc, "is good and composed of a rubble of silex bedded in excellent mortar and rivitted (or faced) with carefully executed face-work and small courses, here and there having alternate courses of red and white stone."[7] When the royal architect saw it complete, he cried, "Comme elle est belle ma fillette d'un an!" ("How fair is this year-old daughter of mine!") But she was a daughter whose parentage was at least as much Arabic and Byzantine as Angevin.

Meanwhile famine and pestilence spread. The misery was increased by Richard's demands for more and more money. Tallage—a term used to cover almost any form of arbitrary taxation—was laid upon towns throughout England and the dependents of each feudal lord, while scutage, nominally at the rate of £1 per knight, was increased on one pretext or another. Nevertheless, Richard was disgusted at the smallness of his revenue from England, and, suspecting malversation, sent over Robert Abbot of Caen, an economic

---

[7] The description of Château Gaillard is taken fromViollet-le-Duc's essay *Military Architecture in the Middle Ages* and Kate Norgate's *Richard the Lion Heart*. Norman fortifications, saysViollet-le-Duc, had nothing in common with the forms adopted by Richard at Château Gaillard—"we may therefore safely conclude that Richard was alone the author of them".

expert from the Norman Exchequer, to see what was going on. Robert reported that he could double the king's income for him. But before he could go into all the sheriff's accounts Robert died. Richard was also bitterly dissatisfied at the small number of men willing to serve in the army.

At a Grand Council at Oxford in December 1197 Hubert Walter gave out that all barons of the realm, both spiritual and temporal, must provide the king with a force of 300 men-at-arms for one year's service abroad and pay the cost of their maintenance till they were killed or crippled—a demand which had no precedent. The justiciar urged compliance for the sake of peace, and so did Richard Fitz Nigel, Treasurer and Bishop of London. But at this point Hugh of Avalon, Bishop of Lincoln, whose favourite companion was a swan, and who had worked as a labourer in the rebuilding of Lincoln Cathedral, refused to comply. He was aware, he said, that the church of Lincoln owed certain military service within the limits of England but not beyond the seas, and concluded: "What I am now asked to do, is contrary to the ancient immunities of the see of Lincoln, and rather than thus fetter and enslave my church I am resolved to return to my own country, and to end my days in the desert solitude from whence I came here."

But the scruples of the unworldly Hugh infuriated the justiciar, who now turned with trembling lips to ask the Bishop of Salisbury his opinion.

"My reply," said Hubert le Poer, "is in entire agreement with that of my lord the Bishop of Lincoln. I could not speak or act otherwise without grave prejudice to the interests of the Church."

At this Hubert Walter abused the Bishop of Salisbury and dismissed the Council. It was, says Stubbs, "the first clear case of the refusal of a money grant demanded directly by the Crown and a most valuable precedent for future times". Several years earlier St Hugh had also refused, on behalf of his diocese, to continue offering the king the customary annual tribute of a furred cloak.

Messengers at once went back to Normandy denouncing St Hugh as the cause of the failure of the Oxford Council. Richard, keeping Christmas at Rouen, in no very Christian spirit summoned the two refractory bishops to his presence and ordered their property to be seized. In the case of the Bishop of Salisbury this was carried into effect, and Hubert le Poer only recovered his lands after the payment of a heavy fine. But no one dared touch anything belonging to the

Bishop of Lincoln, and for the next eight months Hugh of Avalon serenely continued on his way.

"Since our English are such cowards," said Richard at last, "let us send Mercadier who will know how to deal with this Burgundian."

It sounds like Henry II and Becket over again. But the king was strongly advised against resorting to brute force for fear that he might lose the valuable captain of his mercenaries as a result of the bishop's curse. So, instead, he charged Stephen de Turnham, as he valued his life, to carry·out the commission at once. By this time, however, St Hugh, out of compassion for the king's commissioners, who were growing desperate, had set out for Normandy himself.

On his arrival at Rouen, he was met by William the Marshal and the Earl of Albermarle, who both advised him not to brave the king's anger, but to allow them to mediate for him.

"I thank you from my heart for your devotion," replied Hugh, "but I will tell you why I cannot accept it. You are necessary to the king in his present trials and anxieties, for which I feel a true sympathy. To you, more than to any one else, he is bound by ties of gratitude, and for that very reason, I do not wish you to plead my cause with him. In his present state of mind, he will either refuse to listen to you or be angry with you also, so that you will feel less zeal in his service; or he will listen to you, as a very great favour, and so consider himself absolved from any further obligation of gratitude. Therefore, you must content yourselves with telling him, from me, that I have come to Normandy expressly to see him, and hope that he will accord me an interview."[8]

This is hardly a tone one associates with the violence of the twelfth century. The two nobles, we are told, admired this reply and, pressing the bishop no further, returned to the king and told him what the holy man had said. Even Richard seems to have been impressed and replied that he would receive the bishop in three days' time on the Rock of Andelys.

When Hugh arrived at Château Gaillard on 28 August 1198, he found the king in the chapel hearing Mass. As he entered, he heard the choir singing, *Ave, inclyte praesul Christi, flos pulcherime!* (Hail, illustrious pontiff of Christ, flower of spiritual beauty!) and St Hugh's chaplains, doubtless trembling with trepidation for the outcome of the interview, took it as a good omen.

[8] *The Life of Saint Hugh of Lincoln,* translated and edited from the French Carthusian life by Hubert Thurston, SJ.

Richard was seated on his throne near the door, facing the altar, surounded by a group of courtiers, among whom were two arch-bishops and two bishops. The archbishops were seated on the steps of the throne. The king silently awaited the approach of the man who had defied him for nine months, and as St Hugh made his obeisance he glared at him fiercely and then turned his head away.

"My lord," said the bishop, "give me the kiss of peace."

But Richard kept his face coldly averted. So Hugh mounted the steps of the throne and took hold of the king's mantle in both hands and shook him like a sulky boy. "I have come a long journey to find you," he said, "and I have a right to a kiss."

"No," said the king, "you have not deserved it."

"Yes, indeed I have," answered the bishop. "Come now, I insist on your giving me the kiss you owe me." And he shook the king backwards and forwards on his throne, till Richard laughed in spite of himself and gave the salutation demanded of him.

Those who witnessed this scene could hardly believe their eyes, and the courtier bishops respectfully made room for St Hugh to sit down among them. But he shook his head and went to the altar, where he knelt with his eyes fixed on the ground. During the *Agnus Dei* the king also went to the altar steps and knelt to receive the *pax brede*, the little tablet ornamented with a representation of the crucifixion used to transmit to the congregation the kiss of peace, and after kissing it, instead of passing it on to St Hugh, kissed him on the cheek.

After Mass, St Hugh gave the king his version of the Grand Council at Oxford. Richard made no reply, except to blame his justiciar for misrepresenting St Hugh's motives.

"Saving the honour of God, sire," said Hugh, "and the welfare of mine own soul and thine, I have never once even in the smallest particular gone counter to thy wishes."

Then Richard offered St Hugh many presents and begged him to take up his abode at Port-Joie, the royal residence on an island in the Seine connected with the mainland by a revolving bridge which he had just completed. But, taking the king's hand, St Hugh led him behind the altar and began to address him as his spiritual father.

"My lord king," he said, "you belong to my diocese[9] and I feel that I am responsible for your soul to God who has purchased it

---

[9] That is, Richard was born at Oxford, then in the diocese of Lincoln.

with His blood. I want you to make known to me, then, what is really the state of your conscience, that, as your pastor, I may be able, with God's grace, to help you by my counsels. You may remember that a year has already passed since I spoke to you on the subject."

Richard replied that his conscience was fairly clear, except that he felt a bitter hatred of the enemies who were trying to encompass his ruin. Whereupon the bishop urged the king to a more thorough self-examination.

"Your enemies," he said, "will easily be overcome if you yourself are at peace with the King of Kings. You have only one foe to fear, and that is sin—the offences you commit against God, and the injuries you do to your neighbour."

Then Hugh went on to rebuke him for infidelity to his wife and for his persecution of the Church in the matter of the canonical elections and nominations. "I am told," he said, "that you have no scruple in committing the cure of souls to men whose only merit is that they offer you rich gifts, or are your friends. This is a grave crime, and as long as you continue to do such things, assuredly God will never be your friend."

To all this Richard listened patiently, like a bully whose bluff has been called, even excusing himself on some heads and confessing his failing on others. He then asked the bishop to pray for him and Hugh gave him his blessing. Returning to his courtiers, Richard said:

"Truly, if all the prelates of the Church were like him, there is not a prince in Christendom who would dare raise his head in the presence of a bishop!"

His nobles, however, advised him to take advantage of the bishop's blessing and make him the bearer of a note to the barons of England asking them to vote another subsidy. But St Hugh refused. A bishop, he said, was not a courier. In any case, he would not raise a finger to co-operate in such extortion. "Do you know," he said, "that when a king puts out one hand for alms, he holds a drawn sword behind his back with the other?"

When this was told to Richard all he said was that the bishop was welcome to go in God's name. For this delivery, we are told, St Hugh said a hearty Te Deum.

Soon after, on September 28th, Richard won an important victory over the French king at Gisors, which was widely attributed to the prayers of St Hugh. During all this time the usual border raids had been going on, with Philip burning Evreux and Mercadier attacking Abbeville at fair time.

On this occasion Richard, with a small force of about sixty, attacked a French force of five or six hundred, as they were going from Mantes to relieve Courcelles, which he had surprised and captured on the previous day. The victory was not quite so miraculous as it seems at first sight, because the king and his knights had been reinforced by about two hundred other knights as well as by Mercadier and the mercenaries. Nevertheless, the French were many more in number, but, says Hoveden, "on seeing the king of England and his men, after having burned about eighteen towns, [they] retreated with hasty steps". So hastily did they in fact retreat that the bridge over the Epte broke down beneath the weight of the cavalry and men-at-arms as they fled towards Gisors. Philip himself, as Richard jovially put it, "swallowed some water" and twenty of his knights were drowned; three were laid low by Richard's lance, a hundred by his men and a hundred more by Mercadier and the Brabantines. Altogether it was a good show. As for prisoners, they did not bother to count the lower ranks. What was more important, two hundred armoured war-horses were taken. Richard wrote to the Bishop of Durham from Dangu on September 30th:

> Thus have we defeated the King of France at Gisors; but it is not we who have done the same, but rather God and our right (*Dieu et mon droit*),[10] by our means; and in so doing we have put our life in peril, and our kingdom, contrary to the advice of all our people.

Richard's principal aim in this action had been to take the King of France in person. Then he could have bargained with him for a ransom, for his whole system of alliances depended upon subsidies and presents. The building of Château Gaillard had drained his treasury dry and now he had not even enough money to pay the mercenaries to guard the Norman frontier. When he could no longer subsidise them, his allies began to fall away. That, at least, is how he looked at it, as he wrote bitterly to the Dauphin of Auvergne in a *sirvente*:

[10] Adopted after this as the motto of the British Crown.

Your aid vanished hence
When my pay ceased to flow;
At Chinon, well you know,
We've no silver nor pence.
A rich king would suit,
Brave, and faithful to boot;
But I'm miser, paltroon,
Now you've changed your tune . . .

But a word let me say:
If your oath you betray,
A good man by the standard
You'll discover King Richard . . .

Gifts and largesse cut short,
You left tourney and court:
To remember's not hard
That the French are Lombard . . .

What avails a boor's troth,
Or a lout's broken oath?
But he'd better take care
If he would not worse fare.[11]

As a matter of fact, Richard had already surrendered Auvergne to Philip by the treaty of Vaudreuil of January 1196, much to the indignation of the Dauphin of Auvergne and his cousin Guy. He then counselled the Dauphin, if he did not like it, to rebel. When the Dauphin did so and requested Richard's help, Richard pleaded a new agreement with Philip. Indeed, when Count Guy appealed to Richard in person, he gave him "a rough and discourteous greeting" and "bestowed on him neither knights, nor serving men, nor crossbowmen, nor gold: whereat the Count got him home again, poor, and sad, and shamed." But when war with Philip broke out again, Richard nevertheless expected the Dauphin and Count Guy to support him! When they did not, he wrote his *sirvente*. "And the Dauphin made answer in another *sirvente* to all King Richard's sayings, and showed how he was right and Lord Richard wrong, and accused Lord Richard of the evil that he had done to him and to Count Guy, and likewise of all the evil that he had done to others."[12]

About this time, too, Richard hit upon what evidently seemed to him a brilliant scheme for raising money. He broke up his Great

[11] Translated by John Harvey, *The Plantagenets*.
[12] Farnell, *Lives of the Troubadours*.

Seal and had a new one made, announcing that all royal charters and grants would now have to be called in and resealed—for which, of course, payments were exacted. The excuse given for this pre- posterous piece of trickery was that the old seal had been out of the king's possession on two occasions in 1191, when it was temporarily lost in the sea off Cyprus along with the vice-chancellor Roger, and again when the king was a prisoner in Germany. On the new seal, a most beautiful piece of work, the three lions passant-gardant appear for the first time as the armorial bearings of the English kings. Its earliest known impression is that attached to a charter dated La Roche d'Andelys 22 May 1198.

Being unable to wring any more money out of his barons, Richard fell back upon the land with a levy of hidage or dane-geld. This, a new assessment, to replace that of the great Domesday survey, was undertaken by a body composed of the royal commissioners, a clerk and a knight in the presence of the sheriff and four other chosen knights of the shire, who would summon the stewards and bailiffs of the manors, with "four good men" and the reeve from each township, to appear to give evidence. Taxation was still on the basis of the number of hides or plough-teams at work, but the rate of the carucage was raised to 5s instead of 2s a hide—an enormous increase. But this tax also proved to be a failure and was so strenu- ously resisted by the clergy that an edict was passed putting them outside the pale of the law. Some counties paid to be dealt with gently in the matter of carucage; others paid to be relieved altogether of the inquiry.

Somewhat earlier Hubert Walter had issued a fresh set of instruc- tions to travelling justices to remedy any laxity or irregularity in the collection of the revenue, their first duty being to pay strict atten- tion to all the rights of the Crown in such matters as wardship, marriage, escheat and forfeiture. They were also told expressly to see that the savage forest laws were being enforced throughout the realm.

> Our lord the king gives notice, that if any shall commit an offence against him, relative to his venison, or his forests, in any way, he does not wish such to place their confidence in the fact that he has hitherto amerced them solely in their chattels, who have offended against him relative to his venison, or his forests. For if any persons henceforth shall commit any offence against him relative to his forests, and shall be convicted of the same, it

is his intention that the full punishment shall be inflicted on them, as in the days of Henry the grandfather of our lord the king, that is to say, they are to lose their eyes and their virility. The King also orders that his foresters shall make oath that, to the utmost of their ability, they will observe his assize which he has made relative to his forests, and that they will not be guilty of vexatious conduct towards knights or respectable men, by reason of this supervision which the king has given them over their woods."[13]

One good result of the king's desperate need for money was the progressive granting of charters to the towns, by which they paid an annual sum for their freedom. Hence London and the other principal cities set up their self-governing communes composed of the wealthier merchants. The country gentleman, or the smaller knight, acting as justice of the peace in the local affairs also came into his own at this time. That is to say, there was a considerable growth of local self-government throughout the country. Indeed, it has been said that "when History drops her drums and trumpets and learns to tell the story of Englishmen, it will find the significance of Richard not in his crusade or in his weary wars along the Norman border, but in his lavish recognition of municipal life."[14] But it is questionable whether Richard cared tuppence for municipal privilege. The growth of freedom was due to the astuteness of the growing bourgeois class, the business men, who had their eyes on the main chance just as much in the twelfth century as now.

The Pipe Rolls of the reign—that is, the Treasury accounts—do not by any means show all the money taken in the King's name. The appropriation of the effects of deceased ecclesiastics and of other Church property does not appear. This can be seen in the case of the goods of the deceased Bishop of Ely, Geoffrey Riddel. The entry of the sum charged by the sheriff of Cambridgeshire for bringing the goods to London is entered, but not the amount realized by the Treasury on the goods themselves.[15]

Another source of revenue to the Crown was the property and effects of murdered Jews, as well as the property and effects of those who had murdered them. The justices were directed to see that all Jews duly registered the amount of their property and for this pur-

[13] Roger de Hoveden, *Annals.*
[14] J. R. Green, *Stray Studies,* 1876.
[15] Ramsay, *Angevin Empire,* p. 369.

pose registeries were established in four of the chief commercial centres of the kingdom, each with a little staff of officials, half Christian, half Jewish, and a strong box to protect securities and documents. This was done to guard against the wasteful effects of recurrent outbreaks such as those at York, when, much to the king's anger, all the bonds and securities for money on loan were burnt, together with the Jews themselves. Richard protected the Jews because they were a valuable investment. Like sponges, they accumulated money by usury—being debarred from any form of productive work—and were then squeezed dry into the Exchequer. Two purposes would thus be served. Money would be collected and popular resentment at its collection could be turned against the Jews instead of against the Crown.

Generally speaking, Richard's reign does represent a further step towards constitutional government, for the itinerant justices were told to proceed on the findings of local juries, though in this he was only carrying on his father's reform of the law. This advance, however, was due, not to Richard directly, but to his justiciar Hubert Walter, a truly great administrator. Nevertheless, accused or suspected persons had little chance of acquittal, since if the jury found them innocent the jury themselves were presumed guilty for bringing the charge in the first place, and suffered accordingly. Even if acquitted, a suspected criminal had already undergone the barbarous trial by ordeal, which preceded the jury's indictment. But it was in the king's interest that as many cases should be brought into his courts as possible, since they were a most fruitful source of revenue.

V

"THE LION BY THE ANT IS SLAIN"

THE indecisive warfare on the Norman border continued. Richard built a fort on an island in the Seine which he called Boutavant (Push Forward); Philip countered with another called Gouletôt (Swallow All). It was again proposed that the kings should settle their differences by a fight between champions at Les Andelys. But, again, the proposal came to nothing.

In October 1198 Hubert Walter went to the French court to negotiate a treaty. Philip offered to restore all the lands and castles he had taken, except Gisors, the right to which he suggested should be submitted to the judgement of six Norman barons chosen by Richard and six French barons. Richard, however, refused to make any peace which did not include the Count of Flanders and the other feudatories of Philip he had bought over to his side. Philip rejected this condition and the talks were broken off. A truce, however, was declared to last until St Hilary's Day, 13 January 1199.

On that day the kings met for the last time between Les Andelys and Vernon; Richard stood in his boat on the Seine; Philip sat on his horse on the river bank. Negotiations were opened by the Cardinal Legate, Peter da Capua, and a five years' truce was agreed to, each side holding what it then possessed until the termination of the truce. After an exchange of oaths the armies disbanded.

But as Mercadier was returning to Gascony with the mercenaries, four French counts, through whose territories he had to pass, suddenly fell upon him and killed many of his men. Philip disowned the deed. But as soon as Richard left Normandy for Maine, he began to build a new castle near Gaillon and destroyed a neighbouring forest. On hearing this, Richard sent his chancellor to the French court to denounce the truce, saying that he must have a full settlement of the differences between them or no peace at all. Accordingly talks began again and a treaty was drawn up under which Philip promised to restore to Richard all the lands he had taken from him, except Gisors, but as compensation for this strategic castle he granted him the gift of the archbishopric of Tours, promising that he would do his best to get the imperial crown for Richard's nephew Otho, and that his son Louis should marry the daughter of the king of Castille, Richard's niece. But these terms were never ratified.

By the middle of March, Richard had reached Chinon, and it was while living there that news was brought to him of treasure trove turned up by the plough at Chaluz, near Limoges It was described as "an emperor with his wife, sons and daughters all of pure gold, and seated round a golden table", together with some ancient coins, probably Roman work. Achard, the lord of Chaluz, had surrendered part of this treasure to his immediate overlord, Aimar of Limoges, who sent it to Richard. But Richard had a shrewd suspicion that the best part of the treasure was still hidden at the Château-de-Chaluz, and therefore set out at once with Mercadier and his mercenaries to lay siege to the castle. At his approach Achard fled to Limoges, begging for a truce till Easter, when he promised to submit to the judgement of the royal Court of France.

Meanwhile Richard brought up his siege engines and encamped outside Chaluz. It was to be his last and most inglorious siege. The castle, which stands on a low hill above the little valley of the Tardoire, contained no more than about forty souls—peasants and their families who had taken refuge at the approach of the king and his dreaded mercenaries. There were also two sergeants-at-arms of the Viscount of Limoges, Pierre Brun and Pierre Basile. Everyone had shut themselves up in the tower, where they thought they would be safe.

Richard took possession of the town at once and for three days sappers worked away at the base of the tower. On the third day the little garrison—if they can be called that—offered to surrender on condition of safety of life and limb. Richard, who was determined to make an example of all the viscount's castles, replied that he was going to hang them all, including babies at the breast.

On the evening of March 26th the king went with Mercadier to find a suitable place for an assault on the tower. He was wearing no armour except his *casque de fer* and there was nobody visible on the walls or in the crenellations, though great stones continued to fall upon the besiegers. Suddenly Richard noticed a solitary figure on the bastion of the tower. He was told that this man had been standing there all day in utter contempt for danger, that he parried all the missiles of the besiegers with a frying-pan and then collected them and fired them back. Apart from stones, this was probably all the ammunition the defenders had.

As Richard went closer to have a shot at this intrepid bowman, a bolt whistled through the air. The king cried out and ducked behind his shield—too late. The missile at the end of its trajectory, fell heavily from above and struck him in the neck, glanced downwards and embedded itself in the fat of his left shoulder, a veritable bolt from the blue.

With a sharp cry, Richard turned and ran back to his lodging, where he tried to pull the arrow out of his shoulder. But the wooden shaft snapped off and the barb remained stubbornly embedded in the wound.[1] Mercadier sent for his surgeon, who did his best—or rather his worst—by the smoky light of flambeaux. But in his last years

[1] Guillaume le Breton gives a different account. "A noise of the devil" broke out in the camp, the king was carried to his tent, the army laid down its arms and gave itself up to lamentations and the siege was abandoned. It seems, however, that the king was living in the village and that no one saw the incident except Mercadier.

the king had grown so fat that the surgeon had some difficulty in finding the barb and badly mangled the king's neck and shoulder with his probably none-too-clean knife. In spite of plasters and medicaments gangrene set in. But the king would not rest. He had to be forced to remain in his room and four knights stood at his door to prevent anyone from coming in, lest his cries and groans should spread alarm and despondency through the camp and the news of his condition get abroad.

As he lay there in agony, Richard refused to moderate in the least his usual habits of drinking and love-making. The fire in his body only seemed to increase his raging thirst and the fury of his lust. Walter of Hemmingburg (whose account was, however, written in the next century) tells us that though his doctor counselled the strictest abstinence, the king "would not restrain his pleasures, but, burning with the love of women, he desperately adventured his life by taking to himself a lover". Miss Norgate calls him "a difficult patient". But dying or not, true to form, Richard ordered Chaluz to be stormed and everybody inside it hanged—all except the man who had shot him—"whom, as we may reasonably suppose," comments Roger of Hoveden, "he would have condemned to a most shocking death if he had recovered".

But it soon became plain to everyone that Richard was not going to recover and he wrote to his mother at Fontevrault begging her to come to him. He also dispatched troops to besiege the neighbouring castles of Natron and Montagut, "having purposed in his heart to destroy all the castles and towns of the Viscount of Limoges".

He then, we are told, turned his heart to penitence and confessed his sins. He made his nobles swear fealty to John as his successor. To John also he bequeathed three parts of his treasure, the rest went to the poor; his jewels he gave to his nephew Otto of Germany. There was nothing for Berengaria, his absent wife.

Having set his affairs in order, Richard sent for the man who had shot him. He looked at him out of his hard blue eyes and said: "What harm have I done you, that you have killed me?"

"You slew my father and my two brothers with your own hand," replied the man, "and you had meant to kill me. Therefore take what revenge on me you may think fit, for I will readily endure the greatest tortures you can devize, so long as you have met your end, after having inflicted evils so many and so great upon the world."

"I forgive you my death," said the king simply. "You may go free."

But the young man still remained standing at the foot of the king's couch "with scowling features and undaunted neck", dreading pardon worse than death.

"Live on," said Richard, "although thou art unwilling, and by my bounty behold the light of day."

As related by Roger of Hoveden, the scene might have come straight from Shakespeare, though it may never have taken place at all. One rather hopes it did for the sake of Richard's memory, though, of course, he was not prompted by altruism so much as concern for the fate of his own soul, when he came to give an account of himself before God. But still, the gesture is magnificent, and the young man was released with a gift of a hundred English shillings. His wonder at such generosity was to be short-lived. After the king's death Mercadier sent him to the fair Joanna, now Countess of Toulouse, and it was she who tore out his eyes and ordered him to be first flayed and then drawn apart by horses.[2]

The king lingered in pain for twelve days, getting steadily worse. He did not send for his wife. She heard the news of his death at second-hand, from St Hugh of Lincoln, when he called at her retreat at Beaufort-en-Vallée (Maine-et-Loire) on his way to the funeral. We are told that the neglected queen was much affected by the news. As for St Hugh, he had come to France to protest about a new attack on his episcopal property.

On the last day of his life, 6 April 1199, the king made his confession to Brother Miles, his chaplain, who had attended him in all his illnesses both in France and the Holy Land. He admitted that he had betrayed his father in his last days to the king of France, the arch-enemy of his house, and asked that in penitence for that he should be buried at his father's feet at Fontevrault, where his mother could preside over the graves of the husband she hated and the son

[2] The name of the man who shot Richard is variously given as Bertran de Gourdon and Pierre Basile. The Abbé Arbellot in his *La Verité sur la Mort de Richard Coeur de Lion* has shown that de Gourdon could not have shot him and been put to death for it because his name appears in numerous historical documents for some years after 1199. In 1209, for instance, he took part in the Albigensian Crusade. Hoveden, who gives the story of Richard's death that is usually cited, is, in the abbé's opinion, no more than an historical novelist, a forerunner of Scott. Pierre Basile is also mentioned several times in contemporary chronicles. He is mentioned specifically as the slayer of King Richard by Bernard Itier, a Limousin historian, Ralph de Diceto, a usually reliable source, and Matthew Paris.

she loved best. He admitted, too, that he had abstained from the sacrament because of his hatred of Philip of France, but now he put that hate away. Also he had stormed Chaluz and hanged its garrison in the holy season of Lent.

Richard then bequeathed his heart, *"en remembrance d'amour"* to the people of Rouen, but to the people of Poitou for their treachery, he left his entrails, "not deeming them worthy of any other part of him". Finally, he sent his seal to William the Marshal and Hubert Walter at Château Gaillard. Miles gave him absolution and at seven o'clock in the evening, as the sun was setting, he died in his mother's arms.

Miles closed his mouth, shut his eyes and anointed his head and his hands with balm. The ruddy beard and moustache were trimmed, the heart and entrails taken out and what was left was crowned and dressed in coronation robes of pale blue, green and rose. Jewelled gloves were then placed on the dead king's hands and golden sandals on his feet.

The obsequies were arranged in all their details by the abbot of Tourpenay, under the direction of Queen Eleanor. On Palm Sunday, April 11th, St Hugh of Lincoln, assisted by the Bishops of Poitiers and Angers, conducted the funeral service at Fontevrault. John was late for the funeral and Berengaria was missing as usual, but there was a small company of nobles, including the Viscount de Thouars and his son Guy and Pierre Bertin, the Seneschal of Poitou. The dead king's heart was sent to Rouen as a most precious relic to be enshrined in a golden casket. A magnificent tomb was built to contain it, upon which there soon reclined an effigy of the king as he was in life.[3] Over seven hundred years later, the heart was found carefully preserved inside two leaden boxes in a cavity in the wall near the altar of Rouen Cathedral. When the last of these boxes was opened the lion heart was found to have shrivelled to the semblance of a faded leaf. On the lid was inscribed in rudely graven characters:

HIC: JACET

COR: RICAR

DI: REGIS

ANGLORUM

[3] This noble sculpture is mentioned by Alberic of Trois Fontaines. See letter by Albert Way, *Archaeologia*, Vol XXIX, 1842, following its discovery by Achille Deville in 1838. Henry the Young King had also been buried in Rouen Cathedral in 1183. All the royal tombs were smashed to bits during the Revolution.

Richard was buried at his father's feet at Fontevrault and an effigy was placed on his tomb early in the next century. During the Revolution the tombs at Fontevrault were ransacked, and the abbey destroyed, though the effigies of the Plantagenets were left intact. Early in the nineteenth century Fontevrault Abbey was rebuilt as a state prison and the prisoners amused themselves, during their period of recreation, by knocking off the noses and other protuberant parts of Henry II, Eleanor of Aquitaine and King Richard.[4]

A week later, at Easter, the gentle Berengaria visited the tomb of her husband, staying with Eleanor and John at Fontevrault Abbey. But John made his offering at the altar with such an unbecoming levity that St Hugh refused to take it and would not even let him kiss his hand. Instead he led the little goatish man over to a fresco on the chapel wall depicting the tortures of the damned. Quite unabashed John took the bishop over to the opposite wall on which were to be seen the delights of paradise, remarking with a sly smile that it was rather among those that he intended to be after his death. He then rode north to be elected and installed Duke of Normandy, when he again shocked the assembled clergy by his unseemly behaviour, winking at his friends and fooling about during the ceremony in the cathedral.

Queen Eleanor went south with Mercadier to establish her authority in Poitou and next year Richard's only son, the bastard Philip of Cognac, avenged his father's death by killing the Viscount of Limoges.[5] His ill-used wife lived on at Le Mans, where she was known as La Reine Blanche, because of her white widow's weeds, and "La bonne reine Berengère". She lived at Le Mans as Countess for the thirty-one years of her widowhood, until she founded and herself entered the Cistercian Abbey of Espau, where she was buried. Later her body was removed to Le Mans cathedral, where

[4] Fontevrault, "wherein enter all nobles ladies in old age", was the richest abbey in Western France. When he founded it in 1099 Robert d'Arbrissel "overturned the salic law of convents, and brought his monks under the wholesome government of abbesses; and wisely believing that the fair sex must improve the other, under any and every circumstance, he shut up nuns and monks in the same cloister". Leitch Ritchie, *Liber Fluvorum, or River Scenery of France, depicted in sixty-one line engravings from drawings* by J. M. W. Turner, 1853.

[5] Philip Faulconbridge, bastard son of Richard Coeur de Lion, in *King John*, is Shakespeare's invention. Holinshed refers to him correctly as Philip of Cuinac, or Cognac.

her tomb still is. After Richard's death she was, however, so little recognized as his wife that she had to appeal repeatedly to the Pope before she could make good her claim to her jointure, and during this time she was reduced to living on the bounty of her sister Blanche of Champagne. At Le Mans, she is (or was) still remembered for her kindness to the sick and poor. All things considered, Berengaria was hardly the wife for Richard Lion Heart.

As for Mercadier, Richard's Gascon captain, he was murdered in 1200 at Bordeaux by another chief of mercenaries. It was he who stormed Chaluz and committed all the atrocities upon the helpless little garrison of peasants and their families. He was a man after Richard's own heart and had served him faithfully for the last fifteen years.

Epilogue

Richard Coeur de Lion was forty-two at the time of his death. After reigning nine and a half years his titles were: King of England, Lord of Ireland, Scotland and Wales, Duke of Normandy, Aquitaine and Gascony, Count of Maine, Anjou and Poitou, and superior Lord of Brittany, Auvergne and Toulouse; King of Arles, conqueror of Cyprus and, for a time, ruler of the kingdom of Jerusalem. He left no children by his marriage, which appears, in effect, to have been no marriage. He was deeply mourned by his formidable old mother. "I have lost the staff of my age, the light of my eyes," she wrote to the Pope. He was mourned by Abbot Miles and evidently by his son Philip, whom John pensioned off at a shilling a day, and perhaps by Berengaria.

Popular feeling about Richard, as far as it was vocal, is found in a ballad or roundelay sung in Normandy shortly before his death, to the effect that in the Limousin an arrow was making by which the tyrant would die. This story appears in the chronicle of Alberic of Trois Fontaines, a Cistercian, who says that while the smith was forging the arrow-head, passers-by repeatedly saluted him with "Heaven speed you!" Taking these greetings as an omen, the smith engraved a cross upon the metal, and it was with this arrowhead that the king was slain.[1]

[1] Sir Richard Palgrave, introduction to *Rotuli Curiae Regis*, Rolls and Records of the Court held before the King's Justiciars and Justices, Vol I, 1835.

There were of course the usual neat courtly epitaphs such as:

> In hujus morte peremit formica Leonem.
> Proh dolor, in tanto funere mundus obit.
>
> (In this man's death the lion by the ant was slain.
> O evil destiny, in a death so great the whole world fell.)

and Gaucelm Faidit's *planh* from Ventadour, with its "Ah God, the valiant King of the English is no more.... Of all *preux chevaliers* he was the first.... A thousand years shall never see his peer, so open-handed, noble, brave, and generous."[2] But this lacks the personal note of Bertran de Born's lament for Henry the Young King and there is much more conviction in the bitter lines:

> Virus, avaritia, scelus, enormisque libido,
> Faeda fames, atrox elatio, caeca cupido,
> Annis regnarunt bis quinis, arcabalista
> Arte, manu, telo prostravit viribus ista.
>
> (Venom, avarice, crime, unbounded lust,
> Foul famine, atrocious pride, blind desire,
> Have reigned for twice five years. An archer,
> With art, hand, weapon, strength did all these overthrow.)

This, like the Norman ballad, is more likely to have been the general feeling about Richard. After all, *preux chevalier* as he was, Richard and his sort were a poison in the blood of the people.

Gerald of Wales draws a parallel between the deaths of Richard and William Rufus. "Earl Richard who was made king, and succeeded his father in the government of the kingdom, puffed up in his day with tyrannical pride, provoked that avenging wrath which too frequently and too wickedly he was accustomed to abuse, and fell, shot by a bolt from a crossbow as William had fallen by an arrow."[3] Giullaume le Breton finds poetic justice in Richard's death, because it was he, he says, who introduced the devilish crossbow to the French and it was only right that he should feel the effects of it himself. It is difficult not to agree.

In spite of the bitter obituaries written in his own age, Richard

---

[2] Gaucelm Faidit became a *jongleur* because he had lost all he had at dice. He had tasted Richard's bounty and is described in *The Lives of the Troubadours* as "a full and gluttonous eater, and a wine-bibber, wherefore he grew fat beyond measure". He represents Richard as the ideal hero of chivalry.

[3] *The Instruction of Princes.* Gerald is writing a moral work. Elsewhere he is not so severe.

soon became the familiar romantic figure of tradition. He does not appear to have been referred to as the Lion Heart in his own day. The first appearance of the name is in the fourteenth century metrical romance *Kynge Rycharde Cuer du Lyon*, where we learn that it was derived from his exploit of killing a lion in single combat by tearing out its heart. The same ballad credits him with the appetite as well as the heart of a lion, when it represents him as eating a young Saracen prisoner for supper.

"If heroism be confined to brutal and ferocious valour," observes Gibbon, "Richard Plantagenet will stand high among the heroes of his age." Judged by medieval standards, as he should be judged, and not by those of either the eighteenth or the nineteenth centuries, Richard does indeed stand high among the heroes of his age. It is, however, difficult to write about him today, if we are honest, without very mixed feelings. As soon as one looks a little more closely at medieval chivalry the gilt comes off on one's fingers. The highest praise that Froissart can find for the Black Prince is to say that he was "courageous and cruel as a lion". And Gaston de Foix, who to him is the very flower of chivalry, seems to us a monster who stabbed his young son in the throat with a penknife on the mere suspicion that he meant to poison him and then took fifteen of his son's squires and put them to death "right horribly". Yet, we read, "his visage was fair, sanguine and smiling, his eyen gay and amorous... he had great pleasure in harmony of instruments... he could do it right well himself; he would have songs sung before him... nor was there none rejoiced in deeds of arms more than the earl did: there was seen in his hall, chamber and court, knights and squires of honour going up and down talking of arms and armours."[4] Though this was written about two hundred years later, during the final flowering of the Middle Ages, when, under the pressure of commercial and utilitarian interests, men were beginning to feel nostalgic about the ideals of chivalry, it might almost be a description of Richard as Count of Poitou.

But even at the end of the twelfth century, one finds chroniclers contrasting the crusaders of their day unfavourably with the great figures of a more heroic age, for distance always lends enchantment. Still, the twelfth century was not so much the age of a militant faith, of the *Chanson de Roland* (though Richard was probably brought up on it), as of the mystical quest of the Holy Grail and Chrestien de Troyes' *Percival*, *Cligès* and all the refinements of

[4] Quoted by Sir Herbert Read, *The Sense of Glory*.

courtly love. It was also an age of spreading rationalism, scepticism and heresy, an age of empiricism, of histories, of documentary records and classical sculpture, of the growth of great centralized states. It had, in fact, many of the qualities that we usually associate with the Italian renaissance. But the west portal of Chartres, with its elongated, grave and strangely withdrawn figures that seem to look out at us with the light of a secret knowledge in their eyes, is still romanesque in feeling. The twelfth century was an age of many cross-currents and complex influences, when everything was in the melting-pot and free inquiry and a pagan sense of beauty were once again coming to birth. It took the thirteenth century, which begins ominously enough with the Albigensian "crusade", for the Inquisition—which then makes its first appearance in history—to clamp down once more the dogmas of the church. As in communist countries today, orthodoxy could only be maintained by tyranny and fear, by breaking men's spirits with various forms of torture. The black monks of the Dominican Order were the forerunners of the modern political police.[5] The thirteenth century systematized what the wonderful twelfth discovered. But first of all the ancient civilization of Languedoc and Provence had to be stamped out and incorporated in Philip Augustus' new French state.

The twelfth century was just the age to produce a relatively complicated character like Richard Coeur de Lion. No child of such parents as Henry II and Eleanor could be simple and straightforward. For though now chiefly remembered for his battles and exploits in the Holy Land, Richard was after all a poet and a musician, a man with what we should call a keen aesthetic sense, and therefore a sensitive, unordinary and unpredictable man. But that side of him was kept well hidden beneath the chain mail, though it may have taken its revenge in recurrent bouts of fever and boils. As for his morals, all one can say is that they are not such as to be widely condemned by the majority of historians and men of letters today. They do, however, make him rather less suitable as the schoolboys' hero he is usually represented to be. At least he was better than his brother John and no worse than many of his contemporaries. And he was of heroic mould. That is the secret of the

[5] Torture, as we are always unctuously told by comrades, is forbidden in the legal code of the Soviet Union, which has always been most self-righteous in its condemnation of the Nazis' use of it. But so was the shedding of blood forbidden to the Church. They got on just as well, however, with the help of the secular arm.

spell that lies in his name. As Mr John Harvey writes: "But in what goes to make a hero his vices, his anger, his vengeful cruelty even, count for as much as his chivalric virtues and his skill as a poet, the last of an epoch: his qualities were more than life-size. It is here that his secret lay, and that the secret of his lasting fame still lies—he would not be bound by the chains of the average, the mediocre, and the reasonable, and died because the merely possible was not enough for him."[6]

Coeur de Lion remains the second of that long line of Plantagenet kings, several of whom provided Shakespeare with material for plays—and this is possibly their greatest claim to remembrance —which continues unbroken through the golden age of Richard II to "the last English king", who went down fighting on Bosworth Field at the close of the Middle Ages. Yet it is the Lion Heart who has become one of England's national heroes, riding with sword uplifted and stern and noble features at Westminster, his memorable deeds moulded round the base of Marochetti's statue of 1860—how, dying, he forgave the man that killed him and, hurtling like a thunderbolt among them, poleaxed the paynim beneath the walls of Acre.

[6] *The Plantagenets*, p. 40.

BIBLIOGRAPHY

CHRONICLES, POEMS, &c.

Ambroise, *l'Estoire de la guerre sainte*, ed. by Gaston Paris, 1897. Prose translation by E. N. Stone, *Three Old French Chronicles of the Crusades*, University of Washington, Seattle, 1939.

Archer, T. A., *The Crusade of Richard I*, 1888. Fragmentary translations of the chronicles.

Bohardin (Beha ed Din), *Life of Saladin*, ed. by Sir C. W. Wilson. Palestine Pilgrims Text Society Publication XIII, 1897.

Coggeshall, Ralph of, *Chronicon Anglicanum*, ed. Joseph Stevenson, Rolls Series 66.

Devizes, Richard of, *De Rebus Gestis Ricardi Primi*, ed. J. Stevenson, English Hist. Soc., 5. Trans. by Stevenson in *Church Historians of England* 5i, 1858.

Ernoul, *Chronique d'Ernoul et de Bernard le Tresorier*, ed. Mas Latrie, Paris 1871.

Fitz Stephen, William, *Life of Thomas Becket*, English Hist. Documents 1142–1189, ed. David C. Douglas and George W. Greenaway, 1953.

Giraldus Cambrensis (Gerald of Wales) *Concerning the Instruction of Princes*, trans. J. Stevenson, *Church Historians of England*, Vol. 5i, 1858; *Autobiography*, trans. H. E. Butler, 1937.

Grim, Edward, *Life of S. Thomas Becket*, English Hist. Documents, 1142–1189.

Guillaume le Breton, *La Philippide*, 1825.

Guillaume le Maréchal, L'Histoire de, ed. Paul Meyer, Soc. de l'Histoire de France, Paris 1891–1901.

Hemingburgh, Walter of, *Chronicle*, ed. H. C. Hamilton, Engl. Hist. Soc., 14, 1848–9.

Hoveden, Roger de, *Annals*, trans. H. T. Riley, Bohn Antiquarian Library, 2 vols., 1853.

Itinerarium Peregrinorum et Gesta Regis Ricardi, ed. William Stubbs, Vol. I *Memorials of Richard I*, Rolls Series, 38. A poor translation of an inferior text may be found in *Chronicles of the Crusades*, Bohn, where it is attributed to Vinsauf.

Jeanroy, Alfred, *La poésie lyrique des troubadours*, Paris, 1934.

Kynge Rycharde Cuer du Lyon, 1528.

Landon, Lionel, *The Itinerary of King Richard I, with studies of certain matters of interest connected with his reign*. A chronology based on the royal charters. Pipe Roll Soc., 1935.

Lives of the Troubadours, trans. and ed. from the medieval Provençal by Ida Farnell, 1896.

Newburgh, William of (Little William), *Historia Rerum Anglicanum, Chronicles of the reigns of Stephen, Henry II and Richard I*, ed. R. Howlett, Rolls Series 82. A translation may be found in *Church Historians of England* Vol. IV, Part 2, J. Stevenson, 1856.

Stubbs, William, *Chronicles and Memorials of the Reign of Richard I*, 2 vols., Rolls Series, 1864–5.

MODERN WORKS

Adams, Henry, *Mont-Saint-Michel and Chartres*, new edition, 1950.

Arbellot, Abbé F., *La Verité sur la mort de Richard Coeur de Lion*, Paris 1878.

Aytoun, William, *The Life and Times of Richard I*, 1840.

Belloc, Hilaire, *A Shorter History of England*, 1934.

Boase, T. S. A., *English Art, 1190–1216, Oxford History of English Art*, 1951.

Chambers, Frank, Some Legends Concerning Eleanor of Aquitane, *Speculum* XIV, 1941.

Chaytor, H. J., *The Troubadours and England*, 1923.

Coulton, G. G., *Medieval Panorama*, 1945.

Cronin, Vincent, *The Golden Honeycomb*, 1954.

Dingwall, E. J., *The Girdle of Chastity*, 1931.

Davis, H. W. C., *England Under the Normans and Angevins*, 1919.

Fitz Gerald, Brian Vesey, *Winchester*, 1953.

Gibbon, Edward, *The Decline and Fall of the Roman Empire*, chapter on the Third Crusade, etc., ed. Sir William Smith, 1854–5.

Grousset, René, *Histoire des Croisades*, 3 vols., Paris 1935.

Harvey, John, *The Plantagenets, 1154–1485*, 1948.

Hill, Sir George, *A History of Cyprus*, Vol. 2, 1948.

Holbach, M. M., *In the Footsteps of Richard Coeur de Lion*, 1912.

Holland, Vyvyan, The Medieval Courts of Love, a paper read before Ye Sette of Odde Volumes, 22 February 1927.

Kelly, Amy, *Eleanor of Aquitaine*, 1952.

La Monte, J. L., *The World of the Middle Ages*, New York, 1949.

Lindsay, Philip, *The Kings of Merry England*, 1936.

Lloyd, Roger, *The Golden Middle Age*, 1939.

Luke, Sir Harry, *Cyprus*, 1957.

Markham, V. R., *Romanesque France*, 1929.

Norgate, Kate, *Richard the Lion Heart*, 1924; *England under the Angevin Kings*, 1887.

Oman, Sir Charles, *History of the Art of War in the Middle Ages*, 1885.

Painter, Sydney, *French Chivalry*, Baltimore, 1940.

Pound, Ezra, *The Spirit of Romance*, new edition 1953.

Ramsay, Sir James, *Angevin Empire*, 1903; *Revenues of the Kings of England, 1066–1388*, 1925.

Read, Sir Herbert, *The Sense of Glory*, 1929.

Richard, Alfred, *Histoire des ducs et des comtes de Poitou, 778–1202*, 2 vols., Paris 1903.

Richardson, Edward, *Monumental Effigies of the Temple Church*, etc., 1843.

Rougemont, Denis de, *Passion and Society*, a trans. of *L'Amour et l'Occident* by Montgomery Belgion, 1940.

Runciman, Steven, *A History of the Crusades*, vol. 3, 1954.

Scammell, C. V., *Hugh du Puiset, Bishop of Durham*, 1956.

Stenton, C. V., *Norman London*, 1934.

Stothard, C. A., *The Monumental Effigies of Great Britain from the Conquest to Henry VII*, 1817–32. Includes drawings of the Plantagenet tombs of Fontevrault before restoration.

Strickland, Agnes, *Lives of the Queens of England*, 1850–59.

Stubbs, William, *Historical Introductions to the Rolls Series*, collected and ed. by Arthur Hassall, 1902.

Thurston, H., *Life of St Hugh of Lincoln*, trans. and ed. from the French Carthusian life, with additions, 1898.

Way, Albert, The Effigy of Richard I at Rouen, *Archæologia* XXIX, 1842.

Webb, Geoffrey, *Architecture in Britain in the Middle Ages*, 1956.

Wilkinson, C. A., *Coeur de Lion*, 1933.

Viollet-le-Duc (Eugène Emmanuel), *Dict. raisonné de l'architecture*, 1858–68; *Military Architecture*, trans. by M. Macdermot, 1879.

Index